DYING FOR GOD

Figurae

READING MEDIEVAL CULTURE

DYING FOR GOD

MARTYRDOM AND THE MAKING OF
CHRISTIANITY AND JUDAISM

Daniel Boyarin

Stanford University Press, Stanford, California 1999

Stanford University Press
Stanford, California
© 1999 by the Board of Trustees of the
Leland Stanford Junior University

Printed in the United States of America
CIP data appear at the end of the book

AMICAE MEAE

Acknowledgments

In 1944, my teacher Prof. Saul Lieberman published a classic essay in which he treated talmudic martyrology in the context of patristic literature. That article, "The Martyrs of Caesarea," had been written under the inspiration of his meeting and friendship with the Belgian church historian, Henri Gregoire, then a refugee from the Nazis in the Morningside Heights neighborhood in New York, where Lieberman, the Lithuanian Talmudist, had also found refuge. Nearly a half-century later, this student of Lieberman's met another church historian, Virginia Burrus, on Morningside Heights under happier circumstances, when both of us were participants at a conference on asceticism at Union Theological Seminary. This book represents some of the first fruits of that second intellectual encounter and aspires to continue modestly the enterprise begun by the first. I was invited to give the Lancaster/Yarnton lectures on Judaism and the Other Religions while having dinner at the AAR with Prof. Burrus, who had in the meantime become my friend and interlocutor in comparative rabbinic and patristic studies. Accordingly, the subject of these lectures, the issue of similarities and divergences, of indeed common religious and cultural histories of rabbinic Jews and Christians in late antiquity came immediately to mind. I have learned much indeed from this *amicitia* and this *amica*, to whom I hope here to be giving a little bit back.

This book is a revised, expanded, and much annotated version of the lectures which I had the honor and privilege to deliver in January and February of 1998 at Lancaster University and at the Oxford Centre for Jewish Studies. I would like to thank Prof. Paul Morris, lately of Lancaster University and now in the Antipodes, for inviting me, and his successor in the chair of religious studies at Lancaster, Prof. Rebecca Sawyer, for graciously hosting me, and Prof. Bernard Wasserstein, of St. Cross College at Oxford University and president of the Oxford Centre for Hebrew and Jewish Studies, for his gracious hospitality as well. Special thanks are due as well to Profs. Martin Goodman of Wolfson and Christopher Rowland of Queens College for their generous hospitality whilst in Oxford and to Prof. Don Fowler of Jesus College there for inviting us to enjoy the experience of a dinner in college in all its Elizabethan luster and a splendid midnight tour of the old library of Jesus.

I have learned much as I delivered the lectures at these venues and in April 1998 in Jerusalem under the auspices of the Department of Comparative Religion at the Hebrew University as well. The last-named unit is notable in its setting for its openness to new ideas. Among the several questioners who responded on those occasions, Prof. Daniel Schwartz of the Department of Jewish History there stands out for his particularly useful help and support of the general thesis presented here.

I would like to thank the following who have read versions of these lectures and commented to great avail: Carlin Barton, Chava Boyarin, Virginia Burrus, Ruth Anne Clements, Erich Gruen, Galit Hasan-Rokem, Willis Johnson, Karen King, Amy Jill Levine, Harry O. Maier, Joel Marcus, David Satran, Dina Stein (to which good friend I owe the title of the fourth lecture as well), Guy Stroumsa, Mark Vessey, Froma Zeitlin, as well as two anonymous readers for the *Journal of Early Christian Studies* (where some of this material has appeared in an earlier form), and Charlotte Fonrobert, Christine Hayes, Blake Leyerle, and another (anonymous) reader for Stanford University Press, who were both suitably stern as well as encouraging.

I would like to pay a further belated debt of gratitude here. For fifteen years, much in my thinking, teaching, writing, and daily life has been enriched and enabled by what I have learned from Dr. Ruth Cohen and from her philosophy, Theme Centered Interaction. This book in particular, to the extent that it is enriched by an understanding of how human beings can be the same and different at the same time, is an end product of that learning, but there is much, much more than end product.

I am, as always, grateful to the donors of the Taubman Chair of Talmudic Culture at UC Berkeley for the research support that the chair affords me, which enables significantly my scholarly work.

All authors should be blessed with editors like Helen Tartar.

I have written all of my books until now while under the psychoanalytic care of Dr. Ruth Stein. The completion of this book coincides with the end of that decade-long life-transforming therapy. Words cannot express my gratitude or satisfy my debt.

D.B.

Contents

"Problematic distinctions are not binary oppositions."

—DOMINICK LACAPRA

Introduction

When Christians Were Jews: On Judeo-Christian Origins

Not long ago, everyone knew that Judaism came before Christianity. The story would go that Christianity developed out of the "orthodox" Judaism of the first century, rabbinic Judaism, and either deviated from the true path or superseded its ancestor. Interestingly, it was more or less the same story for both Christian and Jewish scholars.

The Old Paradigm: Religions as Kinfolk

In order for this myth to work at all, there has to be an assumption of a self-identical religious organism. Jacob Lauterbach's characterization of Judaism and Christianity as "mother and daughter" is typical of how the myth works.[1] Judaism is the "mother" from which another self-identical religious organism, Christianity, the "daughter," can be "born." As Philip Alexander has described the received opinion: "Two main approaches have been adopted in order to lay down the baseline from which the divergence of Christianity can be measured. The first involves retrojecting rabbinic Judaism into first century Pharisaism and argues in effect that Pharisaism is identical with normative Judaism. . . . The second approach involves trying to determine the essence of first century Judaism, the irreducible common denominator of all, or most of, the Jewish sect[s] or parties."[2]

In other words, in order to imagine a single mother religion that could give birth to a daughter religion, we have to find some way of reducing the diversity of Jewish religious life in the pre-Christian era to a single object that we can then designate as Judaism. This, as Alexander makes clear, has been accomplished in one of two ways. According to the first, one later form of Judaism, the Judaism of the Rabbis, which we know from the second century on and which achieved hegemony quite a bit later than that, is retrojected back onto the Pharisaism of the first century, and that first-century Pharisaism is then treated both as virtually identical with its later "descendant" and as the dominant or even correct and true form of Judaism. According to the second, Pharisaism is not given such anachronistic and theologically determined preeminent status, but all of the known forms of first-century Judaism—except for Christianity—are assumed to have had some common features that joined them all into a single "religion." Out of either of these versions of Judaism in the first century, a different religion was born. Hence, Christianity as the daughter of Judaism.

More recently, scholars have begun to recognize that the historical picture is quite a bit more complicated than either of these approaches allows. In the Jewish world of the first century, there were many sects competing for the name of the true Israel and the true interpreter of the Torah—the Talmud itself speaks of twenty-four such sects—and the form of Judaism that was to be the seedbed of what eventually became the Church was but one of those sects.[3] Abandoning both of the apologetic accounts described by Alexander, scholars have come to see that if we are to speak of families at all, we need to speak of a twin birth of Christianity and rabbinic Judaism as two forms of Judaism, and not of a genealogy in which one—Judaism—is parent to the other—Christianity.

After the destruction of the Temple, the current story goes, two "daughter" religions were born out of this congeries, rabbinic Judaism and Christianity, thus modifying the terms of Lauterbach's conventional metaphor.[4] As Israel Yuval has written of the Lauterbachian commonplace: "The Jewish view [Christian, as well] that sees early Christianity only as influenced and not as influencing certainly has a theological background, namely, thinking of Judaism as the mother religion of Christianity. But historical criticism has to bring us to the conclusion that early Christianity and the Judaism of the Mishna are, in a manner of speaking, sister religions that were crystallized in the same period and the same background of enslavement and destruction."[5] As a figure for this simultaneous birth of Christianity and Judaism, Alan Segal mobilized the verse: "And G-d said to her: there are two peoples in your womb." The two sibling religions are thereby configured now as twin sons, the children of Rebecca, Jacob and Esau.[6]

The purpose of this new family metaphor is clear. Instead of seeing the religious formation(s) that were to become the Church and the religious formation(s) that were to give rise to the Rabbis in a diachronic relation to each other, they are both seen as having arisen more or less together historically out of the old biblical religion of ancient Israel after the crises that attended the people of Israel in the first century.[7]

In the midrash of the Rabbis, Jacob is, of course, Israel, and Esau is frequently simply an eponym for Rome.[8] After 312, Esau, or Edom, his descendant, are most often read as the Christian Church, or as the Rabbis themselves put it: "The Principate turned to sectarianism" [TB Sotah 49b and parallels].[9] This transfer has surely been made by the time of the following Palestinian talmudic statement: "Rabbi Aḥa said in the name of Rav Huna: In the future, Esau the wicked will wrap himself in his tallit and sit with the righteous in the next world, and the Holy Blessed One will drag him and throw him out from there."[10] An Esau who wishes to sit with a prayer shawl and study Torah with the righteous in heaven is almost obviously a Christian, not, I think, a Roman "pagan."

This midrashic equation of Esau with Christianity is very rich, but also very problematic. It is very rich because it incorporates in a powerful symbol the sense of the highly fraught family relationship between Jews and Christians, eventually between Judaism and Christianity, between the Rabbis and the Church. If for the Church Judaism ultimately was a superseded ancestor of the true heir to the promise, for the Rabbis, the two entities were more like constantly struggling twin siblings. This metaphor, however, also is deeply and productively problematic for two reasons. It shifts the gender of the descendants from sisters to brothers, and more importantly, since, according to the biblical narrative, Esau was the elder of the two twins, and Jacob, who is Israel, was born holding on the heel of his elder brother, it implies paradoxically that of the two new religious entities, Christianity is the elder and Judaism the (slightly) younger. The symbolic resonances of the recognition that Judaism and Christianity, or perhaps Israel and Christendom, are not very irenic brothers were abundant, but the chronological paradoxes of making Esau be the elder must have been palpable as well. The Rabbis, it seems, resolved this problem in part by thinking of Esau as an elderly Rome become lately Christian. But some Christian writers saw here other opportunities, naming "the Jews" as the elder son, Esau, and the ultimately dominant Jacob as the younger, "the Christians." If this interpretation seems forced vis-à-vis the text of the Torah, it certainly already would have seemed quite plausible vis-à-vis the historical situation by the third century.

One of the clearest early instances of the patristic tradition of reading Esau as "the Jews" and Jacob as "the Church" is in Tertullian:

> For thus unto Rebecca did God speak: "Two nations are in thy womb, and two peoples shall be divided from thy bowels; and people shall overcome people, and the greater shall serve the less." Accordingly, since the people or nation of the Jews is anterior in time, and "greater" through the grace of primary favour in the Law, whereas ours is understood to be "less" in the age of times, as having in the last era of the world attained the knowledge of divine mercy: beyond doubt, through the edict of the divine utterance, the prior and "greater" people—that is, the Jewish—must necessarily serve the "less;" and the "less" people—that is, the Christian—overcome the "greater."[11]

According to Tertullian's reading of the verse, then, which includes a version of the Hebrew subtly different from the way the Rabbis read the verse, one of the peoples was to overcome the other, and since the greater would serve the less, then obviously, it is the less who overcome. Since the Christians already were both younger and more powerful than the Jews by Tertullian's time (cf. Justin for similar claims), it would have seemed obvious to Tertullian that only the Christians could be read as Jacob, that is, as Israel.[12]

Such patristic claims help us to explain a difficult midrashic passage. In Genesis Rabbah, the midrash wards off the problem of Christianity as Esau's apparent senior (and perhaps, as well, the Christian readings) by reading the awkward verse not about Jacob and Esau at all, but about the twelve tribes that would issue from Jacob:

> And G-d said to her: there are two peoples in your womb. . . . "Two peoples," behold two. And "two nations," behold four. "And one nation will struggle with the other," this makes six. "And the elder will serve the younger," behold eight. "And her days became full for giving birth, and behold there were twins in her stomach," this is ten. "And the first was born ruddy," this is eleven. "And afterwards his brother was born," this makes twelve.[13]

The midrash has thus taken the verse entirely out of its literal sense and entirely out of the usual equation—for this very same midrash—of Jacob with Israel and Esau with Rome. Suddenly, Esau ends up being one of Jacob's twelve sons, since the "two peoples" in Rebecca's womb are translated midrashically as two of the twelve tribes of Jacob, and a displacement effectively erases Esau.

I suggest that it was the difficulty of the stark sequence of elder and younger and the ways that Christian writers could exploit these that led to this drastically distorted reading. Quite astonishingly, but understandably, not one of the three major medieval Jewish biblical commentators, Rashi, Ibn Ezra, and the Ramban, make even an attempt to interpret this verse. Ibn Ezra mysteriously says that "the elder" here is a verb, and that he will explain the verse somewhere else, but doesn't, to the best of my knowledge.

Here, then we have an example of precisely the phenomenon that I wish to begin exploring in this book, the ways that rabbinic Judaism has been influenced by its slightly older brother, Christianity. In some ways and fashions, the midrashic equation of Esau with Rome, which became the Christian Church in the midrashic imagination, as in history, gave rise to a paradox. In what follows, I would like to exploit the temporal paradoxes of the midrashic equation of Esau with Christianity in order to explore a historical problem—to produce, as it were, a midrash that never was.

The central paradox that I have in mind is the following: While Jews and Christians both have thought of something called Judaism as the elder religion and something called Christianity as the younger, the midrashic implications of the verse are that Christianity is the elder and Judaism the younger. This would suggest that rabbinic Judaism was born on the heels, indeed, holding the heel, of its elder brother, the Church.[14] The possibilities hinted at (and suppressed) by the midrashic reading offer a method of investigating both the complicated temporalities of the historical relationship between rabbinic Judaism and Christianity as religious entities and the complex intertwinings of three histories: the history of Israel, the history of Rome, and the history of the Church. Esau and Jacob, I will argue, continued "jostling each other in her womb" at least well into late antiquity, and perhaps will do so forever. Like many twins, Judaism and Christianity never quite formed entirely separate identities. Like closely related siblings, they rivaled each other, learned from each other, fought with each other, perhaps even sometimes loved each other: Esau, the elder, supplanted somehow by Jacob, the younger, who fed him.

If the younger fed the elder, in many ways, the elder served the younger, as well. The image suggests that for at least the first three centuries of their common lives, Judaism in all of its forms and Christianity in all of its forms were part of one complex religious family, twins in a womb, contending with each other for identity and precedence, but sharing to a large extent the same spiritual food, as well. It was the birth of the hegemonic Catholic Church, however, that seems finally to have precipitated the consolidation of rabbinic Judaism as Jewish orthodoxy, with all its rivals, including the so-called Jewish Christianities, apparently largely vanquished. It was then that Judaism and Christianity finally emerged from the womb as genuinely independent children of Rebecca.[15] As Rosemary Radford Ruether put it a quarter of a century ago, "the fourth century is the first century for Christianity and Judaism."[16]

I want to emphasize as well, however, the messiness of the metaphor of Jacob, rabbinic Judaism, born holding on to the heel of Esau, the Church—its refusal to quite work, even the ways that it contradicts itself in its figuring of elder and younger.[17] This messiness serves to plot the untidiness of the train of thought and the train of history in the new midrash proposed herein. It is not a single, unambiguous, clear, linear story, but one of doublings and doublings back, of contradictions and obscurities.

The So-Called "Parting of the Ways"

Even scholars who have recognized that Christianity can hardly be derived as a "daughter" religion from Judaism have still tended to assume a distinct "parting of the ways" sometime in the first or second century, after which there was hardly any contact between the two religions. Philip Alexander has written: "Since there are clearly radical aspects to early Christianity the tendency has been to see the parting of the ways as having taken place early, usually in the first or early second century C.E. Some analyses so stress the radicalism of early Christianity as to suggest that the parting of the ways occurred almost *ab ovo*."[18] Many would place this final break as early as 70 A.C., after the destruction of the Jerusalem Temple.[19] Others put it somewhat later. One of the leading Israeli historians has put it thus:

"With the Bar Kokhba rising the final rift between Judaism and Christianity was complete."[20] And as subtle and critical a scholar as Gerson Cohen writes that "the official establishment of the Christian Church as the religion of the empire made no discernible impression on the Jews of the fourth century, for by that time the chasm between Judaism and Christianity had grown so deep and wide that the alignment of the machinery of state with the Church was of no greater moment than the succession of one emperor by another."[21]

There has been a kind of general collusion between Jewish and Christian scholars (as earlier between the Rabbis and the Doctors of the Church) to insist on this total lack of contact and interaction, each group for its own reasons.[22] This mutual stake has been described, once more by Alexander: "The attempt [to lay down a norm for Judaism in the first century] barely conceals apologetic motives—in the case of Christianity a desire to prove that Christianity transcended or transformed Judaism, in the case of Jews a desire to suggest that Christianity was an alien form of Judaism which deviated from the true path."[23] Indeed, the very distinctness of Judaism has been articulated by Jews as its distance from a "syncretistic" Christianity whose defining feature is that it is somehow a composite of Judaism and Hellenism.[24]

Alexander has provided a simple, graphic metaphor for an alternative approach: "If we picture Judaism and Christianity as circles we can graphically represent how we reached the present state of affairs as follows. Today the circles stand side by side essentially in self-contained isolation. If we move the horizon of time backwards this monadic relationship remains more or less constant until we come roughly to the fourth century of the current era. Then an important development takes place: we observe the circles approaching and beginning to overlap."[25] It is to Alexander's credit that he complicates the picture of a simple "parting of the ways" that took place once and for all, but his Venn diagrams provide too simple a model for the reconfiguring that needs to be done.

Changing Paradigms: Religions and Family Resemblance

The breaking down of the cultural boundaries between groups in close spatial contact is a point at issue not only in the writing of histories of late antiquity, but in our understanding of cultures and their interactions in general.[26] The newly developing perspective on Judaism and Christianity as intertwining cultures is thus dependent on a developing climate of opinion or even Zeitgeist. As Homi Bhabha has written, "The theoretical recognition of the split-space of enunciation may open the way to conceptualizing an *international* culture, based not on the exoticism of multiculturalism or the *diversity* of cultures, but on the inscription and articulation of culture's *hybridity*. To that end we should remember that it is the 'inter'—the cutting edge of translation and negotiation, the *in-between* space—that carries the burden of the meaning of culture."[27] Bhabha, in other words, suggests that cultures are never bounded and singular entities.[28] In accord with much current cultural theory, with its focus on hybridity, and in accord with models of identity construction that are favored today, I will be offering here a revised model for understanding the historical relationship of the two "new" religions of late antiquity, Judaism and Christianity.

First of all, I suggest that the kinship metaphors need to be abandoned, for they imply, ipso facto, the kinds of organic entities and absolute separations that it is precisely the work of this text to displace, or at any rate, to call into question. Instead, I think that we might usefully substitute something like Wittgenstein's notion of family resemblance as a semantic, logical category. All Judaisms and all Christianities share features that make them a single semantic family in the Wittgensteinian sense. This logical category has its historical analogue, as well. Rather than parallel, but essentially separate histories, I propose a model of shared and crisscrossing lines of history and religious development.[29]

In order to make sense of how such developments could take place, we need to imagine the modes by which new religious ideas, practices, and discourses could be shared. I tend to think of Judaism and Christianity in late antiquity as points on a continuum. On one end were the Marcionites, the followers of the second-century Marcion, who believed that the Hebrew Bible had been written by an inferior God and had no standing for Christians and who completely denied the "Jewishness" of Christianity. On the other were the many Jews for whom Jesus meant nothing. In the middle, however, were many gradations that provided social and cultural mobility from one end of this spectrum to the other.

To use a linguistic metaphor, I am suggesting a wave theory of Christian-Jewish history. In one form of linguistic historiography, groups of languages are taken as descended from a common ancestry, a "protolanguage," from which they have diverged as their populations separated from each other. Similarities between the resulting languages are ascribed to their common ancestry. This is called the *Stammbaum*, or family-tree model, which we so often see in handbooks. According to this model, for example, all of the Romance languages are daughter languages of the vernacular spoken Latin of European late antiquity. Notice the kinship metaphor employed, similar to the kinship metaphors used until now for describing the relationship between Judaism and Christianity.[30] In the traditional *Stammbaum* model of Jewish-Christian history, only divergence is possible after 70 A.C., or in some versions, 135 A.C.[31] According to another model, however, the languages in a given group might very well have similarities that are the product of convergence, of new developments in one that have passed to the others, because the languages are still in contact with each other. This is called wave theory, on the assumption that an innovation takes place at a certain location and then spreads like a wave from that site to others, almost in the fashion of a stone thrown into a pond. In this model, convergence is as possible as divergence.

Separate languages, on this theory, are merely artifacts of the official canonization of a particular dialect as the official language of a given group. An example may be helpful. If one were to travel from Paris to Florence speaking only the local dialect in each town or village, one would not know when one had passed from France to Italy. There is no linguistic border "on the ground." The reason that we speak of French and Italian as separate languages is precisely because the dialect of Paris and the dialect of Florence have been canonized as the national languages. Similarly, I would suggest, social contact and the gradations of religious life were such that, barring the official pronouncements of the leaders of what were to become the "orthodox" versions of both religions, one could travel, metaphorically, from rabbinic Jew to Christian along a continuum where one hardly would know where one stopped and the other began.[32]

This model allows us to see Judeo-Christianity (not in its modern sense of a homogenized common culture) as a single circulatory system within which discursive elements could move from non-Christian Jews and back again, developing as they moved around the system. My perspective here is very close to that of Galit Hasan-Rokem, who writes:

> I base my discussion on a cultural model which a) prefers to look at interaction between cultures in terms of dialogue rather than 'influence' (often defined, . . . according to a unidirectional conceptualization) . . . b) deals with exchange rather than polemics (Lieberman's model) . . . c) instead of opposing canonical vs. noncanonical texts, looks at the constant dynamics between them as represented in the interaction between oral/literal, religious/secular. . . .
>
> The discursive model which has been the implicit or explicit basis for most discussions on intergroup relations in rabbinic literature, namely the one which conceptualizes intergroup relations as polemic, stems from a very elitist view of the formation of the texts, and does not reflect the full complexity, multivocality and dynamic points of view introduced in the folk narrative texts themselves.[33]

Following this model, there could be and would have been social contact, sometimes various forms of common worship, all up and down the continuum of "Jews" and "Christians." This social continuity provided for the possibility of cultural interaction and shared religious development. Thus, for instance, H. J. Drijvers has argued that "Christianity" in Edessa had virtually nothing to do with "Judaism" until the end of the third century, when connection with and influence of the Jewish "conversation" expanded dramatically.[34]

A further corollary to this revised model of Jewish and Christian history is that there might very well be a gap between the explicit claims of certain texts that groups are different and separate and the actual situation "on the ground," in which there was much less definition, much more fuzziness at the borders, and thus much more possibility of converging religious and cultural histories than otherwise would seem the case. Such gaps between people's perceptions or articulations of social relations and what can be observed are a commonplace of cognitive anthropology and would be even more expected in the highly charged situation of formative religious groups.[35] Indeed, as both Virginia Burrus and Dina Stein have emphasized to me, denials of sameness are precisely what we would expect in situations of difficult difference.

I am not suggesting, for instance, that there was no distinction at all between "Judaism" and "Christianity" by the second century, only that the border between the two was so fuzzy that one could hardly say precisely at what point one stopped and the other began.[36] "It is monstrous to talk of Jesus Christ and to practice Judaism," thunders Ignatius, thus making both points at once, the drive of the nascent orthodoxy to separation and the lack thereof "on the ground" [Magnesians 10:3].[37] The monster, it seems, was very lively indeed. It is important, moreover, to emphasize that in order to assume convergence as well as divergence, we hardly have to assume noncompetitive or irenic relations between subgroups.[38] As Israel Yuval has written of the intersecting developments of Passover and Easter liturgies: "Parallel development of two different narratives about the same Festival among two rival groups living in close proximity necessarily produces great similarity together with mutual tensions."[39]

All of these considerations raise serious terminological problems, because at the same time that I wish to deny the early existence of separate Judaism and Christianity, I am also speaking of the relationship between two entities that are, in some senses, recognizably different.[40] I shall accordingly try to be careful and not speak of "Judaism" and "Christianity" as single entities in what follows, but of *rabbinic* Judaism and *orthodox* Christianity, or sometimes, when contextually appropriate, of Christian Jews and non-Christian Jews (a reversal of the usual Jewish Christians and non-Jewish Christians) as the two formative entities, in the sense of the ones that were finally "successful" within this system.[41] Finally, in accord with the usage of the third-century Syriac text, the *Didascalia*, I shall (at least erratically) refer to "Judaism" and "Christianity," not as religions, but as "conversations," thus capturing, somewhat anachronistically to be sure, the sense of nondifferentiation that I wish to emphasize.[42]

I think that we need to take seriously the extent to which non-Christian Jews and Christians were themselves "in conversation" with each other at many sites throughout the Roman Empire, including notably in Palestine, Antioch, and Rome itself, for instance, but not only in those places, of course. More scholars are beginning to adopt the perspective articulated so well by Wayne A. Meeks and Robert L. Wilken: "For the understanding of early Christianity, it is necessary to study Judaism, not only as it existed in the so-called 'intertestamental period,' i.e., as 'background' to Christianity, but as a vital social and religious force during the early centuries of the

Common Era. Its presence as an independent religion alongside Christianity during this period helped to shape the context in which Christianity developed."[43] The same is true, of course, in the reverse direction. But I would go even a bit further. These religio-cultural histories were inextricably intertwined to the point where the very distinction between syncretism and "authentic" Judaism, Christianity, and "paganism" finally seem irrelevant.

There are some colorful examples of various types and various weights that support this hypothesis. W. H. C. Frend has noted that, according to a document preserved in Eusebius's church history, the famous martyrs of Lyons of 177 had been eating kosher meat, which they must have been purchasing at "a kosher market established for the Jews, and this in turn indicates fairly close personal relations between the Jews and Christians in the city."[44] Although in this case, we can hardly speak of shared observance, since the Lyonnais Christians were merely following apostolic rules preserved in Acts, nevertheless, if Frend is correct in his assumption that they purchased the meat from a "kosher" butcher, this observance brought them into intimate contact with Jews.

An example of quite a different type is the general observation of both Saturday and Sunday as holy days among fourth-century Eastern monastics.[45] According to Eusebius, this double observance is precisely the marker of the so-called Ebionite heresy: "They observed the sabbath and the other Jewish customs . . . yet, on the other hand, each Lord's day they celebrated rites similar to ours, in memory of the Saviour's resurrection."[46] In other words, in the very heartland of developing Eastern Orthodox Christian life, the monasteries and hermitages of Egypt and Palestine, something that Eusebius would regard as a "Judaizing heresy" and as belonging only to the past was central to the religious actuality.[47] It becomes much easier now to understand why there would be Christians who would attend synagogue services on the Sabbath and church on the Lord's Day. This puts a somewhat different cast on the problem of those who followed such "syncretistic" practices, one faced by both Origen and Chrysostom.[48] Jerome complains as well that the Christians imitate the liturgy of the Jews.[49] In the martyrology of Pionius (the presumedly mid-third-century Asian martyr), a text notoriously hostile to Jews, it likewise seems striking that it is emphasized that the day of the martyrdom is Saturday, and that "they had prayed and taken the sacred bread with water."[50] In spite of Eusebius, here was yet another "orthodox" Christian group who took the Eucharist on the "Jewish" Sabbath.[51] Polycarp's martyrdom, upon which so much of Pionius's is modeled, also takes place on a Saturday.

This brings us to the most important case of Christian-Jewish intimacy in late antiquity, the fact that many Christian groups, the Quartodecimani who observed Easter at Passover, were dependent, symbolically and practically, on Jews to establish the date of Easter.[52] After all of the scholarly discussion of the "Great Sabbath" upon which both Polycarp and Pionius were martyred, does it not seem possible that it is the very Sabbath that is called the "Great Sabbath" by the (latter-day) Jews that is meant, the Sabbath before Passover, which, according to the Quartodecimani, would be the Sabbath before Easter as well, and a most appropriately liturgical occasion for martyrdoms?[53] The only reason for rejecting this interpretation is that given the other indications of dating in the text, it would make Passover come out improbably early in that year.[54] However, if we do not assume that in every respect this was an actual report of the events but a highly stylized, theologized account, then the desire to associate the martyrdom of Polycarp with the Passover becomes compellingly plausible, particularly in the light of the evident associations between martyrdom, the sacrifice of Isaac, and the Passover in the text.[55] These associations are particularly powerful in those churches that continued the older practice and celebrated Easter on the 14th or 15th of Nissan, the day of the Jewish Pesaḥ, because for those churches, the Quartodecimani, the associations between the Crucifixion and the Passover sacrifice were apparently most powerful.[56] For these Christians, Easter or Pascha was simply the correct way to observe the Pesaḥ. The second-century Bishop Melito of Sardis's sermon *Peri Pascha* is perhaps the most compelling Asian example of this nexus.

This is not only of significance owing to the implied analogy between Easter and Passover that I have mentioned, but actually implies that these Christians were in some sense followers of the Jewish religious leadership, as well. We find the following astonishing text attributed to the apostles by the Quartodecimani: "As for you, do not make calculations. But when your brothers of the circumcision celebrate their Passover, celebrate yours also . . . *and even if they are wrong in their calculation, do not worry about it.*"[57] Polycrates, the leader of the Quartodeciman bishops, writes explicitly: "And my kinsmen always kept the day when the people [the Jews] put away the leaven."[58] Since the Jewish festival was movable with respect to the solar Christian year, this would implicate Christians in a kind of inter- action with the Jewish community with respect to the establishment of the date of Easter on a year-to-year basis.

This would, of course, especially be the case if these folks were among those apparently not so rare instances of Christians who attended both Jewish Sabbath worship and Sunday Christian worship. It wasn't until the Council of Nicaea in 325 that this question was settled in favor of the Ro- man (and Alexandrian) practice of setting Easter on the first Sunday after the solar month following the equinox. Not until then was Easter univer- sally perceived as other than a Christianized version of Pesaḥ.[59] At that point, the Quartodecimani became heretics, and like many heresies, theirs, too, was a form of "Judaizing," the description of a process that is almost emblematic for the ways that Christianity and Judaism were finally almost forcibly riven apart from each other.

Some of the most striking examples of Jewish-Christian interaction come from actually shared worship, admittedly rarely attested, but not the less significant for that.[60] In fifth-century Minorca, "Theodore and his rel- atives stood at the head of a community where Jews and Christians had learned to coexist, sharing, for instance, in the same haunting beauty of their chanted psalms."[61] At Mamre, the site of the Abrahamic epiphany, Jews, Christians, and pagans were carrying on a common religious festival, apparently also as late as the fifth century, according to the Palestinian church historian Sozomen, in which

> the inhabitants of the country and of the regions round Palestine, the Phoenicians and the Arabs, assemble annually during the summer season to keep a brilliant feast; and many others, both buyers and sellers, resort there on account of the fair. Indeed this feast is dili- gently frequented by all nations: by the Jews, because they boast of their descent from the patriarch Abraham; by the pagans, because angels there appeared to men; and by Christians because He who has lately revealed himself through the virgin for the salvation of mankind once appeared there to the pious man. . . . Some pray to the God of all; some call upon the angels, pour out wine, or burn incense, or offer an ox, or he-goat, a sheep or a cock . . . [and] all abstain from coming near their wives.[62]

This description presents a remarkable picture. Not only do the three religious groups that Sozomen describes gather together for a common fair, but they celebrate what is essentially the same feast together, a festival in honor of Abraham's angelic epiphany, each with a slightly different explanation for the feast and each with slightly different practices, including practices of one conversation that theoretically would be anathema to the others. We have no reason to suppose that such "regional cults" were common, but this description is certainly indicative, as late as the Sozomen in the fifth century, of social conditions within which religious interaction was possible between the so-called separated religions in Palestine.

In short, without the power of the orthodox Church and the Rabbis to declare people heretics and outside the system it remained impossible to declare phenomenologically who was a Jew and who was a Christian. At least as interesting and significant, it seems more and more clear that it is frequently impossible to tell a Jewish text from a Christian text.[63] The borders are fuzzy, and this has consequences.[64] Religious ideas and innovations can cross the borders in both directions.

These border crossings sometimes can take place where we least expect them. In her Hebrew work *The Web of Life*, Galit Hasan-Rokem has analyzed a fourth-century Palestinian midrash text that tells of the birth of the Messiah in Bethlehem.[65] Hasan-Rokem demonstrates that this story comes from a level that might be called, for want of a less anachronistic term, the folk literature of the Jews of Palestine, and has been adopted and canonized, as it were, in a high Rabbinic text. The choice of Bethlehem as the birthplace of the Messiah is based on the same midrash on the same verse (Micah 5:1) as the midrashim upon which Matthew and Luke based their birth narratives, and indeed, the stories are alike in many narratively significant details: the Messiah is revealed by a traveler, there are three wise men, there are gifts for the mother and the child, and the mother is destitute. In a brief English version of this discussion, Hasan-Rokem emphasizes: "The preservation of this legend both in the Talmud and the midrash attests to the fact that the consolidation of the gospel tradition did not result in an elimination of the legend from the Jewish folk literary corpus, as could have been expected. As far as I can see, the rabbinical inclusion of the tale does not direct itself to the polemical potential of the text. It may rather be interpreted as a folk literary dialogue, an oral intertextuality between two interpretative paradigms of the same plot,"[66] and thus: "[This collection] indicates that there is not necessarily a polemic or imitation here, but similarity of details which is typical of folk narration. It seems to me that this is a parade example of folk traditions that are common to Jews who belong to the majority of the people and to the minority who believe in the Messiahship of Jesus and join the early Christian Church, whose main social base is Jewish."[67]

However, Hasan-Rokem goes even further: "If, however, we prefer to explain the appearance of the legend in the Jewish corpus as ancillary to the gospel tradition rather than parallel to it, then the absence of polemical overtones leads us to a view . . . [that] some of the narrative and idiomatic alternatives developed by ecclesiastical Christianity into dogmas echo folk narrative elements extant in Jewish, both Rabbinical and early Christian, communities in Palestine and its vicinity in the first centuries of the Christian era. The midrash texts include them in their exploration of potential sources of consolation in a troubled era."[68] Hasan-Rokem's analysis suggests strongly that Jews and Christians were not just confronting each other, determined to shore up their identities as well as to triumph over the other. They also were listening to each other and learning, indeed, sharing traditions and even, frequently enough, a common fate.[69]

Living on Borderlines

In this extended essay, I shall be modeling my investigation of the murky and problematic differentiation between rabbinic Judaism and Christianity in late antiquity on some of the subtle research that has been done on the strikingly similar mestizo borderland between Christianity and so-called paganism, as well as on increasingly sophisticated investigations of the ways that Christian orthodoxy produced itself via the making of heresy and heretics.[70] Robert Markus has pithily put it: "The image of a society neatly divided into 'Christian' and 'pagan' is the creation of late fourth-century Christians, and has been too readily taken at face value by modern historians."[71] And Walter Bauer has argued in his study of orthodoxy and heresy: "Thus even into the third century, no separation between orthodoxy and heresy was accomplished in Egypt and the two types of Christianity were not yet at all clearly differentiated from each other."[72]

Similarly, I suggest, through the third century, for much of the eastern Mediterranean, neither was the separation accomplished between Judaic orthodoxy and its prime heresy, Christianity, and the two types of Judaism were not yet at all clearly differentiated from each other.[73] As Ruth Anne Clements has written: "The un-critical use of the terms 'Jewish' and 'Christian' may suggest a uniformity of faith and practice, as well as a self-aware distinction between two different sharply defined faith groups, which is anachronistic if applied to the first three centuries of the Common Era. For a growing number of historians of early 'Christianity,' this realization is leading to a historical-theological reconceptualization of many of the earliest Jesus-believing groups as Jewish in their own self-conception and religious practice."[74]

What is required here is a deconstruction, in the full technical sense of the word, of the opposition between Judaism and Christianity, a deconstruction in which the name "Jewish Christian" is pulled in from the marginal cold of "those who owe something to both religions and set up camp in the territory between the two," in Marcel Simon's words. It needs to be understood as the third term that unsettles the opposition between the "two religions."[75] The evidence that we have for the presence of Christians and other sectarians in the synagogue and the efforts of the Rabbis to detect them and prevent them from serving as precentors suggests that the problem of "Who is a Jew?" was as fraught for the Rabbis as the question of "Who is an orthodox?" was for the Christians. Jerome's important notice that the sect of Nazarenes are to be found "in all of the synagogues of the East among the Jews" and that they consider themselves both Christians and Jews, but are really "neither Christians nor Jews," is highly revealing.[76] Once again, we see that Christianity and Judaism could be kept apart and thus produced as separate religions, only by fiat, whether from Rabbis or Doctors of the Church.

There is no reason, a priori, for instance, why believing that Jesus was the Messiah would be considered as beyond the pale of rabbinic Judaism, any more than Rabbi Akiva's belief in Bar Kolchba as Messiah rendered him a heretic. Only the later success of Christianity determined, retroactively, that in its earlier relations with the Rabbis it was a separate religion. It took the historical processes of what we might call the long fourth century before the "parting of the ways" was achieved, and along that road, there was as much shared religious life and development as partition, as much consensus as dissensus. The religious histories intersect and intertwine.[77]

The set of changes that we refer to as the Christianization of the Empire, the formation of Christian orthodoxy, and other cultural changes entailed by it, made an enormous difference for emerging rabbinic Judaism as well, a difference that in many ways defined the shape of rabbinic Judaism for its entire future existence, just as much, perhaps, as Christianity was fashioned by its ongoing connection with Judaism. The fourth century seems particularly rich in the proliferation of technologies for the production of self and other: Christian orthodoxy versus its other, so-called heresy (including prominently the "Judaizing" heresies);[78] rabbinic Jewish orthodoxy versus its major (br)other, Christianity and Christian Judaism (its "twin"); and even the ongoing issue of the fuzzy separation between Christianity and so-called paganism.[79] Markus has written: "In the religious history of Europe, especially of Western Europe, the half century from 380 to about 430 marks a watershed. On the surface lie the great debates: the debates between pagans and Christians as well as those within the Christian group. In one way or another the debates of these decades all revolved around the question: what is it to be a Christian? What gave the question urgency was the rapid and far-reaching process of christianisation of Roman society which was reaching a climax at this time of dramatic change."[80] This question, for Christians, also had effects on non-Christians: "In so far as a particular section of Roman paganism acquired some sort of homogeneous identity—as did that of some groups of Roman aristocrats in the last decades of the fourth century—it was a response to the growing self-confidence and assertiveness of a Christian establishment."[81]

Not surprisingly, these developments had chain-reaction effects for Judaism as well.[82] It seems reasonable to surmise that it was not until the fourth century, when Christianity became the hegemonic religion of the Empire and Christian "orthodoxy" was set, that rabbinic Judaism solidified and emerged in its own orthodoxy and hegemony, as Judaism *tout court*. Clements has argued: "We may conjecture that by the latter half of the [third] century the Caesarean rabbis had assumed some functions which made them distinctive among their contemporaries, in direct response to the challenge presented by Origen in his role as biblical expositor and disputant. . . . Among Caesarean Jews, the debates helped to consolidate the authority of the rabbis as spokesmen for the larger Jewish community in the realm of religion as well as those of politics and economics."[83] And Tessa Rajak has suggested: "It is probably right to see the development of rabbinic Judaism, and perhaps also its beginnings, as in some way a response to the Christian challenge."[84] Of course, this hardly constitutes a claim on Rajak's part, nor on mine, that every aspect of rabbinic Judaism is a response to formative Christianity; indeed, I shall argue explicitly that the lines of influence and dialogue go in both directions.

The Plan of the Essay

This short book intends to be the beginning of a new investigation of the religious histories of rabbinic Jews and Christians in late antiquity.[85] It is to be read more as a series of hypotheses than as a series of conclusions. Some of these hypotheses already seem well-founded. Some will require much further investigation to test them.

I use two different strategies in order to support the "wave theory" of Christian-Jewish history. In the first three chapters, I employ close and thickly contextual reading of a single extended passage from the Babylonian Talmud, together with its Palestinian and Christian intertexts.[86] After introducing the first chapter with a Christian and then a rabbinic text that directly thematize the Jewish-Christian junction, I try to show how the Talmud text reveals the blurred boundaries between Judaism and Christianity at the very moment that it is trying to insist on the clarity of those boundaries. Much of the discussion in this chapter involves close contextualized reading of a story about a single rabbinic legendary figure, Rabbi Eliᶜezer.[87] This is a story of a martyrdom, or rather of a martyrdom cunningly evaded, and thus prefigures the theme that will be a leitmotif of this book. This story, which is found in different versions in various rabbinic texts from different centuries of the crucial era, also is one important touchstone for rabbinic interactions with Christianity.[88] In this chapter, I try to demonstrate the plausibility of the claim that Christianity held much more attraction for the Rabbis of the talmudic period than our canonical texts are prepared to "admit," and that there was much more contact, and even convergence, between the Rabbis and the Christians long after these contacts frequently are held to have ceased.

Rabbinic literature strikingly, stunningly, seems to ignore the presence and eventual world-shaping growth of Christianity, the Christianization of the Empire. This has been called "the most thunderous silence in Jewish history."[89] Here and there, however, there are texts that construct the reaction of the Rabbis to the enormous religious events that were taking place around them. In order to establish my discussion in the following chapters on martyrdom as a shared historical "invention" of rabbinic and Christian Judaism (which is not the same as Jewish Christianity, but rather an intentionally startling name for Christianity *simpliciter* as the "brother" of rabbinic Judaism, one of Rebecca's children), I focus in this chapter on a complex of stories about this central rabbinic figure, Rabbi Eliᶜezer ben Hyrcanus, otherwise known as Rabbi Eliᶜezer the Great, or just Rabbi Eliᶜezer. What interests me here is the function that the icon of Rabbi Eliᶜezer and this story about him plays in the figuring and negotiations of contact between Jewish Christians and rabbinic Jews in the third, fourth, and even later centuries.

I then continue, in the next two chapters, with an interpretation of the sequel to that passage in the Talmud, by which I hope to show that reading the talmudic text in the light of concurrent Christian writing illuminates it in various ways. This clarification via Christian context supports, I hope, my hypothesis that there was much more going on in the interaction between nascent Jewish and Christian orthodoxies than argument, dialogue, and debate between intellectuals—indeed, much more than confrontation.[90]

Since the entire passage that is read in the first three chapters hovers around the fraught question of martyrdom, in the fourth chapter, I shift gears somewhat, and enter a more directly historiographical mode. The major motif of this chapter is the entanglements of rabbinic Judaism and Christianity with the discourse of martyrdom and its role in helping them invent themselves as separate identities.[91] In this chapter, I test the model offered in the previous ones and show how it enables us to produce an account of the history of martyrology and its Christian and Jewish sources that is different from the ones that are current in the scholarly literature. This essay on martyrology constitutes, therefore, a case study and an experiment toward new ways of thinking about religious histories in late antiquity.

Galit Hasan-Rokem has written of Jewish martyrologies in midrashic texts from the talmudic period: "The intertextual connections that are expressed in these stories do not remain enclosed within the inner-Jewish, Hebrew, and rabbinic borders. In these stories are revealed also the connections with universes of discourse with which rabbinic literature carries out ambivalent, tense and even openly polemic relations."[92] Martyrdom, even more than tragedy, is *Thanatoi en tōi phanarōi*, "deaths that are seen," murders in public spaces.[93] Insofar as martyrdom is, then, by definition, a practice that takes place within the public and, therefore, shared space, *martyria* seem to be a particularly fertile site for the exploration of the permeability of the borders between so-called Judaism and so-called Christianity in late antiquity. Accordingly, I have started there.[94]

CHAPTER I

The Close Call

Or, Could a Pharisee Be a Christian?

A sixth-century Syriac source, the life of the Saint Mar Abba, tells of a Christian who, on his own account, was a crypto-Jew. Mar Abba, originally a fanatical "pagan," upon observing a certain "disciple" embarking on a boat with him to cross the Tigris, decides on the basis of the disciple's "habit"[1] that the disciple is a "son of the Covenant," a usual Syriac term for a Christian. He accordingly beats the disciple and throws him out of the boat. While they are crossing the river, the river becomes stormy, and the boat is threatened with sinking. They return to shore. Twice more the disciple enters the boat; twice more he is thrown out; twice more the boat is in a parlous state. At this point, our potential saint begins to see the light. He expresses himself, however, somewhat strangely. The pagan, examining the disciple's habit and noticing that it is poor and strange, begins to suspect that perhaps the disciple is not "a son of the Covenant of the Messiah" after all:

> But perhaps he is a Marcionite or a Jew.
> And he asked and said to him: "Are you a Jew?"
> He said to him: "Yes."
> He said to him: "Are you a Christian?"
> He said to him: "Yes."
> He said to him: "Do you worship the Messiah?"
> He said to him: "Yes."

It follows, accordingly, that there were three separate religious groups in the area, Jews, "Christians" (the Greek term), and "Messiah-worshipers" or "Sons of the Covenant of the Messiah" (the Syriac terms), and it would seem that it is only someone in the third category that he wishes to throw from the boat. The disciple claims, however, to belong to all three. At this point, our future saint begins to be understandably quite enraged at the disciple and asks: "How can you be a Jew, a Christian, and a worshiper of the Messiah?" he asks, for he "uses the name 'Christian' for Marcionites, in accordance with the custom there," as the narrator informs us. The disciple then provides the following key to his seeming riddle or evasive answer:

> I am a Jew secretly [cf. Rom. 2.29]; I pray to the living God, and I am faithful to his son Jesusmessiah [sic] and the Holy Spirit. And I run away from idol worship and all filth.[2] I am a Christian truly, not like the Marcionites, who defraud and call themselves Christians. For Christian is a Greek word. And the interpretation of "Christian" in Syriac is Messianite. And [therefore] with respect to that which you have asked me: "Do you worship the Messiah?," I worship him truly.[3]

We have no reason to doubt the sincerity of this speaker. He was a Jew and a Christian at the same time.[4] His interlocutor thought this could not be so, because for him, as the narrator insists, "Christian" (the Greek word) meant "Marcionite," those Christians who rejected the name "Israel" completely.[5] This "orthodox" follower of Paul, however, knows that he can be both a Christian and a Jew, for the apostle to the Gentiles has already declared that one who is a Jew ἐν τῷ κρυπτῷ is the true Jew. Indeed, it is the very essence of his claim to be a true Christian and not a fraudulent one that he be both a Jew and a Christian.

Christianity as a Jewish Heresy in Late Antiquity

We see, then, that in the Osrehoene at least, "Christianity" and "Judaism" were not yet separate religions as late as the sixth century.[6] They were still, as for all in the first century, two versions—one "right" and one "wrong," of course—of the same religion, two "conversations," much as they were for the third-century *Didascalia* of roughly the same provenance. "Partings of the ways" have clearly taken place at different paces in different places.

Interestingly enough, the same self-perception seems to hold from the rabbinic side, as well, also in the sixth century or so and also from the Mesopotamian *Kulturgebiet*. In quite a late document, the Babylonian Talmud recollects the following legend of the founding of Christianity:[7]

> When Yannai the king was killing the Rabbis, Yehoshua the son of Peraḥya and Jesus went to Alexandria of Egypt.[8] When there was peace, Shimᶜon ben Shetaḥ sent to him:
>
> "From Jerusalem, the Holy City to Alexandria in Egypt: My sister, my husband is dwelling in you and I am sitting bereft." [Yehoshua] got up and left [taking Jesus with him], and came to a certain inn, where they honored him greatly.
>
> [Yehoshua] said: How beautiful this inn is.

A tragic misunderstanding is about to occur, because the word for "inn," אכסניא can also mean "hostess."

> [Jesus] said: Rabbi, her eyes are bleary.[9]
> [Yehoshua] said: Wicked one. That's what you are busy with?! He brought out four hundred shofars and excommunicated him.

The misunderstanding of the student is followed by the intransigence of the teacher.

> [Jesus] came before him several times and said: Accept me! He didn't pay attention to him.

The teacher now attempts to repair the ill, but it is too late, and another tragic misunderstanding with world-historical consequences ensues:

> One day, [Yehoshua] was in the middle of saying the *Shemaᶜ Yisraʾel*, and [Jesus] came before him. [Yehoshua] wished to receive him, and made a sign with his hands [because he could not interrupt his prayer].
>
> [Jesus] thought that he was rejecting him. He went and erected a tile [or brick: לבינתא] and bowed to it.[10]
>
> [Yehoshua] said to him: Repent!
>
> [Jesus] said to him: This is what I have learnt from you. Anyone who sins and causes others to sin, is not enabled to repent.
>
> And our master has taught: Jesus performed magic, and misled, and corrupted Israel.[11]   Babylonian Talmud Sanhedrin 107b mss,
> censored from printed editions[12]

Scholars who have interpreted this text have read it as either an irenic, somewhat indulgent response to Christianity and to Jesus or as a form of mockery of them. I believe that we can learn something else from it.

One could fairly say, paraphrasing Robert A. Markus, that much of the work of self-definition of Christianity in its first several centuries consists precisely of defining what it is to be a Christian as opposed to what it is to be a Jew. However, it is nearly as true, I would suggest, in the other direction. The social and cultural processes by which Christian orthodoxy constituted itself as such over against the so-called heresies, including so-called Jewish Christianity and perhaps rabbinic Judaism itself, are structurally very similar to the processes through which Jewish orthodoxy (rabbinic Judaism) constituted itself and its authority vis-à-vis other forms of late antique Judaism, in part by defining itself over against early Christianity. This suggests that the Rabbis were reading Christianity as a form of Jewish heresy, and thus as part of Judaism, until well into late antiquity.

In *Orthodoxy and Heresy in Earliest Christianity*, Walter Bauer depicts the stake that Christian "orthodoxy" had in portraying itself as original and the so-called heresies as deviations from the norm.[13] Frequently, it seems, this ideological conviction was presented in the form of biographical legends regarding the fathers of heresies:

> Where there is heresy, orthodoxy must have preceded. For example, Origen puts it like this: "All heretics at first are believers; then later they swerve from the rule of faith."[14] This view is so deeply rooted, and so widely held, that it applies even to such personalities as Mani, who is supposed to have been a presbyter of the church and a valiant warrior against both Jews and pagans, but then left the church because he took it as a personal offense that his students received such scanty recognition. In general, it is an opinion of orthodoxy that only impure motives drive the heretic from the church—indeed, this must be so if the evil-one is at the bottom of it all. . . . Historical thinking . . . recognizes there the same embarrassed, and thus artificial claim, that emanated from Jewish Christianity when it asserted that Paul had sued for the hand of the high priest's daughter and, when it was denied him, began to rage against Torah (Epiphanius *Her.* 30.16).[15]

Bauer reminds us that precisely the same story circulated with respect to Valentinus as well: he became a Gnostic heretic because he had lost an election for the episcopate.[16] As in the stories told by Syrian Christians of the origins of their favorite heresy, Manichaeism, and the stories told by Jewish Christians of the origins *their* favorite heresy, Paulinism, we see here the Talmud presenting in exactly analogous fashion the origins of rabbinic Judaism's bête noire par excellence, Christianity.[17] Jesus was at first a perfectly orthodox rabbinic Jew, and only because of the intransigence of an overly strict teacher and then a tragic misunderstanding did he found the great heresy of Christianity.[18]

Although variations of such stories of the origins of heretical movements can be found outside of the Judeo-Christian orbit as well, this specific tale type of the "stern master and his wayward disciple," in Stephen Gero's formulation, seems more particularly a very specific version of this kind of story, one significantly common to Jews and Christians. In two Christian versions of this story, the disciple notices something about the eyes of a pretty young woman whom the company meet and is sharply rebuked for his own "roving eye."[19] As Gero remarks, "this material provides an unambiguous and interesting instance of the interconnection between biographical narrative in rabbinical sources and in Christian hagiography, the study of which, as the author of a recent updating of a classical survey rightly points out, is potentially important for gaining a more informed understanding of the nature and function of Jewish literature of late antiquity."[20]

The irony of a shared story being the occasion for the narrative insistence on difference will become more and more of a commonplace as we proceed. More to my point, however, the fact that the Talmud, in what seems clearly to be a very late tradition, still reports on the founding and the founder of Christianity in this particular thematological vein connotes that in their eyes, Christianity was still being seen structurally as a Jewish heresy, indeed as a deviant Judaism, just as in the narrative of Mar Saba, Christianity is seen as only a true form of Judaism.[21] Close reading of some rabbinic texts will suggest that a couple of centuries earlier, the boundaries on the ground were drawn even less firmly, for all the desire of the "official" text to obscure this ambiguity.

When Rabbi Eliᶜezer was Arrested by Christianity

A third-century Palestinian text tells the shocking story of a Pharisee who was arrested during the Trajanic persecutions of Christianity:

It happened to Rabbi Eli‘ezer that he was arrested for sectarianism (Christianity),[22] and they took him up to the βημα[23] to be judged.

The ruler said to him: A sage such as you having truck with these matters!?[24]

He said to him: I have trust in the judge.

The ruler thought that he was speaking of him, but he meant his Father in Heaven.[25] He said to him: Since you trust me, I also have said: Is it possible that these gray hairs would err in such matters? *Dimus* [= *Dimissus*]! Behold, you are dismissed.

In order to avoid being martyred as a Christian, Rabbi Eli‘ezer exploits an ambiguity of language. He answers the charge of Christianity, implicitly a charge of disloyalty to the Empire, by indicating his fealty to the Roman *hegemon*. The Rabbi, however, nevertheless is quite distressed. He understands that he would not have been arrested at all were it not for some sin that he had committed, and he cannot rest until he discovers that sin, for indeed, he does have trust in the Judge of the World that he does not do injustice:

When he had left the βημα, he was troubled that he had been arrested for sectarianism. His disciples came in to comfort him, but he was inconsolable. Rabbi Akiva came in and said to him: Rabbi, I will say before you a word; perhaps you will not be troubled.

He said to him: Say!

He said to him: Perhaps one of the sectarians said something to you of sectarianism, and it caused you pleasure.

He said to him: By heaven, you have reminded me. Once I was walking in the marketplace of Tsippori, and I found there Ya‘akov, the man of Kefar Sikhnin,[26] and he recounted a saying of sectarianism in the name of Yeshu‘ the son of Pantiri,[27] and it caused me pleasure, and I was arrested by/for the words of sectarianism, for I violated that which is written in the Torah, "Keep her ways far away from you, and don't come near the opening of her house, for she has brought many victims down!" [Proverbs 5:8].   Tosefta Ḥullin, 2:24[28]

This story beautifully illustrates the hypothesis of simultaneous rabbinic attraction to and repulsion from Christianity. We find here a narrative that, like the letter of Jerome I cited at end of the Introduction, is very anxious to exclude anything Christian from the realm of proper rabbinic Jewish proximity: "Keep her ways far away from you." In this very same narrative,

however, the attractiveness of Christianity to even a centrally located rabbinical hero, Rabbi Eli^cezer, is brought to the fore, and perhaps even more
than this, as we presently shall see.[29]

There is an important interpretative question with respect to this text
that needs to be addressed, namely, why did R. Eli^cezer not simply deny his
Christianity? Why the evasiveness? An accused Christian had to perform
two acts in order to prove his or her "innocence." The first was to sacrifice
to the emperor, and the second was to curse Jesus. We have an excellent
contemporary description of this practice from Pliny the Younger's famous
letter to Trajan:

> Those who denied that they were, or had ever been, Christians, who
> repeated after me an invocation to the Gods, and offered adoration,
> with wine and frankincense, to your image, which I had ordered to
> be brought for that purpose, together with those of the Gods, and
> who finally cursed Christ—none of which acts, it is said, those who
> are really Christians can be forced into performing—these I thought
> it proper to discharge.[30]

Although to be sure, we cannot assume the uniformity and systematization
of the judicial process, this text is certainly evocative of the possibilities
that were available for proof of non-Christianity.[31] The Martyrdom of
Polycarp provides further evidence that this was not, at any rate, a mere
fluke, because the proconsul offers the aged bishop the option: "Take the
oath and I will let you go; revile Christ [λοιδορησον τον Χριστον]."[32]

Although a Jew could not prove his non-Christian leanings by sacrificing to the emperor, he could curse Jesus.[33] Why, then, did not Rabbi Eli^cezer
simply say: "Christianus non sum. Iudaeus sum"? My teacher, Professor
Saul Lieberman, of blessed memory, raised this problem and offered what I,
with due modesty, take as an intentionally tricky answer itself: that Rabbi
Eli^cezer feared further questioning on the "intimate internal affairs of the
rabbinic academies."[34] I wish to suggest in all diffidence and respect that the
very implausibility of the explanation offered by Lieberman is intended to
lead us to a warranted, if highly unsettling, answer: that the text is hinting
that Rabbi Eli^cezer did not *want* to curse Jesus.[35] Rabbi Eli^cezer, the text implies, had more than some sympathy for Jesus and his followers and their
Torah, an implication that is supported as well, of course, by the Rabbi's
irenic Torah conversation with this Ya^ckov/James.[36]

There is a double meaning, a bit of trickster language or indirection in this text that is not directed at the *hegemon*, but at the readers of the text. The phrase that I have translated as "arrested for sectarianism" could just as easily be translated from the Hebrew as "arrested by sectarianism," that is, captured intellectually or spiritually by Christianity.[37] The tradition itself remembers that Rabbi Eliʿezer himself was declared a heretic by the Rabbis for a period of his life. If indeed, there is a sort of repressed motive here of this central rabbinic figure's attraction to Christianity, then the point that I am making against drawing strict lines between the histories of what only *much* later became defined as separate religions is considerably strengthened. In inscribing Rabbi Eliʿezer—one of the most canonical and central of rabbinic culture heroes—in a fictive plot situation that would lead him to extreme marginality and then, in the end, recuperating him, the biographical narrative is inscribing, I suggest, the under-construction, the being-invented nature of the divide between Christians and Rabbis in the third century.[38]

In a very important discussion of the Pseudo-Clementines, Albert Baumgarten has shown from the Christian side, evidence of attachments of at least some Galilean Jewish-Christians (in the strict sense, i.e., Christians who were apparently ethnically Jews) precisely to the Pharisees and their disdain for the Sadducees, because only the Pharisees properly observe the Law. As he writes: "The Pseudo-Clementines therefore do not only think well of the Pharisees in this case, but they reflect a Pharisaic point of view on a particularly sensitive issue," and "describe the Sadducees as the real heretics deserving denunciation" because they did not acknowledge the resurrection of the dead. The denunciation is identical in its terms with similar rabbinic denunciations of the Sadducees, as Baumgarten notes. The text acknowledges the Gospel condemnation of Pharisees as hypocrites, but only to argue that is true of only some Pharisees, no more or less than the Talmud itself would do.

Altogether, the picture of a Christian group with strong Pharisaic allegiances is ineluctable. Baumgarten establishes that when the Pseudo-Clementines argue that were it not for the *kanon*, the Jews would not know how to properly interpret the self-contradictory Bible, the word *kanon* refers to the rabbinic hermeneutical rules. He then concludes that the third-century "Pseudo-Clementine texts exhibit detailed and specific knowledge of rabbinic Judaism. Their awareness is not of commonplaces or of vague generalities which might be based on a shared biblical heritage, but of information uniquely characteristic of the rabbinic world. There can be no doubt that we are dealing with two groups in close proximity that maintained intellectual contact with each other. The authors of the Pseudo-Clementines quite obviously admired rabbinic Jews and their leaders."[39] So, in the third century there were such contacts and such groups.[40] Could our Rabbi Eliᶜezer be a figure for such a group, a group that threatened the neat binary opposition of the world into Jews and Christians? Could the "Gamaliel" of the Pseudo-Clementines, "the head of the people (who was secretly our brother in faith)," be a figure "from the other side" for such groups, as well?[41] Could there have been Christian Rabbis, or Pharisaic Christians among the rabbinic party? How might the rabbinic text provide answers to such questions?[42]

I am obviously not making any claim whatever that this text teaches us anything about the "real" Rabbi Eliᶜezer and any truck that he may or may not have had with sectarianism, magic, or heresy. Instead, I am claiming that we ought to read this text as a historian would read fiction. Keith Hopkins has written, "Serious historians of the ancient world have often undervalued fiction, if only . . . because by convention history is concerned principally with the recovery of truth about the past. But for social history—for the history of culture, for the history of people's understanding of their own society—fiction occupies a privileged position."[43] The method of analysis employed here is close reading of fictional or legendary narrative texts, that is, essentially classical talmudic methodology.

In an earlier version of talmudic studies, one that we might, for want of a better term, call traditional Yeshiva study, such close reading was normative, without being made to do any historical work at all. Rashi (tenth century) or his grandson Rabbenu Tam and myriad others until perhaps the middle of the nineteenth century, when the Jewish early-modern period begins, simply wanted to understand the logic of the talmudic text to the best of their ability, whether it was a legal (halakhic) or a narrative (aggadic) text. "Wie es eigentlich gewesen ist" was simply not a question. Talmudic history, at any rate, simply had not been invented yet. Their methods of questioning and answering questions about the text were substantially the same as those exhibited here. Or, perhaps, better formulated, it would read:

their questions about the text were similar to mine. Their answers might be and frequently would have been very different, in part because they were not motivated by any questions "outside the text." In a sense, they might be comparable to the New Critics of American literary culture, also religious conservatives.

At a later stage in talmudic study—shall we call it the beginnings of *Wissenschaft des Judentums?*—texts such as the ones that I am reading in this essay were simply ignored. Since they were obviously "legendary," or even, "folkloristic," they had "no value" for the reconstruction of events that was the goal of such history writing as that of scholars from Graetz to Urbach. At best, occasionally, such narratives were understood to contain somewhere a "kernel of truth" that could be extracted by very carefully breaking the shell, and by discarding most of the meat, as well. In any case, one did not ask the sort of questions about logical consistency that a Rashi would have asked, or the Talmud itself would have asked, or that I ask above, for instance: "Why didn't Rabbi Eliᶜezer say this and not that?" Since it was understood at best and at least that the likelihood that the "real" Rabbi Eliᶜezer had said anything of the sort at all was virtually nonexistent, there just didn't seem to be any point.

Now we have new methodologies. Rabbi Eliᶜezer no longer is a historical character in the first century, but a "fictional" character in the third century. I return to the methods of questioning the text employed by the traditional learning to ask questions about coherence, internal and external, and draw historical conclusions, not about events but about ideologies, social movements, cultural constructions, and particularly repressions— about the work of the text. Rabbi Eliᶜezer's close call can be uncovered, if indeed it is uncovered and not invented, only by close reading.

Much of the source material analyzed in this and the following chapters consists of what are technically called "legends of the Sages" in the literary-critical and folkloristic work on rabbinic literature. These represent scattered, frequently disjointed, and often contradictory episodic narratives with one or another of the Rabbis (or sometimes other figures in their world) depicted in a single incident. We have no extended biographies or hagiographies in any of the classical rabbinic texts (virtually the only Jewish texts we have between the second and the sixth centuries A.C.).[44]

A naive positivism once regarded these scattered narratives as the elements for a quest for the historical Rabbis. Thus, for instance, in one of the best efforts in that genre, Louis Finkelstein produced a book-length biography of Rabbi Akiva, who will figure centrally in this essay, as well.[45] Such positivism is no longer accepted in the scholarly literature, by and large. The work of scholars from Jacob Neusner to Jonah Fränkel has discredited it.[46] Nevertheless, I believe that one can derive meaning by studying together the stories about a particular Rabbi or other figure because these named characters are themselves a kind of sign or emblem, almost embodied complexes of particular ideas or possibilities for thought (sometimes even impossibilities for thought) within the religious world of the Rabbis and the communities within which they were embedded. So stories about Rabbis Eliᶜezer and Akiva will figure in this book, as well as stories about the marginal figure Papos ben Yehuda.

I am suggesting that through the medium of the legend, the Rabbis are teaching us something of the complexities of their world and their worldview, as they do so often. They are, we might say, both recognizing and denying at one and the same time that Christians are us, marking out the virtual identity between themselves and the Christians in their world at the same time that they are very actively seeking to establish difference.[47] Rabbi Eliᶜezer is thus the character who in his person thematizes the tension between the most "orthodox" space of Rabbinism and the most "sectarian" space of Christianity.[48] He is the very figure of liminality. His story is a representation of the complexities of the relationship between rabbinic Judaism and Christianity in the era leading up to the fourth century.

As Professor Lieberman already pointed out in his unpublished lectures, one can conjecture a strong connection between this story and the well-known talmudic story of the excommunication of Rabbi Eliᶜezer.[49] According to the version of the story that is preserved in the Babylonian Talmud, Rabbi Eliᶜezer refused to accept the will of the majority of the Sages in a halakhic matter and was cursed and sentenced to complete isolation and removal from the rabbinic and even the Jewish community for this relatively minor—if not insignificant—malfeasance.[50] I wish to suggest that rather than the point of halakhic disagreement, in the view of that Talmud at least, it was precisely the manner of Rabbi Eliᶜezer's support for his position, via quasi-prophetic or magical means, that so enraged the Rabbis:[51]

On that day, Rabbi Eliᶜezer used every imaginable argument, but they did not accept it from him. He said: If the law is as I say, this carob will prove it. The carob was uprooted from its place one hundred feet. Some report four hundred feet. . . . A voice came from heaven and announced: The law is in accordance with the view of Rabbi Eliᶜezer. Rabbi Yehoshuaᶜ stood on his feet and said "it [the Torah] is not in heaven."   Baba Metsiᶜa 59a

On a given halakhic question (the question of the purity or impurity of a certain kind of ceramic stove), Rabbi Eliᶜezer initially tried to support his position using the "normal" rabbinic modes of rational argument, the very modes of argument [תשובות] that might be said to define rabbinic rationality. When that failed, however, he didn't accept defeat, but rather turned to another source of authority entirely, miracles and heavenly oracles. According to the Talmud's version of this story, the one that I am quoting here, Rabbi Eliᶜezer was then punished by an extremely harsh version of excommunication, a highly unusual practice in cases of halakhic disagreement: "On that day, all the objects that Rabbi Eliᶜezer had declared clean were brought and burned in fire. Then they took a vote and excommunicated him."

Lieberman suggested that the singular severity with which Rabbi Eliᶜezer was treated was a product of the Rabbis' suspicion that he was intimate with the Christian sectarians, as intimated very clearly and almost openly in the Toseftan story treated here.[52] Alexander Guttmann has argued that it was Rabbi Eliᶜezer's use of magic and prophetic means to argue his halakhic case that so provoked the Rabbis.[53] Through his usage of appeals to forms of authority and authorization that were not rabbinic, Rabbi Eliᶜezer was demonstrating, according to the tellers of this story, that he was "infected" with sectarianism, the most salient case of which was, for them, Christianity.[54] As Guttmann writes, "The employment of miracles, among them the *Bat Ḳol* [voice from heaven], becomes more weighty if we realize that this was done by a personality who appeared to be friendly toward Christianity and its leaders, as was R. Eliezer. . . . Suspicion of Christian leanings combined with the employment of a device which, at this time, was fundamental and successful for Christianity, might have worked almost automatically against R. Eliezer as circumstantial evidence of his pro-Christian sympathies. In this connection likewise, the fact has to be remembered that R. Joshua, leader of the victorious opposition against R. Eliezer, was an outstanding polemicist against Christian influence."[55] My only corrective to Guttmann's formulation would be to translate it from a set of positivist statements about the historical Rabbis Eli'ezer and Yehoshua into a set of considerations of the place of Christians and Christianity in the rabbinic world as represented through these figures as characters.[56] Guttmann's point is particularly cogent when we remember from the above story of the founding of Christianity that in the eyes of the Rabbis of the Talmud, one of the main stereotypes of Christianity was that it was a species of magical practice.[57] The representation of Rabbi Eli'ezer's appeal to magic and prophecy might very well, then, have been precisely the way that the text thinks about the complicated nexus between the rabbinic and Christian forms of Judaism.

That this was the way that rabbinic texts "read" this story can be further supported via another story about Rabbis and their relations with Christians, indeed apparently with the very same Christian who encountered Rabbi Eli'ezer.[58] In the Tosefta Ḥullin, immediately preceding the story of Rabbi Eli'ezer's arrest, we find the following account:

> It happened to Rabbi El'azar Ben Dama that a snake bit him. And Ya'akov the man of Kefar Sama[59] came to cure him in the name of Jesus the son of Panthera, and Rabbi Ishma'el refused to allow him. They said to him: You are not permitted Ben Dama.
>
> He said to him: I will bring a verse from the Torah that proves that this is permitted, but he did not suffice to cite his proof, until he died.
>
> Rabbi Ishma'el said: *Blessed art thou, Ben Dama, for you* left in peace, and you did not violate the fence of your colleagues, for anyone who breaks down the fence of the Sages, terrible things happen to him, as it says, "One who breaks down a fence, let a snake bite him" (Ecclesiastes 10:8).[60]

In this story, we have another instance of a tale about very close contact indeed between the early Rabbis and the same (fictional) apostle of Jesus whom we have already met in the Tosefta above. There, he offered to Rabbi Eli'ezer some pleasant and profitable words of Torah. Here, he offers healing in the name of Jesus, his teacher.[61] The patient dies, however, before the sectarian cure can be effected, and the uncle of the deceased exalts him, saying that he is blessed in that he died before he would have been able to break down the fence, that is, transgress the boundary of rabbinic authority.[62] Receiving the cure of a Christian in the name of Jesus is, accordingly, an offense similar to that of Rabbi Eliᶜezer's receiving Jesus's Torah. In neither case is it the question that the Torah is itself false or wrong, or mutatis mutandis that the cure is ineffective, but since both come from the mouths of sectarians, they must be avoided like a snake bite.[63]

An inconsistency in the story, however, noticed by earlier commentators but not resolved by them, suggests another moment of interpretation here, for according to the cited verse, the snake bite is a punishment for the transgression that Ben Dama had not made—yet—but was only considering making because of the very snake bite that he had suffered. The snake had bitten Ben Dama even before he contemplated making use of the Jesus doctor. Indeed, had he not been bitten, he would not have thought of doing so. So the punishment has come before the crime. As a late gloss in the Palestinian Talmud wonders, "But wasn't he already bitten by a snake?! Rather it means that he won't be bitten by a snake in the next world."

The clumsiness of the answer discloses the validity of the conundrum. I think that once more, by indirection, hint, and insinuation, the story is indicating that this Ben Dama, otherwise a kosher rabbinical Jew, just like Rabbi Eliᶜezer, had been an intimate of the Christians, explaining, by the way, why this Yaᶜkov/James showed up so quickly to cure him. This also explains why Ben Dama is already primed and ready with a halakhic justification for the appropriateness of cures in the name of Jesus. The story is also indicating the work of strict separation that was taking place at the explicit ideological level of the rabbinic text. Rabbi Ishmaᶜel, after all, would rather see him die than be saved by "Christian" magic.

The story thus provides a remarkable parallel to the story of Rabbi Eliᶜezer—indicating the same tensions between manifest and suppressed elements within the narrative—and, in fact, in both early Palestinian sources for this narrative tradition, the Tosefta and the midrash Qohelet Rabbah, we find the two stories, Rabbi Eliᶜezer's near martyrdom and Ben Dama's near cure, together as doublets of each other.

Even though the two stories are not placed together syntagmatically in the Babylonian Talmud, we will find a startling verbal similarity, a sort of rhyming, that suggests that they are doublets there, as well. First, we need to see the version of the Ben Dama story that appears in the Talmud:

> It happened to Ben Dama, the son of the sister of Rabbi Ishmaᶜel that a snake bit him. And Yaᶜakov the man of Kefar Sekhania (= Sikhnin) came to cure him, and Rabbi Ishmaᶜel refused to allow him.
>
> He said to him: Rabbi Ishmaᶜel my brother, let me be cured by him, and I will bring a verse from the Torah that proves that this is permitted, but he did not suffice to finish the matter until his soul left him and he died.
>
> Rabbi Ishmaᶜel cried out over him: *Blessed art thou, Ben Dama, for your body is pure and your soul left you in purity,* and you did not violate the words of your colleagues, who would say, "One who breaks down a fence, let a snake bite him" (Ecclesiastes 10:8).
> Avoda Zara 27b

Now let us look at the end of Rabbi Eliᶜezer's life-story as the Babylonian Talmud relates it:

> It is taught: When Rabbi Eliᶜezer was sick, Rabbi Akiva and his colleagues went in to visit him. He was sitting in his canopied bed, and they were sitting in his anteroom. That day was the eve of the Sabbath, and his son Horkanos went in to take off his [father's] phylacteries. He rebuked him and [the son] went out with a scolding. He said to the colleagues: I believe that Father is out of his mind.

According to rabbinic law, the phylacteries are not worn on the Sabbath. The son wishes to remove the father's phylacteries in order that he should not be in violation, but the father rebukes him. The son concludes that his father is either in a highly irrational state of mind or perhaps that he is following some sectarian practice. "Out of one's mind" is used as a technical term for sectarianism or for *superstitio,* which does not mean a foolish belief to be laughed at, but "everything which opposed the true Roman *religio* such as the activities of astrologers and fortune-tellers."[64]

> [Rabbi Eliᶜezer] said to them: He and his mother are out of their minds. How shall I leave that which is liable for stoning and take care of that which is only a minor commandment?!

Eliᶜezer is apparently exercised that the boy and the mother are not attending properly to their own preparations for the Sabbath while worrying about his apparent "sectarian" practice.[65] Although the aggression toward his wife, the famous Imma Shalom, seems totally gratuitous here, the Rabbi offers a rational, that is, rabbinic explanation for his behavior.[66] He was engaged in preparing for the more stringent aspects of Sabbath observance—and they ought to have been, too—and didn't want to be bothered with the relatively minor stricture to remove his phylacteries. Although by leaving his phylacteries in place he is violating a rabbinic injunction and therefore seemingly still transgressing the boundary, he explains that that is not his intention at all. He simply is angry that his wife and son are concerned with his transgression of a mere rabbinic commandment while they are putting themselves in danger thereby of lighting candles or cooking on the Sabbath, which are much more serious violations. He is neither insane nor insensible of the nuances and details of rabbinic halakha:

> When the sages saw that his mind was clear, they went and sat down four cubits from him.
>
> He said to them: Why have you come?
>
> They said to him: To learn Torah we have come.
>
> He said to them: And until now, why have you not come?
>
> They said: We didn't have time.
>
> He said to them: I will be amazed if they will die a natural death.
>
> Rabbi Akiva then said to him: What about me?
>
> He said: Yours is more severe than all of them.
>
> He took his two arms and placed them on his heart and said: Aiih to these two arms that are like two Scrolls of the Torah rolled up. I have learned much Torah, and I have taught much Torah. I have learned much Torah and I didn't lose from the teaching of my masters even as much as a dog licks from the sea. I have taught much Torah, and my disciples have not lost from my teaching so much as the brush in its case.[67]
>
> And not only that but I teach three hundred laws in the matter of leprosy, and no one ever asked me a question about them, and in the planting of cucumbers, and no one ever asked me about them, except for Akiva ben Yosef. Once he and I were walking on the way. He said to me: Teach me their planting. I said a word and the field was all full of cucumbers. He said to me: Rabbi, you have taught me their planting; now teach me their uprooting. I said another word, and they were all gathered into one place.
>
> The [sages then] said to him: A ball, a slipper, and a cameo that are [made of leather and filled with wool]. He said to them: They are pure.

And his soul left him in purity.

Rabbi Yehoshua stood on his feet and said: The vow is released. The vow is released!

On the going out of the Sabbath, he met Rabbi Akiva on the way [in the funeral procession] from Caesarea to Lydda. He was flagellating his flesh until the blood flowed to the ground.

He opened his eulogy and said: My father, my father, the chariot of Israel and its horsemen (II Kings 2:12).[68] I have many coins and no banker to change them.   TB Sanhedrin 68a

Among its other meanings, this story certainly thematizes the conflicted and conflictual aspect of the representation of Rabbi Eliᶜezer himself. He is a kind of holy man, almost a magic worker, of a type for which rabbinic religiosity harbors a certain constant suspicion.[69] Yet he is the very type of an "orthodox" Pharisee and halakhic authority par excellence. Indeed, even Rabbi Eliᶜezer's response to his original excommunication only confirms his sectarianism, since he, like Jesus with the fig tree, reacted by blasting a third of the olive crop, a third of the wheat crop, and a third of the barley crop, "for everything at which Rabbi Eliᶜezer cast his eyes was burned up."

On one reading at least, for this text, Rabbi Eliᶜezer's magical activity of planting and harvesting cucumbers with a word continues to mark his liminality, indeed, his closeness with "sectarianism." The fact that he uses "halakhot," "laws," to refer both to the "orthodox" issue of purity, that is, to leprosy, and to the suspect planting and harvesting of cucumbers by magic creates an almost comical effect and emphasizes his heterodoxy.[70] This is closely analogous to the attempt to prove a point via the magical uprooting of a carob tree that, according to my reading, precipitated Rabbi Eliᶜezer's excommunication in the first place.[71] As we have seen, early rabbinic texts repeatedly refer to Jesus as a magician.[72]

It could be fairly argued that this is not a particularly telling point, since, as Peter Brown has remarked, "The image of the sorcerer lay to hand in all circles to cut the exceptional and the threatening human being firmly down to size."[73] Indeed, as Brown among others has emphasized, the very distinction between magic and miracles was a function of the evaluation and location of the practitioner, and not a phenomenology of the practice.[74] I am suggesting, nevertheless, that the rhetoric and plot of our narratives suggest that Rabbi Eliᶜezer was accused of being exceptional and threatening when he used language in a certain way to affect "reality" and was deemed to have been cut down to size when he used language in a way that indicated that he, too. believed that "it [the Torah] is not in heaven."

Even Brown seems to allow some measure of "essentialism" in the definition of the sorcerer: "The superstitious man was like the sorcerer. He replicated in his relation to the supernatural patterns of dominance and dependence that were best left unexpressed."[75] This sounds like a fair enough representation of the character of Rabbi Eliᶜezer in these stories. Note, of course, the tight association of *superstitio* and sorcery, both threats to a kind of civic order. The precise issue between Rabbi Eliᶜezer and his colleagues is "the difference between legitimate and illegitimate forms of supernatural power."[76] Hence, perhaps, his insinuated association with Christians, Christians who did boast à la Eusebius of "foreknowledge of the future, visions, and prophetic utterances; laying on of hands," healing the sick, and even raising the dead.[77]

In contrast to the commonplace characterization of Rabbi Eliᶜezer as a figure for extreme conservatism, he begins to look like a harbinger within Jewish society of the same cultural changes that were "the making of late antiquity," according to Brown.[78] Indeed, some of the same conflicts within Christian groups that led to such movements as Montanism, the "new prophecy," and its opponents might very well have been motivating the tensions within Rabbinism between prophetic and rabbinic modes of authority and authorization for halakhic practice.[79] As Christine Trevett has remarked: "The matters at issue between the earliest New Prophets and the developing Catholic tradition . . . concerned not heresy but *authority*."[80] One might easily conclude the same as to the issue between Rabbi Eliᶜezer and his former fellows.

The Rabbi's seeming refusal to obey the laws of the Sabbath in his apparent desire to retain his phylacteries seems also to mark him as being "out of his mind," that is, suspect, in a mystical and perhaps sectarian state. His answer, belligerent as it is, thus marks him as "within" because it is a rational answer based on a good halakhic principle. He is saying "Do not risk a major violation of the Sabbath, a violation that results in the punishment of stoning, in order to see about the removal of my phylacteries, since the wearing of phylacteries on the Sabbath is only a very minor violation." Since his answer behaves according to the laws of ordinary rabbinic rationalities, the Rabbis conclude that he has "returned" from his mystical, sectarian, perhaps ex hypothesi Christian deviance.[81] He is sane again, a proper Pharisee in his worldview. It is not, then, about cucumbers that the Rabbis ask him, but a perfectly ordinary question in the everyday laws of purities, and it is his appropriate answer to this question that repatriates him into the rabbinic community, that releases the vow of excommunication. It doesn't even finally matter whether his answer is correct or not, but only that it obeys the structure and strictures of rabbinic authority. From a literary point of view, the fact that the last word out of his mouth is "pure" serves iconically to signify his repurification.

In addition to the fact that, as I have mentioned, both of these Palestinian sources, the stories of Rabbi Eliᶜezer's arrest and of Ben Dama's near fall into heretical behavior, appear as doublets, the formal similarity between the two death stories in the Babylonian Talmud—the use of the phrase (attested in only one other place) "his soul left him in purity"—also suggests that the two were once a pair in an earlier corpus, apparently a variation of the two forms in which the stories appear together in the early Palestinian texts. In any case, the formal echoes suggest that it is legitimate to read them together.

What do we learn from reading these stories together? Ben Dama was genuinely tempted to engage in some kind of medical sorcery offered by a disciple of Jesus in order to be cured from his snake bite, just as Rabbi Eliᶜezer had been genuinely tempted to enjoy and render definitive the Torah that he heard in the name of Jesus. However, I have already pointed to a telling inconsistency in the story as it is recounted. The implication is that Ben Dama was saved from heresy entirely through his timely death. However, there is more than an implication in the cited verse that the cause of death, the very snake bite that brought him low, was itself a punishment for his *prior* engagement with Christianity. The death by snake bite is precipitated, according to the story's interpretation of the verse, by the very same breaking down of fences from which he ostensibly was saved by that death. His death in purity was therefore a kind of atonement or reparation for his earlier sin, a recuperation, and the idea of death as atonement for one's own sins is a familiar rabbinic concept. Since the death was by snake bite, we have prima facie evidence that the narrative implicates Ben Dama in antecedent involvement with the Jesus sect.

Similarly, then, we can understand the death of Rabbi Eliᶜezer and the lengthy and total isolation and excommunication into which he had been placed. Rabbi Eliᶜezer was also suspected by his fellows of untoward closeness to the Christians, and if my argument above about his refusal to curse Jesus is cogent, it is not entirely surprising that he was so suspected. He was, indeed, an adjunct, or perhaps a fellow traveler of Jesus, the narrative seems to suggest, and his death "in purity" represents the same kind of recuperation or salvation from heresy that Ben Dama's does. The text thus records both the intimacy of the Rabbis with Christianity and the explicit cultural work of separation that was being undertaken. As we proceed through the texts being read in this essay, we will understand more and more, I hope, precisely why such exertion was necessary.

As we move in the coming chapters into the fourth century, we will see more and more that the story of the so-called parting of the ways is a much more ambiguous and complicated narrative than is usually imagined. Jews and Christians, however much they tried to convince themselves and others differently, traveled indeed along similar paths for a long, long time— if not always. Indeed, paradoxically, with respect to certain discourses and practices, far from a "parting of the ways," we will observe a startling convergence of roads taken.[82] It is not accidental that the story of Rabbi Eliᶜezer with which this investigation begins involves an arrest and near martyrdom for Christianity, nor that it forms the first episode in the longest cycle of talmudic martyr stories. The Talmud thus brings together the questions of Jewish-Christian definition and martyrology. Martyrdom and the conversation around it are thus provided by the Talmud itself as a pertinent case study for examining the question of Judeo-Christian origins.

CHAPTER 2

Quo Vadis?

Or, The Acts of the Tricksters

Put bluntly, the "power" of the martyr was unambiguous: but the life
expectancy of such a wielder of power was, by definition, severely limited.

—*Peter Brown*

In the previous chapter, I engaged in a reading of an early rabbinic
legend in which one of the most central (and at the same time, most
marginal) of the Pharisees was arrested by the Romans on suspicion of
Christianity and escaped martyrdom through a double entendre, at once
denying and admitting his attraction to and perhaps partial complicity
with the Nazarenes. I asked why Rabbi Eliᶜezer did not simply deny Christian leanings, and answered that it was because to do so would have required him to curse Jesus, an act in which, the story hints on my reading,
he did not want to engage.

We could ask, however, the opposite question. Let us imagine for the
moment that a historical narrative and not a work of virtual fiction is
before us: If Rabbi Eliᶜezer were indeed a Christian, would he not have
proudly admitted this, as eagerly seeking martyrdom as did his contemporary Ignatius, who wrote to the Roman Christians begging them not to do
anything that would impede his path toward martyrdom?[1] Perhaps not. I
would like to suggest that Christians and Rabbis, similarly and in some
sense together, if not equally so, were engaged in contest and reflection
about the new-fangled practice of martyrdom. In this chapter, I shall begin
exploring how comparative study of rabbinic and patristic literature can
yield surprising insight into both.

Quo Vadis?

More than fifty years ago, my teacher, Professor Saul Lieberman, of blessed
memory, wrote: "There is also a genre of Greek and Latin literature which

can be very helpful in clarifying *realia*, popular concepts and practices referred to in the Palestinian Talmud and midrashim, namely, lives of saints and acts of martyrs. Written in vulgar *koine* and vulgar Latin, this literature employs a wealth of popular terms and homely expressions which have their counterparts in rabbinic sources. And the more polished patristic literature proves exceedingly useful for our purpose when it deals with *realia*, popular concepts and practices."[2] I do not disagree with my teacher, but only add to his words, if I say that the "more polished patristic literature" has much to offer talmudic studies, even when it is not dealing with so-called "popular concepts and practices," but with the most prized and pivotal religious discourses and practices, such as martyrology itself.[3]

Indeed, the very distinction between high and low culture has to be called into question. Scholars from Arnoldo Momigliano to Robert A. Markus and from Peter Brown to Averil Cameron have been vigorously engaged in rejecting this opposition for the very Christian literature with which we deal. Momigliano has written: "Thus my inquest into popular beliefs in the Late Roman historians ends in reporting that there were no such beliefs. In the fourth and fifth centuries there were of course plenty of beliefs which we historians of the twentieth century would gladly call popular, but the historians of the fourth and fifth centuries never treated any belief as characteristic of the masses and consequently discredited among the elite. Lectures on popular beliefs and Late Roman historians should be severely discouraged."[4] Peter Brown has well articulated this perspective with respect to the contemporary Fathers of the Church: "Yet it is remarkable that men who were acutely aware of elaborating *dogmas*, such as the nature of the Trinity, whose contents were difficult of access to the 'unlettered,' felt themselves so little isolated for so much of the time from these same 'unlettered' when it came to the shared religious *practices* of their community and to the assumptions about the relation of man to supernatural beings which these practices condensed. In the area of life covered by religious practice—an area immeasurably wider and more intimately felt by ancient men than by their modern counterparts—differences of class and education play no significant role."[5] What is true of the historians and true of the Fathers is no less true of the Rabbis. It follows from Lieberman's point that the areas of shared cultural and religious creativity might be much broader than we have previously thought, as well.

A case in point is the dialogue about martyrdom. Not only rabbinic Jews, but Christians were thinking very similarly about this practice and its value in the third century, and in texts of different genres. I find one important context for my talmudic passage in the Apocryphal Acts of the Apostles, a group of texts that frequently has been read as popular. Cameron has written of this literature, however: "Within the wide range of Christian literature, it was possible to cut across the barriers of class and genre in a way not open to classical writers. . . . The apocryphal literature did that too."[6] In one of these texts, nearly contemporaneous with the earliest version of Rabbi Eliᶜezer's trickster escape from martyrdom,[7] we find an ideological issue being raised that is very similar to the one implicitly invoked by that story: the value of martyrdom (and especially the martyrdom of a teacher), as opposed to his continued life and instruction.[8]

I am referring to the "Quo vadis?" sequence from the Apocryphal Acts of Peter. Here is that text. Several Roman officials have become exasperated by the apostle's convincing their wives to stop sleeping with them:

> So there was the greatest disquiet in Rome; and Albinus put his case to Agrippa, and said to him, "Either you must get me satisfaction from Peter, who caused my wife's separation, or I shall do so myself"; and Agrippa said that he had been treated in the same way by him, by the separation of his concubines. And Albinus said to him, "Why then do you delay, Agrippa? Let us find him and execute him as a troublemaker, so that we may recover our wives, and in order to give satisfaction to those who cannot execute him, who have themselves been deprived of their wives by him."
>
> But while they made these plans Xanthippe discovered her husband's conspiracy with Agrippa and sent and told Peter, so that he might withdraw from Rome.[9] And the rest of the brethren together with Marcellus entreated him to withdraw, but Peter said to them, "Shall we act like deserters, brethren?" But they said to him, "No, it is so that you can go on serving the Lord." So he assented to the brethren and withdrew by himself, saying, "Let none of you retire with me, but I shall retire by myself in disguise."

Peter thus begins his retreat from Rome in disguise. One of the options for resistance on the part of dominated peoples is disguised identity. Such tricksterism is a time-honored practice of colonized and otherwise subjugated people. In his analysis of the modes of resistance of dominated populations, James C. Scott has articulated the concept of the trickster's speech. Scott argues against a notion of hegemony whereby the dominated always comply with domination,[10] claiming that the appearance of hegemony is only the "public script" that serves the purposes of both the colonizer and the colonized in situations of nearly total domination: "In this respect, subordinate groups are complicitous in contributing to a sanitized official transcript, for that is one way they cover their tracks."[11] It follows that what might appear as accommodation to the culture of the dominating population might be, in fact, the very opposite. Although such tricksterism is common among oppressed populations, the Christian text in the end will have none of it:

> And as he went out of the gate he saw the Lord entering Rome; and when he saw him he said, "Lord, whither (goest thou) here?" And the Lord said to him, "I am coming to Rome to be crucified." And Peter said to him, "Lord, art thou being crucified again?" He said to him, "Yes, Peter, I am being crucified again." And Peter came to himself; and he saw the Lord ascending into heaven; then he returned to Rome rejoicing and giving praise to the Lord, because he said, "I am being crucified"; (since) this was to happen to Peter.
>
> So he returned to the brethren and told them what had been seen by him; and they were grieved at heart, and said with tears, "We entreat you Peter, take thought for us that are young." And Peter said to them, "If it is the Lord's will, it is coming to pass even if we will not have it so. But the Lord is able to establish you in your faith in him, and he will lay your foundation on him and enlarge you in him, you whom he himself has planted, so that you may plant others through him. But as for me, so long as the Lord wills me to be in the flesh, I do not demur; again, if he will take me, I rejoice and am glad."
>
> And while Peter was saying this and all the brethren were in tears, four soldiers arrested him and took him to Agrippa. And he in his anger ordered that he be charged with irreligion and be crucified.[12]

We see from this text that the question of the proper behavior under persecution was an active issue among Christians at the time of the production of the first versions of the Rabbi Eliᶜezer's story. We can see dramatized within the text the competing ideological voices and their reasons: Shall we run away to continue doing the Lord's work, or be crucified with Christ? This text makes its conclusion absolutely clear: the Christian teacher must accept martyrdom in accord with the exemplum of his Lord.

Torah as Hidden Transcript

According to Scott, the discourses of dominated populations fall into four categories. The first is the "public," within which they are actually working within the terms of the discourse of the dominators. The second is the "hidden, offstage, where subordinates may gather outside the intimidating gaze of power" and "where a sharply dissonant political culture is possible." A third is the realm of the trickster tale, within which the "hidden transcript" is encoded in a public one. Finally there is the speech of open rebellion, the martyr's speech. As Scott remarks, we rarely have access to the hidden transcript itself and most often must determine it from suspicious readings of the trickster material.[13] The talmudic discourse, however, gives us direct access to the "hidden transcript," frequently thematizing the doubleness of its own trickster language, as in the story of Rabbi Eliᶜezer discussed in the previous chapter, where the Talmud openly relates what the Rabbi said and what the *hegemon* understood / was meant to understand. This literature, composed in a language that the conquerors did not know,[14] provided a safe and private space within which to elaborate the transcript hidden away from the colonizer.[15]

In the apocryphal Christian story, the conflict between the hidden and the public transcript, between tricksterism and martyrdom, is implicit. A text from the Palestinian Talmud, however, explicitly thematizes open resistance versus accommodation as the appropriate response to oppressive power. Two different interpretations of a verse in Deuteronomy lead to two almost directly opposed practices vis-à-vis the Roman overlords (or more likely, vice versa: two different practices with respect to Rome lead to two readings of the verse), one of direct alienation and one of (seeming) accommodation.[16] The verse itself is explicitly about Esau, who (through his alternative name, Edom) is always an eponym for Rome (and then for Rome as Christendom) in rabbinic literature.

Seeing the verse in its immediate context will illuminate the interpretative controversy and its political/cultural meanings: "And He commanded the people, saying, 'You are passing within the border of the Children of Esau who dwell in Seᶜir, and they will be afraid of you, so be very careful. Do not provoke them, for I will not give you their land, not even to stand on, for I have given the Mount of Seᶜir to Esau as an inheritance. You shall buy food from them for money, and eat, and also buy water from them for money, and drink."

> They said to Rabbi Ḥiyya the Great: Rabbi Shimᶜon bar Yoḥai teaches, "'You shall buy food from them [Edom = Rome] for money, and eat, and also buy water from them for money, and drink' (Deut. 2:6): Just as water [is that] which has not been modified from its original state [lit. its creation], so also everything that has not been modified from its original state."   Shabbat 1:3, 3c

Rabbi Shimᶜon bar Yoḥai, whose opposition to any rapprochement whatever with Rome was proverbial,[17] pulls the verse completely out of its context—well-respected midrashic practice—and accordingly reads it formalistically and technically as a limitation on the possible forms of interaction between Jews and Gentiles. You can only acquire certain types of foodstuffs from them, he says, those that have a characteristic of water, namely, that they are unprocessed. One can see immediately that such a regulation would have two powerful effects: a restraint on trade between Jews and Gentiles, as well as a powerful chill on eating together or sharing food, commensality, in addition to the chill that the kosher rules already prescribe.

Rabbi Ḥiyya, however, is quite opposed to this view, both politically and midrashically. His notion is that Jews may purchase any sort of foodstuff from Gentiles, as long, of course, as it is kosher. The Talmud asks, then, how he would go about interpreting the same verse that Rabbi Shimᶜon has read as strongly limiting of commensality between Jews and Gentiles. Rabbi Ḥiyya develops a whole political philosophy of Jewish-Gentile interaction—actually of Jewish-*Roman* interaction, a procedure justified by the fact that the verse actually does refer to the proper behavior of Israel toward the children of Esau, or Edom.

The Bible explicitly says not to provoke them. An alternative to provoking them is also offered by the verse, which Rabbi Ḥiyya understands in a way that takes it out of its immediate biblical-historical context and gives it new cultural power as a suggestion to use gifts to turn Roman hearts favorably to their Jewish subjects. This is derived from the verse by typically clever midrashic punning, in addition to the mobilization of the foundational intertext, the story of the original Jacob and Esau:

> How, then does Rabbi Ḥiyya the Great explain the verse: "You shall buy food from them for money, and eat"?—If you feed him, you have bought and defeated him, for if he is harsh with you, buy/defeat him with food, and if [that does] not [work], then defeat him with money.

The phrase "buy food from them" can also with only relatively modest stretching of the syntax—well within the bounds of midrashic practice—and none whatever of the lexicon, be read as "defeat them," since the word "buy" and the word "defeat" are homonyms, sharing, as they do, the root שבר. The verse is thus read as: "With food, buy them, and [if that doesn't work], break [= defeat by suborning] them with money." This is an obvious allusion to the situation within which the weak, "feminine" Jacob bought the favor of the "virile," dominant Esau by giving him food.

Baksheesh itself becomes institutionalized as a discursive practice of opposition to oppression. Various "dishonest" practices and deceptions are valorized by rabbinic and other colonized peoples in direct opposition to the "manly" arts of violent resistance. As an Indian untouchable phrased it: "We must also tactfully disguise and hide, as necessary, our true aims and intentions from our social adversaries. To recommend it is not to encourage falsehood but only to be tactical in order to survive."[18] Rabbi Ḥiyya's philosophy is to follow the biblical injunction not to provoke authority by standing up to it, but to attempt to oblige it, with the result that the authority will favor the entire people and act justly toward them. The trick is to defeat them by seeming to go along with them. "Kill them with kindness" is the lesson.

This "hidden transcript," preserved before our eyes in the Talmud, provides an elegant demonstration of Scott's argument that "what may look from above like the extraction of a required performance can easily look from below like the artful manipulation of deference and flattery to achieve its own ends."[19] A neat comparison is afforded by the injunction of an African American grandfather to his grandson in Ralph Ellison's *Invisible Man*: "I want you to overcome 'em with yesses, undermine 'em with grins, agree 'em to death and destruction, let 'em swoller you till they vomit or bust wide open. . . . Learn it to the young 'uns."[20] If flattery fails, says Rabbi Ḥiyya, then defeat them by bribing them. And the text concludes: "They say: That is how Rabbi Yonathan behaved. When he saw a powerful personage come into his city, he used to send him expensive things. What did he think? If he comes to judge an orphan or a widow, we will find him propitious towards them" (Yerushalmi Shabbat 1:3; 3c).

If Esau was the legendary ancestor of Rome, Jacob, his brother, was the exemplary rabbinic male. It is important to emphasize to what extent Jacob already in the Bible is a virtual "trickster," that figure of folklore all over the world who "represent[s] the weak, whose wit can at times achieve ambiguous victories against the power of the strong."[21] Twice in his life, as described in the Bible, Jacob, the weak emblem of Israel, achieved victory, respectively over Laban, the ancestor of the Aramaeans, and then—and this is much more relevant for our text—over Esau, the eponymous ancestor of Rome and thus of Christendom.[22] These figures and their stories were paradigmatic for the self-fashioning of the Jewish male and for collective self-fashioning.

The diasporic Jew throughout history is a trickster par excellence.[23] That social system enabled the continued existence of the Jews as a deterritorialized cultural entity for nearly two thousand years.[24] Part of the durability of the political, and thus cultural system that the Rabbis built was founded on antiphallic modes of resistance and the exercise of power, the use of the "weapons of the weak."[25] I am not, of course, claiming uniqueness for the Rabbis in this. Catherine Edwards remarks that "Cicero warns against the slippery ways of Greeks and Asiatics, which are to be connected, he says, with their lack of political power (*Ad Q. fr. I.16*). By implication, those who have been conquered behave like other dominated groups, women and slaves."[26] In Chariton's first-century (?) A.C. novel, *Chaereas and Callirhoe*, we read, as well, that Persians love truth, as opposed to the lying slanders of the clever Greeks.[27] What we learn from Jewish texts of late antiquity is that this was not only an accusation from without, but a valorized representation from within at least one dominated group.[28] Such modes of resistance, moreover, were coded from within the Jewish cultural system as feminized. We need only to think of the Book of Esther, the paradigm book of Diaspora politics, to see that this is so.[29]

Acts of Tricksters and Martyrs

The Babylonian Talmud presents us with two paradigmatic stories of response to Roman power with directly opposing ideologies. One is an indirect echo of the story of Rabbi Eliᶜezer that we already have encountered, a tale of a Rabbi's witty escape through a kind of tricksterism from the threat of martyrdom for teaching Torah, while the other, a tale of a Rabbi who bravely goes to his death in order to deny publicly the authority of the Romans, is the model of the defiant martyr par excellence. These two figures of resistance, the trickster and the martyr, are known from dominated populations all over the world. As James Scott has remarked: "Those who did assert themselves defiantly won themselves a place in black folklore—that of the 'baaaad Nigger'—that is one of both admiration and fearful awe. Admiration, for having acted out the hidden transcript and fearful awe, for having often paid for it with their lives. . . . The more common folk hero of subordinate groups—blacks included—has historically been the trickster figure, who manages to outwit his adversary and escape unscathed."[30]

In the context of late antiquity, the trickster is indeed a trickster, but the "baaaad Nigger" is, of course, the martyr. As the historian Brent Shaw has written: "These [martyr] stories have embedded in them paradigms of how to confront power in situations where silent scripts, both individual and collective, become public."[31] The two figures actually are pitted against each other in the same story here, thus thematizing more directly the question of appropriate modes of resistance.[32] Although the narrative does not directly and unambiguously oppose martyrdom, it raises powerful questions about the validity and value of dying for God as opposed to living for God.[33]

In Tractate Avoda Zara, 16b–19b of the Babylonian Talmud, we find a very complicated and fascinating discourse having to do with Roman power, different modes of cultural resistance to it, and issues of sexuality and gender. Unwinding the intricately interwoven halakhic and aggadic expression of this text will help us understand how gender and the situation of a subjugated male population are entangled within the cultural formation of talmudic Judaism. Reading this text through this and the next chapter also will help us to begin to sort out the similarities and differences between the rabbinic and Christian discourses of gender, martyrdom, and resistance in late antiquity.

The Talmud begins by presenting us with an elaborated version of the story of Rabbi Eliᶜezer's near martyrdom and escape through the use of trickster language, through double entendre. Reading it against the martyrdom of St. Polycarp, one of the earliest of Christian martyrologies, already illustrates some fundamental similarities and differences between the two discourses. First of all, like Rabbi Eliᶜezer, Polycarp also initially escapes from his threatened martyrdom by running away at the urging of his flock. However, while at his place of refuge, he dreams that his pillow is burning and concludes that "I must be burned alive," and indeed, in the end, after a series of near misses, he does succeed in getting himself burned alive.[34]

Even more pertinent is a comparison between the use of double meaning in the two texts. Rabbi Eliᶜezer, it will be recalled, exploited double meaning in order to trick the *hegemon* into releasing him without the Rabbi actually compromising his faith. He said: "I have trust in the judge," and only the Talmud lets us know that he meant God and not the Roman *hegemon*. Not so Polycarp. He uses double language in order to insure that his desired martyrdom will actually take place. When he is asked, in order to save his skin, to say "Away with the atheists," by which the proconsul means, of course, the Christians, the aged bishop "looked sternly at the whole crowd of lawless heathen in the stadium, indicating them with a wave of his hand, groaned and looked up to heaven, and said, 'Away with the atheists!'"[35] The gesture of the bishop disambiguates precisely what the Rabbi leaves purposely ambiguous. The Rabbi plays the trickster; the bishop enacts the "baaaad Nigger." Had Polycarp not gestured at the crowd and thus exploited the double meaning to avoid being killed, or alternatively, had Rabbi Eliᶜezer looked heavenward as he spoke, clueing the *hegemon* into his "true" intention and gotten himself killed, we would have had the same theme being used in the same way. As the texts are, however, we find the same theme, the double language used by Christians and Jews, employed for exactly opposite ends, one to escape, one to ensure a martyr's fate.

This pattern of similar plots with different ends (and to different ends), when employed by Christians and Rabbis, could serve as an emblem for this and the next chapter. Playing on the usage of folkloristics, we could refer to the varying usages of a story within different religious groups as religious ecotypes of the tale. However, we must observe one important caution. One could conclude from this, too hastily, that the Rabbis always will opt for tricksterism, the Christians for defiance. The matter, however, is not quite that simple.

In fact, the Talmud is quite unsure of its mind on this matter, as it shows immediately. After this story about Rabbi Eliᶜezer, the talmudic narrative continues via the double narrative of two Rabbis arrested by the Romans to thematize explicitly the contest between escape from martyrdom through tricksterism and manfully provoking death:

> Our Rabbis have taught: When Rabbi Elᶜazar the son of Perata and Rabbi Ḥanina the son of Teradyon were arrested for sectarianism, Rabbi Elᶜazar the son of Perata said to Rabbi Ḥanina the son of Teradyon: "Happy art thou who has been arrested for only one thing. Woe unto me who has been arrested for five things." Rabbi Ḥanina the son of Teradyon said to him: "Happy art thou who has been arrested for five things and will be rescued. Woe unto me who has been arrested for one thing and will not be saved, for you busied yourself with Torah and with good deeds, while I only busied myself with Torah."—This is in accord with the view of Rav Huna who said that anyone who busies himself with Torah alone is as if he had no God.

The story of Rabbi Eliᶜezer that appeared in the beginning of this text and that was discussed in the previous chapter provided only one option, but now the options are multiplied and confronted in the form of dialogue between the two rabbinic protagonists. As in the case of Rabbi Eliᶜezer with which the whole cycle opened, here, also, the Rabbis are very anxious about justifying God's punishment of apparently righteous men via their arrest by the Roman authorities. There were both Jewish and Christian thinkers at the time who believed that martyrdom was "an atonement for sin committed in this or a previous life."[36] The notion, not by itself remarkable, that the oppressive Empire is God's whip, raises the question of resistance to a high theological pitch at the same time that it reinstates a rather simple theodicy, as we shall see. The Rabbis, like Job's friends, cannot stand the thought of a God who punishes without cause.[37]

The text goes on with the details of the trials of the two prisoners:

> They brought Rabbi Elᶜazar the son of Perata. They asked him: "Why did you teach and why did you steal?"[38] He answered them: "If book,

no sword and if sword, no book! Since one must be absent, the other must as well."

Rabbi El^cazar the son of Perata uses trickster wits to get himself out of trouble. He declares that there is a self-contradiction in the charges against him, for one cannot be both a scholar and a thief. Since, he says, the two accusations contradict each other, they cancel each other out.

The premise of the argument itself makes sense in terms of contemporaneous cultural norms. The occupations of robber and scholar were considered logically incompatible within the cultural frame of this text, as we learn from the Hellenistic novel *Leucippe and Cleitophon*, in which the hero reports a beating in which he was passive and then remarks: "He grew tired of thumping me and I of philosophizing." Philosophy is thus equivalent to nonthumping, ergo violence and sagacity are incompatible.[39] The logic also is a particularly typical form of talmudic reasoning according to which, when a statement includes two propositions that are mutually exclusive, they are both considered to be untrue. At the same time that it functions in the plot to establish Rabbi El^cazar's cleverness, this proverbial utterance of the Rabbi's announces a theme of the text. Torah is incompatible with the sword, thus repeating the theme established through the typology of Esau, the Roman, and Jacob, the Jew.[40]

This was apparently a Christian topos as well, as we learn from a story in Eusebius's *Ecclesiastical History*. According to this text, a centurion named Marinus confessed himself a Christian and was given several hours to reconsider his confession or be martyred:

> There is a certain mark of honour among the Romans, the vine switch, and those that obtain it become, it is said, centurions. A post was vacant, and according to the order of promotion Marinus was being called to this advancement. Indeed he was on the point of receiving the honour, when another stepped forward before the tribunal, and stated that in accordance with the ancient laws Marinus could not share in the rank that belonged to Romans, since he was a Christian and did not sacrifice to the emperors; but that the office fell to himself. And [it is said] that the judge (his name was Achaeus) was moved thereat, and first of all asked what views Marinus held; and then, when he saw that he was steadfast in confessing himself a Christian, gave him a space of three hours for reflection.

This Caesarean text, however, exactly contemporary with our talmudic text, does not abide the notion of a Christian who is a soldier, just as the Talmud implies the incompatibility of book and sword:

> When he came outside the court Theotecnus, the bishop there, approached and drew him aside in conversation, and taking him by the hand led him forward to the church. Once inside, he placed him close to the altar itself, and raising his cloak a little, pointed to the sword with which he was girded; at the same time he brought and placed before him the book of the divine Gospels, and bade him choose which of the two he wished. Without hesitation he stretched forth his right hand and took the divine book. "Hold fast then," said Theotecnus to him, "hold fast to God; and, strengthened by Him, mayest thou obtain that thou hast chosen. Go in peace." As he was returning thence immediately a herald cried aloud, summoning him before the court of justice. For the appointed time was now over. Standing before the judge he displayed still greater zeal for the faith; and straightway, even as he was, was led away to death, and so was perfected.   *Ecclesiastical History* VII: 15[41]

Clearly, the notion of incompatibility of the book and the sword was common to both Rabbis and bishops.[42] The stories have dramatically different endings, for Rabbi El⁽azar escapes from being martyred via this proverbial utterance, while Marinus, of course, is propelled toward martyrdom via the same topos. This is not an incidental difference.

The Rabbi's tricksterism is rewarded with miraculous divine interventions, signaling the text's approval of his tactics. The Romans next ask him:

> Why do they call you Rabbi [Master]? He answered them: "I am the master of the weavers." They brought before him two spools of thread and asked him: "Which is the warp and which is the weft?" A miracle took place for him. A male bee came and sat on the weft and a female bee came and sat on the warp.[43]
>
> "And why did you not come to the House of Avidan [the local pagan temple]?"[44] He said: "I am old, and I was afraid that you would trample me with your feet." They said to him; "Up until now how many old men have been trampled?" A miracle took place for him, and that very day an old man was trampled.
>
> "Why did you release your slave to freedom?"[45]

"It never happened!"

One got up to testify against him [that he had released his slave]. Elijah came and appeared like one of them. He [the disguised Elijah] said to him [the potential witness]: "Since a miracle has happened for him in the other cases, a miracle will happen this time as well, and something bad will happen to you [lit. that man]."[46] That man [who was betraying him] did not pay attention and got up to tell them. A letter had been written to the House of Caesar. They sent it with him [the informer]. [Elijah] threw him four hundred parasangs, so that he went and never came back.

This is obviously a highly comic, even grotesque story of resistance, a trickster tale par excellence. Rabbi Elᶜazar the son of Perata repeatedly uses rhetorical methods involving "double meaning [and] ambiguous intentions," precisely those tactics that a Roman polemicist of the second Sophistic would deride as Greek, Asiatic, or effeminate, and the text justifies him every time.[47]

There is little doubt in my mind that we are in the realm of folk literature here, by which I do *not* mean a literature that is not of the Rabbis themselves, but rather a literature that exemplifies the close connections between the rabbinic class and the "folk." In the typical fashion of the folk narrative, three miracles take place for our hero. In the first, a male bee sits on the weft, the insertive, "male" thread, and a female bee on the warp, the receptive, "female" thread, and the Rabbi is thus able to determine the difference and convince the Romans that he is, indeed, a weaver. In the next the miracle again convinces the Romans of the truth of a lie. Similarly, in the third case. Here a Jew is prepared to denounce the Rabbi as having indeed freed his slave, which apparently in the world of the story was both illegal and a sure mark of adherence to Judaism or Christianity, and through a highly improbable combination of circumstances and miracles, the denouncer is removed so far from the scene that he will never be heard of again. The values of this "folk legend" are clear. Any sort of deception is legitimate, as long as it gets you off the hook with the oppressor, because his rule is absolutely illegitimate. Our protagonist here is a veritable Brer Rabbi.

The debate between tricksterism and martyrdom as the most honored and most valuable response to oppression was in the air as a living and active cross-confessional issue at the time that the talmudic literature was being composed. During the Decian persecution, there were even many Christian *libellatici* who "prided themselves on their cunning and their escapes," that is, Christians whose *libelli* (certificates of having sacrificed) had been obtained by trickery.[48] How different, after all, is this from Rabbi El'azar's claim that he doesn't sacrifice because he's old and afraid of getting trampled in the temple? As Glen Bowersock has phrased it, "The debate over flight is striking in its fundamental assumption that escape—as opposed to apostasy—might be a possible alternative for a Christian."[49] The debate was in common, the accent of the decision, however, less so. These *libellatici* had to be readmitted to the Church as penitents after the persecution, whereas the rabbinic tricksters are heroes.[50]

Again, however, I must emphasize that the Talmud text is not decisive on this question. It never quite rules for tricksters or for martyrs. Our next talmudic hero, in any case, is anything but a trickster:

> They brought Rabbi Ḥanina the son of Teradyon, and said to him: "Why did you engage in Torah?" He said to them: "For thus the Lord my God has commanded me!"
>
> They immediately sentenced him to burning, and his wife to execution [by the sword], and his daughter to sit in a prostitute's booth.[51]

In contrast to the tricksters, the hidden-transcript players, Rabbis Eli'ezer and El'azar the son of Perata, this Rabbi, like Polycarp, plays the role of the "baaaad Nigger." This is a paradigmatic martyr story: Martyrdom is witness to the greater jurisdiction of God's power and justice, which supersedes that of the mere temporal authority. "For thus the Lord my God has commanded me!" This admirable sentiment—analogous to the "Christianus sum" of the martyrs—is the precise antithesis to that of Rabbi Eli'ezer's duplicitous "I have trust in the J/judge."

What is the function of this oppositional story here? At first glance, we could conclude that it is cited in order to refute and displace the trickster model that the text seemingly valorized up to this point. In the light of the antithetical echo story of Rabbi Ḥanina, we might begin to wonder if Rabbi Eli'ezer's statement is, in fact, not a lie, not only with respect to the *hegemon*, but with respect to the *Hegemon* as well, for by seeking to escape the judgment that the Roman wishes to impose on him, is he not also seeking to escape the judgment that God wishes to impose on him? In other words, to put it sharply, could we not say that Rabbi Eli‘ezer confesses by this action that he trusts *neither* judge? At first glance, then, and given the predilections of our own culture toward "manly" *virtus* and *honestas*, predilections that are themselves a product of a Romanized Christianity,[52] we might very well understand that Rabbi Ḥanina's story is being presented as a hermeneutical key to reading the stories of both Rabbi Eli‘ezer and the farce of Rabbi El‘azar the son of Perata, and the latter two come off badly.

The text, however, immediately disables such a reading in the sequel, actually an alternative version of the story of Rabbi Ḥanina's arrest:[53]

> Our [ancient] Rabbis have taught: When Rabbi Yose the son of Kisma
> became ill, Rabbi Ḥanina the son of Teradyon went to visit him. He
> said to him: "Ḥanina, my brother, don't you know that this nation
> was set to rule over us by Heaven,[54] and it has destroyed His house,
> and burned His temple, and killed his saints, and destroyed his goodly
> things, and still it exists, and I have heard that you gather crowds
> together in public, with a Scroll of the Torah in your lap, and you sit
> and teach!"[55] He [Ḥanina] said to him, "From Heaven they will have
> mercy." He [Yose] said to him, "I say logical things to you, and you
> answer me: 'From Heaven they will have mercy!' I will be surprised if
> they do not burn you and the Scroll of the Torah with you."

Rabbi Ḥanina, according to this version, not only bravely answered "Because my Lord has commanded me" when questioned by the Romans, he actively provoked his arrest by provocatively gathering groups to study Torah in public. In order for seditious discourse to be formed, Scott shows, there have to be "autonomous social sites," either hidden from the eyes of the dominating population or hidden from their ears because of "linguistic codes impenetrable to outsiders."[56] The study of Torah in general in sites such as the Bet Hamidrash, or even more in public "crowds," would provide precisely such an arena, and it does not matter, according to Scott, what the discourse is in that arena. Insofar as it maintains the possibility of a hidden transcript, of a place within which the dominated Jews could elaborate their true views of their Roman (and Sassanian) overlords, it would serve the function. This is even more the case, of course, when the content expressed in the study of Torah itself incorporated encoded or open contempt for the rulers, as was frequently enough the case with the study of Torah. The response of the "Romans," their efforts to prohibit the study of Torah, and in particular to prohibit it in crowds, would indicate their understanding—or at any rate, the narrator's understanding—of the role of such gatherings in the maintenance of the "hidden transcript."

This argument is especially cogent in the light of Lieberman's demonstrations that the Romans never forbade the exercise of the Jewish religion per se, but only of particular practices that they considered offensive (such as circumcision) or politically dangerous. Teaching Torah in public as a site of potential sedition certainly would have been one of them, as would also another of Rabbi Ḥanina's practices, the pronouncing of God's name in public, which the Romans would see as *maleficium*.[57] At the same time, there is more than a hint here, in the voice of Rabbi Yose the son of Kisma, at a quietist theological position exactly antithetical to that of a martyr. It is God who has sent the Romans to rule over the Jews, and the rebellious act of provocatively gathering crowds to study Torah in public is thus rebellion against God's will. Rabbi Ḥanina's act is the rabbinic Jewish analogy, therefore, to the early Christian practices of provocatively inviting martyrdom known, somewhat misleadingly, as "voluntary martyrdom."[58]

The text sends us, it must be said, some very ambivalent messages. Note the irony in the following incident:

> They said: there did not pass many days until Rabbi Yose the son of Kisma died and all of the great of Rome went to bury him. On their way back, they found him [Rabbi Ḥanina] sitting and studying Torah and gathering congregations in public with the Scroll of the Torah placed in his lap. They wrapped him in the Scroll of the Torah and surrounded him with sticks of firewood and lit them and they brought wool swatches, soaked them in water, and placed them on his heart, in order that he not die quickly.

Rabbi Yose's prophecy that Rabbi Ḥanina would suffer greatly because of his provocative behavior came true exactly as predicted—the Scroll of the Torah is burned, as well—but it was in a sense Rabbi Yose's accommodating practice (his conformity to the public transcript) that occasioned the tragedy. Had he not been so accommodating, the "great of Rome" would have not been attending his funeral and Rabbi Ḥanina would not have been arrested. This text simply will not settle down in one place and take sides on the issue of tricksterism versus martyrdom.

Together with the thematic homology between the Rabbinic text that I have been considering and roughly contemporary Christian texts of various genres, there is a significant difference, as well.[59] In the Christian texts, whatever the initial hesitation and contestation, there finally seems to be a decision made, a resolution drawn.[60] Let us have a brief look now at a "polished patristic" text of the third century, the life of Cyprian, the martyr and bishop of Carthage, written by his deacon, Pontius, some time in the second half of that century.[61] What is significant here is that Cyprian, in spite of his exhortations to martyrdom, upon being given the chance had himself withdrawn from Carthage in order to escape being martyred.[62] One can hear in his deacon's account some rhetorical dancing in order to defend this:

> And therefore for such merits he at once obtained the glory of pro-scription also. . . . He might, indeed, at that time, in accordance with the rapidity wherewith he always attained everything, have hastened to the crown of martyrdom appointed for him, especially when with repeated calls he was frequently demanded for the lions, had it not been needful for him to pass through all the grades of glory, and thus to arrive at the highest, and had not the impending desolation needed the aid of so fertile a mind. For conceive of him as being at that time taken away by the dignity of martyrdom. Who was there to show the advantage of grace, advancing by faith?

Although a cynic might see here merely a faithful or even sycophantic disciple defending his beloved bishop's honor, there is more going on than that, for the argument being offered is a serious one, one so serious that it provided the basis for the antimartyrdom discourse of the Gnostics, for whom the Christian never could be perfected through dying, but only through living a life of ever-increasing spirituality. Precisely for that reason, the "orthodox" Christian could not finally choose this option.

After detailing all the losses to the community that would have occurred if Cyprian had been martyred too soon, the good deacon demonstrates that even the bishop's initial flight and dodging of martyrdom was only for the sake of—martyrdom:

> Who was there to raise up such great martyrs by the exhortation of his divine discourse? Who was there, in short, to animate so many confessors sealed with a second inscription on their distinguished brows, and reserved alive for an example of martyrdom, kindling their ardour with a heavenly trumpet? Fortunately, fortunately it

occurred then, and truly by the Spirit's direction, that the man who
was needed for so many and so excellent purposes was withheld from
the consummation of martyrdom. Do you wish to be assured that the
cause of his withdrawal was not fear? To allege nothing else, he did
suffer subsequently, and this suffering he assuredly would have
evaded as usual, if he had evaded it before. It was indeed that fear—
and rightly so—that fear which would dread to offend the Lord—
that fear which prefers to obey God's commands rather than to be
crowned in disobedience. For a mind dedicated in all things to God,
and thus enslaved to the divine admonitions, believed that even in
suffering itself it would sin, unless it had obeyed the Lord, who then
bade him seek the place of concealment.

This is a riveting text. Every argument against martyrdom that was mobilized by Rabbi Yose in the Talmud is cited here, as well. God does not in-
tend or desire that those who could teach his Torah should die before their
time, and it is far, far better to withdraw, appearing pusillanimous, as Cyprian clearly did, to judge from the defense, than to be killed prematurely
and cease doing the Lord's work. This was the argument used by the apostle's friends in the Apocryphal Acts, as we saw above, as well, however the
embarrassed and defensive tone of these explanations is entirely different
from that of the Talmud.

But finally, the patristic text, like the apocryphon, makes its burden
clear. The only thing that justifies Cyprian's temporary evasion of martyrdom is the fact that in the end he was, like Peter, martyred.[63] In short, in
the Cyprianic *Life*, we have a virtual instant replay of the "Quo vadis?"
story. This is no mere conceit. The letter of the Roman clergy attacking
Cyprian for his "retirement" explicitly provided a negative comparison between him, "the hireling shepherd," and Peter, "the good shepherd, who
fed his sheep 'by the very manner of his death.'"[64] As G. W. Clarke emphasizes, in this letter: "The value of making a steadfast stand is highly
stressed. Indeed the confessors (*fratres qui sunt in vinculis*) take pride of
place before the presbyters in the concluding salutation. By corollary, their
attitude toward *fuga* (and that includes Cyprian's), with their sermonizing
on the good and the hireling shepherd and their frequent references to de-
sertion (*deserentes, dereliquimus, reliciti*) is plainly critical and scarcely
veiled by the decency of innuendo."[65] Since Peter was the good shepherd,

it would not be entirely surprising to find Cyprian's panegyrical thanatographer implicitly referring to this intertext. Both theoretical options, escape from martyrdom as a means to maintain the teaching of the Christ and the exhortation to martyrdom, are raised in both texts, but the decision is finally clearly in favor of the latter.[66] Christian discourse needed to render a decree on the matter, just as developing Christian orthodoxy needed finally to settle theological questions, and disagreement leads repeatedly to schism.

The exception that proves this rule is Clement of Alexandria in the late second century and early third. For a Tertullian, the contemporary founding voice of Latin Christianity in Carthage, Clement would be a heretic, no more, no less. As W. H. C. Frend has put it so pithily, "It is perhaps fortunate for the Church that Clement and Tertullian never met. If they had, or if the view of Clement and Origen had been propagated in Africa and Italy, the schism between East and West might have occurred in the third and not in the eleventh century." All this because "To Clement the Christian Gnostic was the type of perfect Christian. To Tertullian it was the martyr."[67]

Here is Clement's most explicit statement on the subject:

If the confession to God is martyrdom, each soul which has lived purely in the knowledge of God, which has obeyed the commandments, is a witness both by life and word, in whatever way it may be released from the body, shedding faith as blood along its whole life till its departure. For instance, the Lord says in the Gospel, "Whosoever shall leave father, or mother, or brethren," and so forth, "for the sake of the Gospel and my name," (Matt. xix. 29) he is blessed; not indicating simple martyrdom, but the Gnostic martyrdom [i.e., true witnessing], as of the man who has conducted himself according to the rule of the Gospel, in love to the Lord (for the knowledge of the Name and the understanding of the Gospel point out the gnosis, but not the bare appellation), so as to leave his worldly kindred, and wealth, and every possession, in order to lead a life free from passion. "Mother" figuratively means Country and sustenance; "fathers" are the laws of civil polity: which must be contemned thankfully by the high-souled just man; for the sake of being the friend of God, and of obtaining the right hand in the holy place, as the Apostles have done.

Up until this point in the text, Clement reveals his own ideological stance on the question of martyrdom as against gnosis. As Frend writes, Clement provides a link between Philo's Therapeutae and the first Christian monks and is the first Christian writer who "placed the ascetic ideal on the same level as that of the martyr."[68] All that would be well and good when there was no one making martyrs of orthodox Christians anymore, that is, in the fourth century, when indeed the "white martyrdom" became central in orthodox Christian practice. In Clement's time, however, for a Christian writer to argue at last against martyrdom and for asceticism and gnosis would be to mark him as a heretic. And therefore the text continues, achieving its now-familiar denouement:

> Then Heraclitus says, "Gods and men honor those slain in battle;" and Plato in the fifth book of the *Republic* writes, "Of those who die in military service, whoever dies after winning renown, shall we not say that he is chief of the golden race? Most assuredly." But the golden race is with the gods, who are in heaven, in the fixed sphere, who chiefly hold command in the providence exercised towards men. Now some of the heretics who have misunderstood the Lord, have at once an impious and cowardly love of life; saying that the true martyrdom is the knowledge of the only true God (which we also admit), and that the man is a self-murderer and a suicide who makes confession by death; and adducing other similar sophisms of cowardice. To these we shall reply at the proper time; for they differ with us in regard to first principles. Now we, too, say that those who have rushed on death (for there are some, not belonging to us, but sharing the name merely), who are in haste to give themselves up, the poor wretches dying through hatred to the Creator. These, we say, banish themselves without being martyrs, even though they are punished publicly. For they do not preserve the characteristic mark of believing martyrdom, in as much as they have not known the only true God, but give themselves up to a vain death, as the Gymnosophists of the Indians to useless fire.[69]   Stromateis, IV, 4

Clement was clearly not opposed to martyrdom, per se. He could hardly have been so and been an orthodox Christian at all in his time, but his attitude was ambivalent in the extreme, to say the least.[70] His sympathies, one suspects from this text, are clearly with the Gnostic position on dying for God, or rather, we should say, with the Gnostic opposition to dying for

God. Although Clement could not then take up a position as directly opposed to martyrdom as that of the trickster Rabbis, his stance seems not
very different from, say, that of Rabbi Yose ben Kisma. Indeed, his riposte
to those who rush into voluntary martyrdom is much more enthusiastic
than his promised but deferred refutation of the Gnostic position.[71]

In contrast to both the Peter of the apocryphon and the Cyprian of the
Life, Clement, in the time of Severan persecution of 202, left Alexandria
never to return,[72] thus voting, as it were, with his feet for the trickster or escape option that we find so prominently in the Talmud, too. For Clement,
the very "rabbinic" Matthew 10:23, "When they persecute you in this city,
flee ye into another," was the defining text. Clement writes in good rabbinic fashion:

> For He, in a way, bids us take care of ourselves. But he who disobeys
> is rash and foolhardy. If he who kills a man of God sins against God,
> he also who presents himself before the judgment seat becomes guilty
> of his death. And such is also the case with him who does not avoid
> persecution, but out of daring presents himself for capture. Such a
> one, as far as in him lies, becomes an accomplice in the crime of the
> persecutor. And if he also uses provocation, he is wholly guilty, chal-
> lenging the wild beast. And similarly, if he afford any cause for con-
> flict or punishment, or retribution or enmity, he gives occasion for
> persecution.   Stromateis, chapter 10

He could be echoing Rabbi Yose ben Kisma.[73]

In contrast to Clement, Tertullian represents the conviction of the
Latin Church, according to Frend.[74] If, for Clement, martyrdom was one
means of Christian fulfillment and not to be actively sought or provoked,
for Tertullian, martyrdom was the only sure means to salvation.[75] There are
only martyrs in Perpetua's vision of heaven. Tertullian's view is thus closer
to that of Rabbi Ḥanina, who actively provoked the Romans to martyr
him, and even closer to that of Rabbi Akiva, whose story we shall encounter in the final chapter, and who proclaimed that being martyred was
the *only* way to fulfill the commandment to "love the Lord with all one's
soul."[76] Frend's penchant is to identify strongly the Tertullian, North African tradition with a kind of Judaistic, Maccabean archaizing versus the
more civilized, Platonized East, but there is another way to think of this.[77]
One could hypothesize tentatively that the Greek tradition of cunning,

metis, as a value, versus the Roman supreme value of *virtus* is at play here, thus suggesting once again the enormous convolutions of cultural multi-causation, Hebrew, Greek, and Roman, in the production of the multifold discourse of martyrdom.[78]

On another scale, one would put Tertullian with Rabbi Shimᶜon bar Yoḥai, the most radical rejector of Rome, its culture, its legitimacy, and its value among the Tannaitic figures.[79] Rabbi Shimᶜon is also represented as having visited Rabbi Akiva in prison and having demanded that his teacher teach him Torah there, almost surely an attempt to share his fate as "confessor" and martyr.[80] Paradoxically, these two great rejectors of Rome seem most strongly to be representing the Roman value of honor,[81] while figures like Rabbi Yose ben Kisma and Clement in the Christian world, in their accommodations to Rome, represent more Hellenistic or old Jewish value systems. Compare, for instance, the following texts. The North African Christian Minucius Felix writes:

> All that the Romans hold, occupy, and possess is the spoil of outrage; their temples are all of loot drawn from the ruin of cities, the plunder of gods and the slaughter of priests.[82]

The Talmud relates that Rabbi Shimᶜon bar Yoḥai had very similar views to those of Minucius Felix. They were opposed, however, by Rabbi Yehuda:

> Rabbi Yehuda, Rabbi Yose, and Rabbi Shimᶜon were sitting, and Rabbi Yehuda the son of converts was sitting before them. Rabbi Yehuda opened: How beautiful are the deeds of this nation [Rome]. They have established markets, bridges, and bathhouses. Rabbi Yose was silent. Rabbi Shimᶜon the son of Yoḥai said: Everything they established, they established only for themselves. Markets to seat prostitutes in them; bath houses to pamper themselves; bridges to take tolls. Yehuda the son of converts went and reported the matter and it was heard by the rulers. They said Yehuda who praised, will be praised. Yose who was silent will be exiled to Sepphoris.[83] Shimᶜon who condemned, will be killed.   TB Shabbat 33b and see Avoda Zara 2b

We could almost imagine such a conversation between Clement and Tertullian. Tertullian also shared with this same Rabbi Shimᶜon bar Yoḥai an absolute opposition to engaging in gainful employment. According to legend, when the latter was released from eleven years' hiding in a cave, he came out and saw Jews plowing and blasted them in his anger.[84] A Tertullian could have done no more.[85]

This instance of the discourse of martyrdom turns out to be almost emblematic for the textual forces that eventually, in my view, would mark the greatest cultural difference between rabbinic Judaism and the Church. As "orthodox" Christianity developed its definitive corpus of patristic literature, dissenting voices gradually were either eliminated or homogenized into the "single-authored" text of the Church—emblematic of this is Tertullian's exclusion from that canon—while in the rabbinic texts, the chorus of heterogeneity (certainly on this, as on many questions) remained loud and cacophonous in the carnivalesque Talmud.[86] The formation of these two different types of canon at about the same time, in approximately the fifth century, finally, I think, provided one of the dividing points that would mark off a hegemonic rabbinic Jewish culture very different from what achieved hegemony as orthodox Christianity. In rabbinic Jewish textuality, the very fact that both options remain enshrined in the same text with the same consequent authority produces a religio-cultural situation in which schism can be avoided while nearly opposing ideological options both remain active.

Several scholars, working from very different disciplinary foundations, have pointed to this aspect as characteristic, and even determinative of rabbinic Judaism. As Gerald Bruns insightfully put it, "From a transcendental standpoint, this theory of authority is paradoxical because it is seen to hang on the heteroglossia of dialogue, on speaking with many voices, rather than on the logical principle of univocity, or speaking with one mind. Instead, the idea of speaking with one mind . . . is explicitly rejected; single-mindedness produces factionalism."[87] Keith Hopkins has analyzed this difference from the point of view of historical sociology, arguing that "unlike Judaism after the destruction of the Temple, Christianity was dogmatic and hierarchical; dogmatic, in the sense that Christian leaders from early on claimed that their own interpretation of Christian faith was the only true interpretation of the faith, and hierarchical, in that leaders claimed legitimacy for the authority of their interpretation as priests or bishops."

Hopkins describes this phenomenon historically: "Admittedly, individual leaders claimed that their own individual interpretation of the law was right, and that other interpretations were wrong. But systemically, at some unknown date, Jewish rabbis seem to have come to the conclusion, however reluctantly, that they were bound to disagree, and that disagreement was endemic."[88] Shaye Cohen, on the other hand, analyzes it functionally: "The great achievement of Rabbinic Judaism is not that it triumphed over competitors, organized and unorganized, but that it created a framework which tolerated, even encouraged disputes, but did not create sects."[89] Cohen is precise here: rabbinic Judaism did not engage in the formation of schisms.[90] Indeed, as Frend makes eminently clear, the conflict between rigorist approaches vis-à-vis martyrdom versus accommodation to the Empire and ones more similar to those of a Rabbi like Yose the son of Kisma repeatedly led to schism in the late ancient Church. Novatianism, Donatism, and the Meletian schism were all products of such conflicts.[91] It just seems right in this context that the Donatist schism began, or at least was prefigured, according to Frend, in the conflict between a trickster, Bishop Mensurius of Carthage, who had handed over heretical books to the Roman authorities for burning during the Great Persecution, and the primate Secundus of Numidia, who "took his stand on the example of the martyr-priest Eleazar in 2 Maccabees and claimed to have defied them."[92] The Talmud, as we have seen, comprehends both of these seemingly mutually exclusive options on the same page.

Rabbinic Jews and Christians were debating the same question of deception, flight, or martyrdom through the third century, but only Christian textuality seems bound to answer the question "Quo vadis?." For the Rabbis, the destination can remain open. It is not finally the issues themselves, or even the positions taken on them, that divide the traditions, but the forms of textuality and authority that they generate and venerate.[93] Ambrose (and other patristic "authors") control their texts in ways that the unauthored rabbinic text does not. A useful analogy would be to Bakhtin's distinction between Tolstoy and Dostoevsky, with Ambrose playing Tolstoy to the Talmud's Dostoevsky. This analogy should make clear, as well, that this typology does not imply a hierarchy. It should also be emphasized that "tolerance" for diversity is *not* what was at issue here. There is no reason to see the Rabbis as any more tolerant than the Fathers. The issue is rather the elasticity or plasticity of the discourse of the different traditions in their ability and desire to allow heterogeneity on certain kinds of questions.

CHAPTER 3

Thinking with Virgins

Engendering Judeo-Christian Difference

"The glory of women is always twisted."

—*Nicole Loraux*

"Charlotte, we're Jewish," says Cher in the opening scene of *Mermaids*, as she passes her adolescent daughter, Wynona Ryder, genuflecting ecstatically at her private shrine to St. Perpetua. Charlotte abandons her worship of the martyr, with a rather dramatic effect on her nascent sex life. What might it be about a young Christian woman tortured to death in the arena in third-century North Africa that would so attract an American Jewish teenager as a model and ego ideal?

In fact, virginity and martyrdom have been intimately connected in Christianity from the fourth century on, and the virgin girl is a topos in both Judaism and Christianity for thinking about male bodies and their spiritual states. Here, I will investigate the figure of the virgin girl in the traditions of both rabbinic Jews and Christians in late antiquity, first as an ego ideal for men, and then as one for women, with strikingly different conclusions to the two analyses.[1]

Virgin Rabbis; or, the Empire as Brothel

At the end of the story about Rabbi Eliᶜezer and the disciple of Jesus that we read in the first chapter, the Rabbi declares that his sin was violating the injunction encapsulated in a verse of Proverbs to stay far away from sectarian heresy, namely, Christianity. When the Talmud cites this story, the text continues directly with a halakhic passage that draws on the citation from Proverbs that was used in the story about Rabbi Eliᶜezer: "Keep her ways far away from you, and do not come near to the opening of her door"

(Proverbs 5:8). The issue begins with a typical midrashic exploration of the precise referent of "her" in the verse:

> "Keep her [the "Strange Woman's"] ways far away from you!"—This [refers] to sectarianism. "And do not come near to the opening of her door"—This is the government.
>
> There are those who say: "Keep her ways far away from you!"— This is sectarianism and the government. "And do not come near to the opening of her door"—This is the prostitute. How far [must one keep away from the prostitute's door]? Rav Ḥisda said: "four cubits." Babylonian Talmud Avoda Zara 17a[2]

From here until the end of the text, these three themes, heresy, collaboration, and prostitution will be intertwined. Sectarian heresy, prostitution, and collaboration with Roman power had become associated in the cultural "unconscious" of rabbinic Judaism, no doubt at least in part simply because all three are seductive and dangerous.[3] The seemingly literal reading, that one must be wary of the sexual lure of the "strange woman," is tacked on here, almost as an afterthought. However, as we shall see, there are overtones to this nexus that go far beyond this rather obvious and trivial observation. The association of negative Jewish behavior with the lust of the male customer of the prostitute is crucial to the main theme of the text, the transformation of the chaste Jewish male—and indeed the Jewish people— into female virgin as the one most fit to resist such sexualized enticements.[4]

The gendering of sectarian heresy, which here is Christianity, is supported by the fact that in the Proverbs verse what one is enjoined to keep away from is "her ways."[5] The literal subject of the verse is the seductive "strange woman," whose lips drip honey, but whose aftertaste is bitter. It is important to recognize here a major metaphorical shift. For the Prophets, the dominant metaphor is of a female Israel gone awhoring with myriad lovers, while here, we find Israel figured as a lustful male tempted sorely by a seductive female. This shift of the metaphor of a straying Israel from female to male is accomplished by repeatedly reading figures of sexual danger from Proverbs as if they were allegories for religious temptations and dangers. Foreign whores and seductive daughters are transformed, as we shall see below, into heresies and seductions of collaboration, thus rendering the errant Jews their illicit male partner.[6]

At first glance, this claim may seem strange, since I and others have been arguing so strenuously that the Rabbis saw themselves as feminized.[7] However, on further reflection, there is no paradox here at all. If the negative, the abjected image of self is the lustful male, the valorized image is the virgin female. We can find an explicit modern pendant for this theory in Ramakrishna's exhortation to his disciples to "become woman" in order to transcend their own sexual desire to be with women: "A man can change his nature by imitating another's character. By transposing on to yourself the attributes of woman, you gradually destroy lust and the other sensual drives. You begin to behave like women."[8] By the time we reach the end of the talmudic narrative, we shall see that the female virgin is indeed an object of identification for the Rabbis, in much the same way that Virginia Burrus has taught us that the virgin performed symbolically for contemporary Christians such as the fourth-century Bishop Ambrose of Milan. As we shall see below through a reading of her work, at a time contemporaneous with the Rabbis, Ambrose also urged self-feminization as an antidote to the perceived evils of the male psyche. In both late ancient Christianity and Judaism, ideal male identity was secured in part via cross-gender identification with female virgins. Affinities run strong and deep.

Following this small bit of halakhic discourse, the Talmud goes on with the stories of tricksters and martyrs that I have analyzed in the previous chapter. I wish now to go back and interpret a part of the talmudic martyrology that I passed over in that reading. Close reading of this passage will strongly support the interpretation that I have been giving and amplify its meanings. Immediately after describing the punishments of the three members of Rabbi Ḥanina's family, the text explains why God has allowed them to be so maltreated:

> Him to burning, for he used to pronounce the Holy Name literally. How is it possible that he did such a thing?! For we have a tradition that Abba Shaul says that also one who pronounces the Holy Name literally has no place in the World to Come. He did it for the purpose of self-instruction, for as another tradition says: "'Do not learn to do' [pronouncing God's name; Deut. 18:9], but you may learn in order to understand and to teach." [If that is the case], why was he punished? Because he used to pronounce the Holy Name literally in public, and

it says "This is my eternal name" [Exodus 3:15], but the word "eternal" לעולם is spelt as if it meant "for hiding" לעלם.

And his wife for execution [by the sword], because she did not censure him.

And his daughter to sit in a prostitute's booth, for Rabbi Yoḥanan said: She was once walking among the great of Rome, and they said, "How beautiful are the steps of this maiden!" And she immediately became more meticulous about her steps.

The narrative explains the punishments of the three members of the martyr's family and provides a version of a theodicy. The explanations of the punishment of the Rabbi and of his daughter are doublets and highly gendered in their implications. Rabbi Ḥanina himself was condemned for doing something in public that he should have done in private. The two explanations for his punishment, the "realistic" one, that the Romans had arrested him for illegally teaching Torah in public and the theodical one, that God had arrested him for revealing His name to the public, have to be read as comments upon each other.

It was appropriate, indeed, for him to be pronouncing God's name as it is written and together with its vowels in order to instruct himself, but this activity needed to be carried in private, just as his study and teaching of Torah ought to have been in private, according to Rabbi Yose the son of Kisma. God's name was given for hiding, not for public exposure to the eyes of the hostile Romans. In other words, the text is proposing a homology between the reasons for Rabbi Ḥanina's capture by the Romans at both the pragmatic and the theological levels. God has meant the teaching of Torah to be a private, internal activity for the Jewish people in a hostile world, a "hidden transcript," and not a matter of provocation and defiance, just as a chaste maiden is meant to keep herself hidden from the eyes of lustful males and certainly not to encourage and willfully attract their gazes. The Torah is a bride for the Rabbis: "Rabbi Ḥiyya taught: Anyone who studies Torah in front of the one of the 'people of the land' is like one who has intercourse with his fiancee in front of them" (TB Pesaḥim 49b).[9] By teaching Torah in public, therefore, Rabbi Ḥanina was engaged in an act as provocative and as immodest as that of his daughter.

Resistance, according to this view—the trickster party in rabbinic Judaism—consists of doing what we do without getting into trouble and using evasiveness in order to keep doing it. Interestingly enough, in defying the Romans and thus courting a martyr's death, Rabbi Ḥanina was behaving in a way culturally intelligible to the Romans[10]—behaving like a "real man," a muscle Jew—while Rabbi Yose the son of Kisma through deceptive, "womanish" complicity with the Romans, *resisted* their cultural hegemony.[11]

As I have suggested, however, Rabbi Ḥanina's own sin, the sin of public exposure of the Torah to the gaze of outsiders, whether Jewish or Roman, is doubled by the sin of his daughter, which then enables us to interpret the father's transgression. She, like the Torah "bride" of her father, reveals herself in that same marketplace.[12] Exposed to the predatory male gaze, ethnicized as both "Roman" and the province of the powerful males of Rome, she does not evade the gaze, but seeks to enhance her object status further.[13] Having thus rendered herself a sexual object, she is punished by being turned into a whore, the ultimate depersonalized sexual object. Although the text is couched in the form of a critique of the woman here, and that (unfair) judgment, that blaming of the victim if you will, ought not to be papered over in our reading, at the same time, there is also encoded here a critique of the male gaze itself. It is no accident that it is the important men of Rome who are represented at this moment. They are the proverbial (or stereotypical) "construction workers" in this text. And Rashi comments, citing the biblical verse: "A respectable king's daughter remains indoors," at one and the same time a "sexist" demand for a kind of purdah for women and, since the daughter of the king is Israel, a comment on the proper behavior of Jews in general in the world. The daughter's story then doubles the critique of her father's provocative behavior. Through this doubling, the approved practice for Jews is gendered feminine, while the behavior of the Romans is gendered masculine. The violence of their gaze is congruous with the greater violence of their bloodshed, and the resistance of the Jews is to be veiled: "eternal" through being "in hiding," as the double meaning of the verse implies. "Remain indoors. Continue to live, continue to maintain Jewish practice, but do not behave in ways that draw attention to us or provoke the hostile intervention of the ruling powers. It is God who has sent them to rule." Thus, if we return to the terms of the contestation encountered in the last chapter, the text once more seemingly endorses the view of Rabbi Yose the son of Kisma (and the practice of Rabbi Elᶜazar ben Perata, as well) that the trickster is to be preferred over the martyr, but it does not by any means entirely erase or delegitmate the way of Rabbi Ḥanina, either.

The end of the daughter's story reprises the issue of hidden transcripts and tricksterism, this time, however firmly gendering it by incorporating it in a version of the folk tale of the virgin in the brothel. In her ultimate redemption, and via the mode by which she preserves herself, this girl will be installed as an archetypical female virgin, as a positively marked, valorized model for Jewish masculinity:

> Beruria, the wife of Rabbi Meʾir was the daughter of Rabbi Ḥanina. She said to him: It is painful to me that my sister is sitting in a prostitute's booth. He took a *tarqeva* of dinars and went, saying if she has done nothing wrong [i.e., if she is sexually innocent], there will be a miracle, and if not, there will be no miracle. He dressed up as a soldier and solicited her. She said: I am menstruating. He said: I can wait. She said: There are many here more beautiful than I. He said: I understand from this that she has done nothing wrong. He went to her guard: Give her to me! The guard said: I am afraid of the king. He [Meʾir] took the *tarqeva* of dinars, and gave it to him, and said: Take the *tarqeva* of dinars. Keep half and use half for bribing anyone who comes. He [the guard] said: What shall I do when they are gone? He [Meʾir] said: Say 'God of Meʾir save me' and you will be saved. He [guard] said: How do I know that this will be so? He [Meʾir] said: [Now you will see.] There came some dogs that eat people.[14] He shouted to them, and they came to eat him. He said: 'God of Meʾir save me,' and they let him go.
>
> He let her go.

In contrast to a Polyxena or a Perpetua, the archetypal Greco-Roman-Christian martyrs for chastity, the daughter of Rabbi Ḥanina does not stand up to her oppressors and defend her virtue in a demonstrative way, thus bringing upon her their wrath and her death. Rather, she tricks her way out of the situation through lies and wiles (rather like the Three Billy Goats Gruff and their troll from European folklore). All that is necessary for God to perform miracles and for her to be saved, however, is that she succeed at the task. The "dishonorable" means are totally irrelevant. At the same time, though, the text is thematizing the vulnerability of the people without power. Without the miracle, they would be eaten alive by the "dogs."

Lest we think that the counsel of tricksterism is intended only for women, the text immediately goes on to disable such a reading:

> The matter became known in the house of the king. They brought him [the guard] and crucified him. He said 'God of Meʾir save me,' and they took him down and asked: What was that?[15] He told them: This is how the events took place. They wrote it on the gates of the city, and they engraved Rabbi Meʾir's face on the gates of Rome and said: If a man who looks like this comes, arrest him! When Rabbi Meʾir came there, they wished to arrest him. He ran away from them and *went into a whorehouse.* Elijah came in the guise of a whore and embraced him. *Some say that he put his hand in Gentile foods and tasted them.* They [the Romans] said: God forfend! If that were Rabbi Meʾir he wouldn't do such a thing.[16] Because of these events [Rabbi Meʾir] ran away to Babylonia.

The most striking aspect of this sequence is, of course, the escape via entering into the whorehouse and, moreover, disguising himself, once more, as a customer of the prostitutes. This time, however, it is not to test the chastity of someone else, but to save his own skin. Just as it was considered by the Jewish text entirely proper for the young woman to pretend to acquiescence in prostitution in order to preserve her life, so it is entirely proper for Rabbi Meʾir to disguise himself and pretend to (or maybe actually) violate the Jewish law in order to keep himself alive, in accord with the principle that the commandments are given to live by, and not to die by. The trickster option is reopened, and Rabbi Meʾir runs away to Babylonia, a safer place for the study of Torah, and not so incidentally the place where this story was formulated.

In the end, then, there is a perfect analogy between the male Rabbi and the young female Jew, and the thematic material of the entire text is brought together in a culminating fashion. The association between the Roman government and its blandishments and dangers and the house of prostitution is reprised, and the text opens up to its final moral and nearly allegorical meanings in which the Jewish people are figured no more as a man, Jacob, even a feminized man, but as a woman.[17] It is now Rabbi Meʾir, the paragon of male virtue, who preserves his chastity in the whorehouse.[18] As Laurie Davis has phrased it, "the rabbis see themselves as virgins in a brothel."[19]

Virgin Fathers; or, Androgyny and the Lion

In this collection of martyr stories from the Talmud Avoda Zara, a text that insists on the representation of the Christian heresy as a beautiful prostitute who tempts the male Jewish people away from God, the Rabbis seem very close to those Christian ascetics who at exactly the same period also were using the female virgin as *their* most valorized exemplar.[20] The harlot, moreover, was a privileged metaphor for heresy among fourth-century Christians, as well.[21] These Christians were tangled up with power and prestige in the Empire in highly complex and nuanced ways that have been explored by Virginia Burrus: "To state the thesis in general terms: post-Constantinian Christianity lays claim to the power of classical male speech; yet at the same time late ancient Christian discourse continues to locate itself in paradoxical relation to classical discourse through a stance of feminizing ascesis that renounces public speech."[22] As Burrus here unveils, within the discourse of such figures as the late fourth-century Christian writers Ambrose and Prudentius, there are knotty and intricate elements of resistance to the dominant (Roman) discourse of masculinity, and of masculine sexuality in particular. This resistance or reconception of masculinity is achieved in no small measure by "thinking with" virgins.

For example, in Ambrose's *On Virgins*, we find such countermasculinity thematized and symbolized in a story that issues in an array of paradoxical gender identifications. In one crucial episode, Thecla, the apocryphal female associate of Paul, has entered the martyrological ring. She is the proverbial Christian who has been thrown to the lions. As Ambrose structures his recounting of this episode, the lion "initially represents the sexual violence signalled by both the 'rage' of Thecla's would-be husband and the 'immodest eyes' of the male onlookers who gaze upon the spectacle of her nakedness."[23] The would-be martyr, Thecla, voluntarily presents to the lion her "vital parts," an obvious eroticized displacement of the offer of her sexual parts to her rejected fiancé. Male sexuality is figured as devouring of the woman, and the lion represents the rapacity of a husband, as well as that of the Empire.[24] As Gillian Clark has written, "Christians inherited a discourse of sexuality as invasive and violent."[25] The text draws an explicit analogy between the hunger of the male lion to eat the virgin's flesh and the lust of her husband to consummate the marriage. Even the

lion, a mere beast, however, is led to transform its bestial and violent maleness in the presence of the virgin martyr, and by her example.

We find an important shift taking place in fourth-century Christian
discourse. As is well known by now, earlier Christian texts frequently represented the possibility of a virilization of the female, whether as martyr,
Perpetua, or as apostle, Thecla.[26] It could be argued, indeed, that in the
earliest periods of Christianity, there was a radical critique of Greco-Roman
gender discourses and sexual dimorphism *tout court*. This critique is represented in large part through "gender-bending" attacks on female subordi-
nation such as the famous early story in which Jesus promises to make
Mary male.[27] Although, obviously, we should be very chary of ascribing
"feminist" motives to such representations, it seems that the stance of dras-
tic alienation from the Roman world and all of its works, including marriage, led to at least this burst of imagination, this envisioning of female
power and autonomy.[28]

In the second century, we find Perpetua, who is marked as the Christian resister to the Roman culture of gender through her "ability to stare
directly back into the faces of her persecutors, not with the elusive de-
meanour of a proper *matrona*," but with a returned gaze that, in Brent
Shaw's words, "broke with the normative body language in a way that signalled an aggressiveness that was not one of conventional femininity."[29]
Slightly before her, there is Blandina, whose "fortitude and endurance were
compared to those of a victorious male athlete."[30] In contrast to these virile, masculinized female martyrs of the second century, in the fourth century, we have a much more complex structure of gender in which both the
masculinized aggressivity of the female martyr as *virago* and an almost contradictory feminized passivity as *virgo* are produced simultaneously.[31] In
the Acts of Paul and Thecla, Thecla is saved by a *female* lion, who herself
dies in the arena protecting the virgin from the attack of a male lion and
serves as a powerful icon not only of resistance to the family values of the
ancient city, but of female autonomy and solidarity.[32] In Ambrose's narrative, the male lion "becomes female" and abandons his attack on the girl.[33]
In other words, what was once unambiguously countercultural and sub-
versive with respect to Rome and its gendered hierarchies and representations had now become highly ambiguous, almost fluid in its meanings. No
longer simply the victorious, valorous, virilized gladiator, à la Perpetua, the

fourth-century virgin martyr was now partially rewritten via the intertexts as a model of passive, female virtue.[34]

Burrus traces the discursive modes through which is achieved "the literary transformation of would-be 'manly' women—*viragines*—into femininely docile *virgines*."[35] The most vivid example of this is in her reading of Prudentius's poem on the death of the martyr Agnes. In this text, the virgin presents her breast to the persecuting executioner's sword, but in the end is executed by decapitation. This is a highly marked shift, as Burrus argues, employing the work of Nicole Loraux. Death by sword to the breast is a masculine death, the death of a warrior; death by sword to the neck is a feminine death, the death of a sacrificial victim.[36] Loraux has shown how shifting versions of the story of the death of the Trojan virgin Polyxena from Euripides through Virgil differently construct this symbol.[37] In various of these versions, Polyxena is either given the choice of the virile death by sword to the breast or denied that choice and forced to accept the feminine death. Burrus demonstrates how the variations of the death of this virgin as it moves from Euripides through Ovid and Seneca are vital for understanding its Christian version in Prudentius. In the Greek, Polyxena offers the executioner the manly breast or the womanly throat, and the latter chooses the throat. Ovid and Seneca, on the other hand, "unlike Euripides, are willing to grant the virgin at least the outward sign of a noble and manly death, admittedly still controlled by bridal and sacrificial interpretations." Prudentius's variation, however, is even more chilling than Euripides' because this virgin offers only the manly breast, but the text has her killed nevertheless via the suppliant bend of the neck for decapitation.

As Burrus concludes: "Prudentius does not fail to exploit the exaggerated boldness of the Latin Polyxena as she shapes his portrait of Agnes, but like the Greek tragedian he compromises his portrayal of manly womanhood at the final, fatal moment. Refocusing the narrative gaze on the vulnerability of the female neck, Prudentius provides Agnes with the place of death which for him, as for ancient Greek tragedy, reestablishes her essential femininity in sexualized subjugation. But the message now rings more harshly. Euripides' Polyxena offers both breast and throat only to die by the more feminine death of the throat. But Prudentius's still more virile Agnes offers *only her breast*, so that it is in complete and chilling disregard of her words that her *neck* is severed. More violently even than Euripides' Polyxena, the Christian Agnes must be wrenched back into her womanly place."

"She is not after all audacious *virago* but docile *virgo*,"[38] not, that is, triumphant warrior, but sacrificed virgin. There is, however, yet one more wrinkle to be added to this analysis, for the submissive neck for decapitation does not carry precisely the meaning of the feminine death via piercing the throat, either, but suggests rather the reclaiming of a variety of masculinized honor, like the submission to death of a defeated gladiator. Thus all of the ambiguities of gendering, honor, and death remain in play while clearly restraining the audacity, the representation of female martyr as *victorious* gladiator, as *virago*, that characterized the second-century texts.[39] As Burrus concludes, "Perhaps we should resist the temptation to seek a 'final word' which would resolve the tensions and ambiguities of the late fourth-century tale into one all-too-neat judgment."[40]

The female martyr remained a highly charged symbol, owing to her subversions of sexuality and gender, but she functioned now most readily as an example for the male ascetic. As virilized woman, she could have functioned as an ego ideal for Christian women, an ideal that conduces to the overturning of gendered hierarchies and even of gender itself, as signified by Thecla's lioness and her own androgynous mien.[41] Burrus shows that as passive virgin, mirrored by the feminized male lion Thecla is no longer primarily a figure for the virilized female, but rather for the feminized male, the male who upon perceiving her is inspired, like the lion, to a complete renunciation of his "naturally" violent, leonine, male sexuality—which is not to say that he achieves it. The masculinization and pluralization of the lions in the Ambrose version is significant of their transformation into an icon of the audience watching the martyrdom (and the audience reading the martyrology), at least insofar as these are male.[42] This audience (and the writers/readers) are thus called upon to identify both with the lion and with the victim of that lion, with both the figure of an oppressive male and that of a resistant virgin. One way of saying this would be that in the earlier version, one could imagine at least a female subjectivity in some sense behind the text. The implied author *could* be female.[43] The implied author of Ambrose's text is unambiguously, if complexly, gendered male.[44] Thus, the virgin becomes available for male identification.[45]

Burrus sums up her reading of this passage by remarking that "through the manipulation of the figure of the lion, the subjugating force of male sexual violence has not been defeated so much as sublimated. On one reading at least, the lion's averted, feminized gaze continues paradoxically to restrain the virgin; the very gesture of honoring her—indeed of freely mirroring her feminine subjugation—becomes itself the vehicle of her constraint."[46] In the era of "imperial Christianity," the resistance to male sexuality, understood as "naturally" violent because of its cultural construction within the dominant Roman formation to which most Christians had belonged, remained an important part of Christian male self-construction, but it no longer could accommodate such resistance through figurations of female "achievement" of maleness.[47] Gender hierarchy had to be preserved, but not at the cost of reinstating an ideal of invasive phallic maleness. The point was to "sublimate" it. Subjugation was to be retained, but without violence. This is the moment that Burrus refers to as "the veiling of the phallus." A paradoxical relation of these men to their own male selves is paralleled in their paradoxical relation to classical discourse (figured as "male") and even to Roman imperial power itself. It is precisely through their stance of self-feminization that the Fathers produced and maintained their discourses of subjugation of women.

In this respect too, the Fathers are quite similar to both early Rabbis and later rabbinic tradition. These also subjugated women through a discourse of self-feminization.[48] Both early rabbinic Jews and early Christians performed resistance to the Roman imperial power structure through "gender bending"—males consciously renouncing the markers of masculinity and adopting practices that signified them as female within the economy of Roman gender models—thus marking their own understanding that gender itself is implicated in the maintenance of political power. Various symbolic enactments of "femaleness"—as constructed within a particular system of genders—among them asceticism, submissiveness, retiring to private spaces, (ostensible) renunciation of political power, exclusive devotion to study, and self-castration[49] were adopted variously by Christians or rabbinic Jews as acts of resistance against Roman culture and the masculinist exercise of power.

This point is made by Burrus about early Christianity: "For men, the pursuit of Christian ascesis entailed the rejection of public life and therefore of the hierarchies of office and gender; in this respect, their opponents were not far off the mark when they insinuated that male ascetics were 'feminized' through their rejection of the most basic cultural expressions of male identity."[50] Sulpicius Severus, a Gallic ascetic synchronous with our talmudic text, like Ambrose, his contemporary and associate explicitly identifies women, and especially virginal women, as his models for the ascetic life of retirement and withdrawal from public exposure and activity. "Sulpicius' special interest in virginal women is in large part attributable, I think, to the fact that it is women in general and virginal women in particular who traditionally model the life of complete retirement and avoidance of public exposure," Burrus writes. Thus, "Sulpicius puts forth the radical suggestion that the male must indeed 'become female' through his ascetic renunciation of public life" and "presents the virgin as an ideal of which Martin [of Tours, the soldier-monk who brought Christianity to much of fourth-century Gaul] acknowledges himself to fall short, compromised by his episcopal office and also, I would add, by his very maleness."[51] The male must become female in order to escape the moral dangers of his masculine state.

This parallels the becoming female of the Rabbis through their ascetic renunciations of intercourse with alluring Christianity or participation in the Roman state. The Rabbis, as well, adopted distinctly feminized stances of renunciation of political power.[52] In the talmudic text, the Rabbis are close, mutatis mutandis, to those ascetics for whom the virgin was a model for a life of withdrawal from public exposure—mutatis mutandis, for the withdrawal of a Roman aristocrat from the public could not be identical to the withdrawal of a Jewish Sage. Insofar as the female virgin was being utilized by male cultural products as a mode of negotiation of their critical, resisting, accommodating, alienated, envious, and other stances toward Roman power and cultural prestige, different positionings with respect to "Rome" would result in different virgins.

As a tentative hypothesis, I would offer the following: Identification with the female virgin was a mode for both Rabbis and Fathers of disidentification with a "Rome" whose power was stereotyped as a highly sexualized male. Both groups were engaged in complex, tangled, and ambivalent negotiations of self-fashionings in response to their attraction and repulsion from that Rome. Each, however, occupied a different space within the economies of power and ethnic emplacement in the Empire. Christian writers, even as late as the fourth or fifth centuries, frequently were former Roman "pagans," sons of power and prestige in imperial society who were highly educated and who identified with classical culture. It is telling that both Ambrose and Prudentius were former provincial governors.[53] Their renunciation of such identification and certain forms of power and prestige is thus both more dramatic (for being voluntary and "expensive"[54]) and more ambivalent than that of the Rabbis, who were always already outsiders to a certain extent by virtue of birth into a minority ethnic and religious group and by virtue of socialization into a different language and literary tradition.

Christian culture, with its powerful, but by no means univocal critique of marriage, continued to represent a much more radical rejection of Roman cultural values than did that of the Rabbis. I find here, nevertheless, a remarkable example of sharp cultural convergence. This is analogous, in Burrus's subtle readings, of the ways that power and prestige were both subverted and maintained, even by such ascetic figures as Sulpicius (a fortiori by bishops such as Ambrose) through their rhetorics of seclusion, withdrawal, and "feminizing ascesis."[55]

This analysis of Burrus's proves strikingly productive, therefore, for our understanding of the rabbinic text, as well, for parallel to the development of a discourse of male identification with female virgins among the Fathers, a similar discourse was developing among the Rabbis. The Rabbis also obviously stood in a highly ambivalent position vis-à-vis their version of "Rome." As we have seen, for them, being male represented a species of danger, danger of being "seduced" into pursuing one of two prostitutes, heretical sectarianism in the form of Christianity (which was becoming the dominant religion of the Empire) or collaboration with Roman power.[56] Thus, also for them, the female virgin was to become symbolic of a virtual ego ideal.

Another way of saying this would be to mark the gap between the explicit and implicit meanings of the rabbinic text. On the explicit level, the text represents the purity of rabbinic culture, its efforts to remain entirely different and other from Christianity. However, at the same time, via its use of the figure of the female virgin to symbolize its valorized male self— the self that resists Christianization—it is indicating, at this distance at least, the convergence of rabbinic culture with that of the Christians, or, perhaps better put, their common cultural history and development. In her habitation of "private" indoor spaces, the talmudic virgin is the figure who is construed as most able to resist the "sexual" seductions of both sectarianism and accommodation to Roman power. To reprise: It is behaving as a male with respect to the "female" blandishments of heresy or collaboration that gets one into trouble. Behaving as a "female," then, would get one out of it.

Virgin Brides, Virgin Martyrs

For all this convergence, however, there are differences, as well. As Burrus has written: "Both the continuity and the 'otherness' of rabbinic Judaism in relation to Christianity are revealing, as Jewish and Christian men are seen to deploy strikingly different rhetorics of sexuality for the construction of counter-masculinities within the context of late ancient Greco-Roman culture."[57] One source of such differences, I would suggest, is that the use of the virgin as a male identificatory symbol is highly dependent on the posture of a given society toward actual virgin girls, and this was crucially different for the Rabbis and for the Fathers of the fourth-century Church. Up until now, I have focused entirely on the identification of the Rabbis with the female virgin in the brothel as a symbol of their tricky resistance, their playing of the hidden transcript, within the brothel of the Empire.[58] As such, my strategy has been to downplay the gendered differences of the text, emphasizing instead the ways that the genders are homologized in the narrative, that Rabbi Me'ir doubles the daughter of Rabbi Ḥanina, who doubles Rabbi El'azar ben Perata in his trickster escape, who doubles Rabbi Eli'ezer in his. All these males are feminized figures finally metaphoricized as the virgin in the brothel. The tricksterism of the virgin daughter thus at one level reprises and spotlights the openness of the talmudic text on the question of tricksters versus martyrs. Even in the very narrative in which martyrdom is being valorized, there is a favored instance as well of tricky escape. But even this is compromised by the fact that both the daughter and Rabbi Yose ben Kisma seem engaged in pleasing "the great men of Rome." Both the defiance of the father and the trickster escape of the daughter seem equally valorized, or at any rate, once more, the text just won't settle down to a univocal position on the acts of the tricksters and the martyrs.

However, if we reread its ending, now emphasizing gendered differences rather than disavowing them, we will find very different meanings emerging from the text. In other words, if we look at the virgin as a representative of Jewish female subjectivity, rather than as a transgendered symbol of identification for the Rabbis and for the people of Israel, we suddenly discover not a narrative that opens options for Jewish *people*, but a narrative that shuts them down for Jewish *women*.

To put it bluntly: In the rabbinic world, there can be no virgin martyrs.[59] The daughter has to escape from the brothel, not only to reopen and revalorize the trickster option, but also because she must not die a virgin. The female virgin provided a highly valued model of rabbinic and patristic resistance to certain "Roman" cultural values and practices, as we have seen. But this Jewish virgin, insofar as she is a girl and not a mere device for the exploration of male selves,[60] is subtly different from her Christian sisters.[61] She escapes her fated sexual violation, not through open resistance, resistance that ultimately costs her her life, like the second-century Perpetua, whose continued marital life is interpreted as sexual violation, or even like the fourth-century Agnes, but instead through the use of trickster methods, "feminine" wiles, which allow her to escape both fates, rape as well as death. If the paradigmatic virgin for the fourth-century Fathers was the virgin martyr, the paradigmatic virgin for the Rabbis was the virgin in the brothel, who will, in the end, be a virgin bride.[62]

The sequel to the story of Thecla in Ambrose forms a remarkable parallel to the talmudic story that we have just read and will help sharpen this point dramatically.[63] It is so close to the talmudic narrative that it must clearly count as a variant of the same folktale type, but, the differences between the two culturally localized versions (ecotypes) are as instructive as the similarities. Since the text is rather long, I will paraphrase it, quoting only excerpts.

Ambrose tells of a virgin in Antioch who avoided being seen in public and who, knowing of the desire of many men for her, declared herself a perpetual virgin, whereupon "she was no longer loved, instead she was betrayed." The virgin, insisting on her chastity and not afraid of death, prepares herself for it. However, her persecutors have a more nefarious plan. They will allow her neither the crown of martyrdom nor virginity. After she refuses to sacrifice to the emperor, they send her, like Rabbi Ḥanina's daughter, to a brothel:

> At this the young woman, not in doubt about her religion but fearing for her chastity, said to herself: "What shall I do? Today I shall be either a martyr or a virgin. One of the two crowns is begrudged us. But the title of virginity has no meaning where the author of virginity is denied."

Virginity itself is worthless unless it is virginity of God. She will not sacrifice in order to preserve her chastity, any more than she would to preserve her life. Rather than risking giving up her religion, she chooses to enter the brothel, assuming that, like Rahab, she will be forgiven for this. Ambrose continues:

> All at once my discourse is ashamed and fears, as it were, to enter upon and relate the wicked course of events. Stop your ears, virgins of God: a young woman of God is being led to a brothel. But open your ears, virgins of God: a virgin can be made to prostitute herself but she cannot be made to commit adultery. Wherever a virgin of God is, there is a temple of God. Brothels not only do not bring chastity into disrepute, but chastity even does away with the disrepute of a place.
>
> A huge crowd of curiosity seekers surged towards the bordello. (Learn the miracles of the martyrs, holy virgins, but unlearn the vocabulary of these places.) The dove was shut up inside, while outside the hawks were loud, contending among themselves as to who would be the first to seize the prey.

In an echo of the lions, who were metaphorical representations of male sexual desire in the Thecla sequence, here we find the desiring male represented as a raptor. The virgin prays, invoking the miracle that saved Daniel from the lion's den, and indeed, God vouchsafes her a miracle in the form of a trickster:

> She had hardly completed the prayer when all of a sudden a man with the appearance of a fearsome soldier burst in. How the virgin trembled before him. . . . "A sheep too may lie hidden in this lair of wolves. Christ, who even has his legions (cf. Matt. 26:53), has his soldiers as well. Or perhaps the executioner has come in.[64] Do not be afraid, my soul: he is used to making martyrs." O Virgin, "your faith has saved you" (Luke 8:48).

The virgin here considers the possibility that the fierce soldier who has come in is not a lustful customer, but her potential executioner. Perhaps she will be saved by her faith, granted the two crowns of virginity and martyrdom after all. But not quite, for

> the soldier said to her: "I beg you not to fear, my sister. I have come here as your brother to save my soul, not to destroy it. Heed me, so that you may be spared. Having come in as an adulterer, I shall, if you wish, go out a martyr. Let us exchange our clothing; yours fits me and mine fits you, but both fit Christ. Your garb will make me a true soldier; mine will make you a virgin. You will be clothed well and I shall be stripped better, so that the persecutor may recognize me. Put on the garment that will hide the woman and hand over the one that will consecrate the martyr." . . . While saying this he removed his cloak, which was a garment that until this time was suspected of being that of a persecutor and an adulterer. . . . When she had changed her clothing the maiden flew out from the snare, but no longer with her own wings, inasmuch as she was borne by spiritual wings. And—what had never been seen before—she left the brothel a virgin, but Christ's.

Ambrose's rhetoric here is very deft. The virgin in the brothel, so far from being a sight that the ages never had seen, is practically a topos in this type of literature, but Ambrose (with a wink and a nudge) informs us that this was a sight that never had been seen before.[65] The blind and rapacious audience cannot see the *thauma edestai* that there is before their eyes, an intact virgin leaving the brothel:

> Those, however, who were looking with their eyes but did not see (cf. Matt. 13:13), were like wolves overpowering a lamb, raging at their prey. One who was less modest went in. But when with his eyes he had grasped the situation he said: "What is this? A maiden went in but a man is here. This is not that famous story of the hind substituted for the virgin.[66] Rather it is a case of a maiden transformed into a soldier. I had heard and did not believe that Christ changed water into wine (cf. John 2:1–10), but now he has begun to change sexes as well. Let us get out of here while we still are what we were. Have I myself, who see something else than I can believe, been changed too? I came to a brothel, I see a pledge.[67] And yet I shall depart changed, I shall go out chaste—I who came in unchaste."[68]

Here are more violent figures for male desire, but it is also a very clever moment, indeed. The shameless pagan who went in sees a woman changed into a man and fears that he, too, will be transformed. His sex will change, and he will exit the brothel a female virgin—that is, a Christian. Once more, Ambrose has produced the virgin girl as the type of the Christian male.

The Christian soldier disguised as virgin gets caught, of course: "He who had been seized in place of the virgin was condemned in place of the virgin. Thus it was not just a virgin but martyrs who came out of the brothel." Here we have another effective rhetorical move in which the identification of the female virgin as male role model is made explicit. The folkloristic figure of the man disguised as woman is explicitly thematized as an appropriation of the name "virgin" by the male martyr, an appropriation that is doubled by the identification of the Fathers with female virgins, both martyred and not. In other words, the male Christian cross-dressed as a Roman soldier and then once again cross-dressed as a virgin martyr produces the same effect of identification with a virgin for a male audience as that produced through the cross-gendering of the lion/ess in Ambrose's retelling of Thecla's story. The transformation of the second customer makes a perfect double of the transformation of the lion. He also goes in as a hypermale predator—a wolf—and is transformed into a celibate, feminized Christian. The point of identification is made even more palpable here, however, and thus serves as a further interpretative key, guaranteeing Burrus's reading, for the "female" object, the "virgin" who produces this second conversion, is, in fact, this time literally, a cross-dressed man.

The story goes on to report that the escaped maiden, however, returns to the place of punishment. The virgin insists that she must be martyred, also, using the very reasonable argument that it was chastity she sought, and her chastity is equally in danger now. Moreover, if the soldier is martyred in her place, then she would be guilty of his blood. "A virgin has a place to bear a wound, even if she had no place to bear an affront. . . . I have changed my clothing, not my profession. If you snatch death from me, you have not saved me but circumvented me."[69] In the end, of course, both achieve the crown of martyrdom together.[70]

The typological connection, perhaps even the genetic connection, between this story and the story of Rabbi Meʾir's martial disguise is palpable. In both cases, the male rescuer disguises himself as a Roman soldier, a typical customer of the prostitute's, in order to reveal himself to her as her rescuer. The stories have very different endings, however. Rabbi Meʾir's sister-in-law escapes, and that is the end of her story. The narrative of the virgin of Antioch, however, reprises the by now familiar Christian plot of the escaped martyr who returns to fulfill his or her destiny as martyr. We have seen this in the narratives of both Polycarp and Cyprian, the plot that I have referred to as the "Quo vadis?" plot.

The virgin of Antioch is, indeed, not circumvented by being rescued. We have here, then, a narrative of female autonomy: she gets to choose her fate, the double crown of virginity and martyrdom. However, we also have here a narrative of the most extreme form of social control. As Burrus elucidates, the function of the narrative of the virgin of Antioch is to "obscur[e] the awkward narrative fact of Thecla's triumphant survival of persecution. It is by juxtaposing Thecla's story with that of the Antiochene martyr that Ambrose brings Thecla directly . . . under the control of the late fourth-century tale of the virgin martyr, with its necessary fatal conclusion."[71] Conversely, the rescue of the rabbinic virgin is as necessary in terms of the rabbinic discourse of gender as the death of the patristic one is for theirs, for were the Jewish virgin to die then, her calling as woman would have been destroyed, not preserved. Whereas for much of the Christian tradition the perpetual virgin girl is perfection itself, for the Rabbis, she is a chrysalis, not yet fully formed. As Chrysostom well put it: "The Jews disdained the beauty of virginity. . . . The Greek admired and revered the virgin, but only the Church of God adored her with zeal."[72] For Chrysostom, by the fourth century, rabbinic Judaism, with its anti-ascetic tendency, simply *is* Judaism.

For Ambrose, the primary issue in the symbolization of the virgin as ego ideal is precisely her virginity—her literal continence, interpreted as a model for male celibates, that is, as an abiding sign of Christian resistance to the regimes of heteronormativity and natalism of the Greco-Roman world.[73] Rabbinic Judaism, in contrast, for all its alienation from certain aspects of late classical culture, strongly accepted and identified with the ideologies favoring marriage and child-bearing that were current in their time in the Roman world.

Early Christianity, it could fairly be argued, was in large part a powerful resistance movement to this facet of Roman culture. In the Ambrose text about Thecla, her near martyrdom is caused entirely by her resistance to the dominant Roman cultural norm of marriage and procreation. There is virtually nothing in the story about her belief in Christ, her rejection of pagan gods, or even her rejection of emperor worship that leads her into the ring with the lions. To be sure, her commitment to virginity was generated by her conversion to Christianity, but the content of that conversion is seemingly more about virginity than about any other religious practice or belief.[74]

This is typical of virgin-martyr acts in general. As Elizabeth Castelli has characterized this type of text, "The formulaic character of many of the accounts suggests not an audience expecting novelty, but one finding a compelling spiritual idiom in the repetitions of the triumph of virginal virtue over scurrilous and scandalous male desire,"[75] including I would add and emphasize, the scurrilous and scandalous desire of "legitimate" husbands.[76] To be fair, this text comes from Ambrose's treatise "On Virginity," so it is not entirely surprising that this should be the focus, but the story as it appears in the apocryphal Acts of Paul and Thecla is not all that different in content, although told not nearly so well there.

Early Christian sainthood, I wish to suggest, is as much about sexuality and about the resistance to, critique of, and oppositional positioning with respect to a certain regime of power/knowledge about sex as it is about anything else. That regime is found in the discourse shared by both pagans and Jews in the late antique city: the foundation of human good is the formation of reproductive families. Rabbi Hanina is the perfect model of a family man, and in every respect, other than his commitment to the study of Torah, a fine support for the late antique city. The virginity of his daughter, preserved miraculously in the brothel to which she is sent, will certainly fit her by the end of that story for a proper marriage to a scholar of Talmud, just like her father (although perhaps a more prudent one).[77]

The Rabbi's daughter cannot, therefore, die a virgin.[78] Although there are, of course, stories within the Jewish and even the rabbinic traditions of youths and maidens who commit suicide rather than sacrifice their chastity to Gentile oppressors, the point about reproductive families is, in fact, strengthened by that very narrative because the fact that they die unmarried is considered to add to the tragedy of the situation, not as, in itself, a religious triumph.[79] Another extraordinary story has a large group of married Jewish couples who have been separated for purposes of sexual exploitation and die bloodily rather than violate their marriage vows. In the story, the blood of the husbands and the blood of the wives joins into one stream.[80] Thus, even though we don't literally have the end of the story, by all normative rabbinic traditions, the Rabbi's daughter in the story we have been reading will have to end up a bride.[81]

Were this all there were to say about the issue, we would simply have two exactly equally violent systems of oppression of women: one dictating marriage for all, and one dictating universal virginity. Indeed, one could argue that the very *longuer* of the Ambrosian narrative is generated by its necessity to transform a trickster-escape tale into a tale of a virgin martyr, just as we have seen in the narratives of Peter and Cyprian. By the time of Ambrose's writing, however, the Christian girl could choose to be a virgin or a bride, for all that the virgin remained more honored.[82]

Thus, although the Rabbi's daughter cannot die a virgin because she must end up a bride, the Christian girl has two choices open to her: bride or virgin.[83] In this respect, early Christianity, even in its post-Constantinian phase, reflects a much more radical revision of Greco-Roman mores than does rabbinic Judaism. Kate Cooper has written: "The romance of late antiquity takes [among Christians] the form of a saint's life, in which the chaste desire of the legitimately married hero and heroine has metamorphosed into the otherworldly passion by which a Christian saint embraces a childless death."[84] If we accept the current view that one major function of the Greek novels was to reinforce marriage and the reproductive family as the foundation of civic society, as has been argued by Cooper, among others,[85] and that the apocryphal Acts, including especially the Acts of Paul and Thecla, were about parodying and resisting that romantic ideology, then the rabbinic text—even this rabbinic martyrology—is ideologically closer to those Hellenistic novels than it is to the apocryphal Acts. As Judith Lieu has described them, these last "create a world in sharp conflict with contemporary social structures, rejecting marriage and family life, anticipating and valuing suffering and death."[86] One would hardly describe rabbinic culture in these terms.

Elizabeth Clark, and with her, several other feminist scholars, have emphasized that the "otherwordly passion" represented a real, if also direly compromised avenue of autonomy for early Christian girls and women.[87] Castelli has made the point that "in a tradition where self-representation is a virtual impossibility for women, [Blandina's martyrdom] stands as a remarkable moment of spiritual assertion and refusal to be fully defined by

the terms she did not accept."[88] Even this sort of highly compromised option did not exist for our talmudic virgin, however. Her escape is not only
an escape from oppression but also, an oppressive escape, signified in that
she has to pass a chastity test before even being deemed worthy of rescue
by Rabbi Me'ir. Her escape is not a sign of her freedom. She is constrained
to escape precisely because her virginity is being preserved, like that of
Leucippe, *for* her husband, while the Antioch virgin's, like Agnes's, is being
preserved *from* her husband, or rather for her true chosen husband, Christ.
In Prudentius's hymn to Agnes, that virgin's telos is rendered with compelling eroticism. Miracles prevent her from being sexually violated, but
none will circumvent her desire for martyrdom. As the executioner approaches her, she speaks:

> I revel more a wild man comes,
> A cruel and violent man-at-arms,
> Than if a softened youth came forth,
> Faint and tender, bathed in scent,
> To ruin me with chastity's death.
> This is my lover, I confess,
> A man who pleases me at last!
> I shall rush to meet his steps
> So I don't delay his hot desires.
> I shall greet his blade's full length
> Within my breast; and I shall draw
> The force of sword to bosom's depth.
> As bride of Christ, I shall leap over
> The gloom of sky, the aether's heights.
> Eternal King, part Heaven's gates,
> Barred before to earth-born folk,
> And call, O Christ, a virgin soul,
> A soul that aims to follow thee,
> Now a sacrifice to Father God.[89]

At the point of Prudentius's writing, however, Christian women were
hardly being martyred anymore. The virgin martyr was now the model and
type of the ascetic life of the Bride of Christ, the nun,[90] while, of course,
the option of carnal marriage also was available for women.[91]

Burrus paraphrases this text: "Invoking a potential tale of liberation only to subvert that narrative, the poet compromises Agnes' rescue from sexual violation and indeed undermines her very resistance through his spectacular scripting of her climactic speech."[92] There is no escape offered from male domination.[93] At the same time, however, the power of the virgin martyr never can be completely eclipsed: "Only by explicitly problematizing female audacity can the tale of the virgin martyr attempt to restrain the heroism of women. And because the tale must therefore become engaged in the construction and contemplation of the heroic *virago*, its message of virginal docility always carries with it the potential for its own subversion."[94] If, moreover, we remember that medieval Christianity did offer intellectual and spiritual vocations for religious women, however much under the hierarchical superiority of males, while medieval Judaism offered none, then we can, again following Burrus, see this as an incompletely subverted potential tale of liberation (or a partially subverted tale of virginal docility), and not one that is unequivocally compromised and undermined. As Burrus writes, "[Agnes] is not after all audacious *virago* but docile *virgo*," but insofar as she is an ego ideal for Christian girls, she presents the possibility of choosing a life path, however compromised, however limited, that rabbinic society had shut down completely.[95]

Only a naive, highly apologetic, or triumphalist voice—of which there are unfortunately many—would claim that Christianity bears a feminist message vis-à-vis a misogynist Judaism.[96] To be sure, it is a caricature that regards the lives of Jewish wives in antiquity as peculiarly worse than those of their Christian or traditionalist Greco-Roman sisters, or that sees early Christianity as a "feminist" movement, or ignores the "patriarchal" control of even religious women in the Church.[97] As Charlotte Fonrobert has argued: "We have to ask whether in a discourse which builds up an elite of sexual renunciation, in which women are allowed or even encouraged to participate, married women might perhaps fare worse than in a culture in which everybody is required to marry."[98] And Fonrobert further remarks that "because of its focus on doctrinal questions on the one hand, and on sexual *askesis* primarily for the Christian leadership, on the other, early Christian discourse often neglected to consider the everyday life of those who failed to rise to prominence as hailed ascetics," that is, to produce a Christian sexual ethic for them.[99] She maintains that observance of "Jewish" menstrual-purity rules provided an avenue of spiritual fulfillment, of *askesis,* analogous to virginity for the Christian married women of the community of the *Didascalia.*[100]

This is a different Christian solution to the problem than emphasis on marriage as a form of martyrdom and suggests different interpretations of possible meanings of menstrual purity for rabbinic Jewish women, as well. The use of a claim of menstruation as a means of "self-defense" in the story of Beruriah's sister above suggests this motive also, a motive that goes back as far as Rachel claiming to be menstruating in order to trick her father out of his household gods in the Bible.[101] Fonrobert's discussion of the *Didascalia* suggests as well that perhaps the exclusion of women from the study of Torah among rabbinic Jews was not as total as imagined. There is a passage from the Tosefta, also preserved in the Palestinian Talmud, that reads: "gonnorheics, menstruants and parturients are permitted to read the Torah, to study Mishna, midrash, religious law and aggada, but men who have had a seminal emission may not" (Berakhot, ch. 2, para. 12). Even those who have taken this passage seriously as an original halakhic text have understood it as reflecting only a utopian possibility, not a reality of women studying Torah in antiquity.[102] However, the converted Jewish women of the *Didascalia* openly claim that they are not allowed to study Scripture when they are menstruating, suggestive at least, of the possibility that their practice represents another halakhic tradition, the one that the Tosefta speaks against, and that we thus have some real evidence that at least some Jewish women did study Torah in antiquity. The *Didascalia,* it should be emphasized, is almost exactly contemporaneous with the Tosefta.[103]

This is surely the other side of the coin.[104] It nevertheless remains the case that Perpetua, Thecla, Agnes, and Eulalia paved the way for Hildegard, Julian, and Teresa, all of whom, in medieval Jewish society, would have been only someone's wife and somebody's mother. They also could have been prominent businesswomen, of course, like Glikl, or my great-grandmother, but not abbesses, writers, theologians, or poets.[105] As Castelli has written, "the decision to remain a virgin and to renounce marriage and the world did provide some virgins with an opportunity to pursue intellectual and spiritual activities which would otherwise have been unavailable to them. Especially among educated aristocratic women who wished to pursue a life of study, the life of ascetic renunciation was the only institutionally established means of pursuing intellectual work."[106] It is not entirely surprising, therefore, that Cher's American Jewish daughter, Charlotte, might have fixed on Perpetua as a heroine and model of female spiritual self-realization.[107]

It would seem, then, to continue the conceit with which these chapters have all found their endings, that in contrast to the dilemma of the trickster and the martyr, where the Christian text seemed to feel it necessary to provide only one honored road, while the Jewish text left both ways open, in the matter of the virgin and the bride, it is the Christian text that permits two life paths, neither, of course, presenting anything like full autonomy for women, while the rabbinic text firmly shuts the gate in front of perhaps the only way available in antiquity for females to achieve any measure of spiritual or intellectual autonomy at all.

Rabbinic Judaism and Christianity thus can perhaps be most richly read as complexly related subsystems of one religious polysystem, well into late antiquity and even beyond. I am inspired here, as frequently before, by the words of Mieke Bal. "Dichotomies have two inevitable consequences: They subsume all relevant phenomena under only two categories, thus restricting the possibilities and paralyzing the imagination, their centripetal quality. And they turn hierarchical, shedding off one pole as negative in favor of the other, which needs to establish its value, their centrifugal quality."[108] Such is the dichotomy between a reified Judaism and a reified Christianity. Unsettling this binary opposition and upsetting the almost ineluctable invidiousness accompanying dichotomies is thus not only a matter of rectifying the historical record, but also of mobilizing new ways to imagine and conceive of well-known texts and cultural events. I will conclude this book with a case-study application of this principle with regard to the religious discourse that is my primary theme, the discourse of martyrology.

CHAPTER 4

Whose Martyrdom Is This, Anyway?

It would be fair to say that at present there are two major theses with regard to the origins of Christian martyrology, which, for the sake of convenience, we can refer to as the Frend thesis and the Bowersock thesis, although neither of these scholars is the originator of "his" thesis. According to W. H. C. Frend, martyrdom is a practice that has its origins securely in "Judaism," and the Church "prolongs and supersedes" the Jewish practice.[1] For G. W. Bowersock, on the other hand, Christian martyrdom has virtually nothing to do with Jewish origins at all, It is a practice that grew up in an entirely Roman cultural environment and then was "borrowed" by Jews.[2] It will be seen, however, that both of these seemingly opposite arguments are founded on the same assumption, namely, that Judaism and Christianity are two separate entities, so that it is intelligible to speak of one (and not the other—either—one) as the point of origin of a given practice.[3] The proposition that I have been putting forth is that it is precisely this fundamental assumption that needs questioning. If Christians are Jews, and if even Rabbis sometimes can be—at least almost—Christians, as we have seen, then the whole question of who invented martyrdom takes on an entirely different character. I shall be trying to show indeed that the making of martyrdom was at least in part, part and parcel of the process of the making of Judaism and Christianity as distinct entities.

In Bowersock's view, "Martyrdom was not something that the ancient world had seen from the beginning. What we can observe in the second, third, and fourth centuries of our era is something entirely new. Of course, in earlier ages principled and courageous persons, such as Socrates at

Athens or the three Jews in the fiery furnace of Nebuchadnezzar, had provided glorious examples of resistance to tyrannical authority and painful suffering before unjust judges. But never before had such courage been absorbed into a conceptual system of posthumous recognition and anticipated reward. . . . Martyrdom, as we understand it, was conceived and devised in response to complex social, religious, and political pressures, and the date and the circumstances of its making are still the subject of a lively debate."[4]

On some current definitions, Bowersock's point, which underlies the relatively late and uniquely Christian conception of martyrdom, would be simply nonsense. Thus, Jan Willem van Henten, in his work on 2 and 4 Maccabees, has defined the "martyr text" in the following fashion:

> A martyr text tells us about a specific kind of violent death, death by torture. In a martyr text it is described how a certain person, in an extreme hostile situation, has preferred a violent death to compliance with a decree or demand of the (usually) pagan authorities. The death of this person is a structural element in such a text, and the execution should at least be mentioned.[5]

If this is the definition of martyrdom, then it is obvious that the pre-Christian 2 Maccabees already contains a martyr text, and we must certainly date martyrdom prior to the second century after Christ.[6] Following van Henten's minimalist definitions, Bowersock's claim that "what we can observe in the second, third, and fourth centuries of our era is something entirely new" hardly can be entertained, let alone sustained. Bowersock has correctly, in my view, challenged such generic characterizations as "emphasiz[ing] banal coincidences in various narratives of resistance to authority and heroic self-sacrifice as if every such episode constituted martyrdom."[7] However, he substitutes for this generic cliché a notion of martyrdom as a single thing, an essence, and that makes it effectively impossible to perceive the complexities and nuances of its history.

Rather than taking it as a thing, "something entirely new," I propose that we think of martyrdom as a "discourse," as a practice of dying for God and of talking about it, a discourse that changes and develops over time and undergoes particularly interesting transformations among rabbinic Jews and other Jews, including Christians, between the second and the fourth centuries. For the "Romans," it didn't matter much whether the lions were eating a robber or a bishop, and it probably didn't make much of a difference to the lions, either, but the robber's friends and the bishop's friends told different stories about those leonine meals. It is in these stories that martyrdom, as opposed to execution or dinner, can be found, not in "what happened."

As I have already hinted above, I am in agreement with Bowersock on his major point. A new discourse appeared in late antiquity, one that was different from what had gone before. Indeed, I have made a similar point with reference to Jewish martyrologies.[8] But in order to make this point, we need to be more specific about what we mean by martyrdom. There must be new constituents of this discourse, elements that define late antique martyrology, elements that we cannot find in 2 Maccabees, at least. Oddly, the characteristic that Bowersock cites, "the conceptual system of posthumous recognition and anticipated reward," is perhaps the oldest, most clearly pre-Christian element of martyrology. This element is already well attested in 2 Maccabees: the notion that the martyr is immediately "saved," and it appears markedly in 4 Maccabees, as well.[9] In the later language, this would be expressed as a conviction that he or she has "earned salvation in a single hour." I would suggest, rather, that the following are the closely related elements that constitute the novelty of late antique martyrdom as a practice of both rabbinic Jews and Christians, without yet taking a stand on the order of their precedence:

1. A ritualized and performative speech act associated with a statement of pure essence becomes the central action of the martyrology.[10] In rabbinic texts, this is the declaration of the oneness of God via the recitation of the "Hear O Israel." For Christians, it is the declaration of the essence of self: "I am a Christian." In both, this is the final act of the martyr's life. For Christian texts, this is new with the *Martyrium Polycarpi*. For rabbinic Jews, it begins with the stories about Polycarp's contemporary, Rabbi Akiva.[11]

2. In late antiquity, for the first time the death of the martyr was conceived of as the fulfilling of a religious mandate per se, and not just the manifestation of a preference "for violent death" over "compliance with a decree."[12] For Christians, beginning with Ignatius, it was a central aspect of the experience of Imitation of Christ. For Jews, it was a fulfillment of the commandment to "love the Lord with all one's soul."[13]

3. Powerful erotic elements, including visionary experience, were in-

troduced into martyrology at this time.[14] In earlier versions of martyrdom, other passions were dominant. Elᶜazar in 2 Maccabees is "glad to suffer these things because I *fear* him" (2 Macc. 6:30).[15] In 4 Maccabees, the whole proposition is that the piety of Elᶜazar enabled him to prove that "devout reason is leader over our passions" (7:16). Indeed, as Tessa Rajak has emphasized, "for the author it is the Stoic virtue of the mastery of the passions by the agency of reason which enables a person to subordinate himself or herself to the rule of divine law, living temperately, displaying piety, and ultimately, if necessary, mastering fear and dying with fortitude before abandoning those same principles."[16] Rabbi Akiva was anything but a Stoic.[17] He and some of his Christian brothers and sisters, in direct opposition to both Maccabean works, are said to suffer torture and death because they are passionately in love with God, not because they fear his punishment or to demonstrate their Stoic fortitude or apathy. These eroticized elements produce effects that have to do with sex and gender systems, as well.

All of these elements were new in the martyrologies of both Christians and Jews of late antiquity.[18] In a sense, the gap between the earlier and the later forms could be encapsulated in the gap between the title of Tessa Rajak's essay on the early material, "Dying for the Law," and the title of the present work.

Given these definitions, the possibility of Christian origins for martyrology is, at least, intelligible. I am not sure that Bowersock's historical claim for precedence can be maintained. Nor am I sure that it can be refuted. My argument with Bowersock is not with respect to the historical validity of his chronological arguments, however, but with the model of historical relations between Christians and Jews, Christianity and Judaism, and Jews and Rome that it presupposes. That model is based on the assumption of phenomenologically, socially, and culturally discrete communities of Jews and Christians and of an absolute opposition between Judaism and Palestine on the one hand, Christianity and the Greco-Roman world, on the other.[19] By posing the issue in the way that he does, Bowersock is reinscribing a phenomenological boundary between Jews and Christians, a sort of pure Christianity, pure Judaism, and indeed pure Greco-Romanness. Thus, Bowersock writes at one point: "Christianity owed its martyrs to the *mores* and structure of the Roman empire, not to the indigenous character of the Semitic Near East where Christianity was born. The written record suggests that, like the very word 'martyr' itself, martyrdom had nothing to do with Judaism or with Palestine. It had everything to do with the Greco-Roman world, its traditions, its language, and its cultural tastes."[20] The vector of my argument throughout this essay points in exactly the opposite direction—not to a history based on inviolable boundaries, but to a history based on border crossings so fluent that the borders themselves sometimes are hard to distinguish.

Let us come back once again, to the story that is the leitmotif of these chapters, the story of when Rabbi Eli^cezer was arrested by and for Christianity. In the talmudic version of the story (ca. fourth century), which portrays the controversy between Rabbi Eli^cezer and the Christian, we see the point of the inseparability of Christians and Jews even more clearly than in the earlier version:

> When he came to his house, his disciples came to comfort him, but he was inconsolable. Rabbi Akiva said to him: "Allow me to say to you one of the things that you have taught me" [an honorific euphemism for the student teaching the teacher]. He said to him: "Say!" He said to him: "Rabbi, perhaps you heard a Christian word, and it gave you pleasure, and because of that you were arrested for sectarianism." He said: "By heaven, you have reminded me. Once I was walking in the upper market of Sepphorris, and one of the disciples of Jesus the Nazarene, a man by the name of Jacob of Kefar Sekhania, met up with me.[21] He said to me, 'It is written in your Torah: "Do not bring the wages of a prostitute or the proceeds of a dog [to the house of your Lord]" (Deut. 23:19). What about using them to build a latrine for the High Priest?' And I said nothing to him. And he told me that thus had taught Jesus his teacher: "'It was gathered from the wages of a prostitute, and to the wages of a prostitute it will return [Micah 1:7]"—it comes from a place of filth, and to a place of filth it will return' [i.e. for building a latrine one may use the proceeds of a prostitute], and the matter gave me pleasure, and for that I was arrested for sectarianism, since I had violated that which is written: Keep her ways far away from you!" (Proverbs 5:8).   Babylonian Talmud Avoda Zara 17a, ms Rabbinowitz 15, JTSA

As I have already argued , Rabbi Eli'ezer is inconsolable not because he has had to use tricksterism to escape being martyred, but because he was arrested at all, as the continuation makes clear. The strongest clue to the meaning of this narrative is the fictional character and apparent arbitrariness of the particular halakhic discussion between the Rabbi and the Christian, for there is no special reason why it would be this specific issue that a disciple of Jesus would raise with a Pharisee.[22] It is obvious, moreover, that this conversation is the work of the later editor,[23] since it is absent in the earlier Tosefta, and since, moreover, it is consistent with the patterning of stories about Jesus in later texts, especially in the Babylonian Talmud, that portray Jesus as a virtual "Rabbi."[24]

The choice of an interlocution having to do with prostitution and the Temple thus must be laid at the door of the talmudic "author" of this legend, and its significance sought within the context of Jewish culture in general and of this talmudic passage in particular.[25] Although some scholars have seen in this discussion about latrines and prostitutes that is placed here in the mouth of Jesus an attempt at mockery of Jesus and his followers, I do not think that such an interpretation is necessary, or even warranted. As the traditional talmudic commentators have pointed out, the question is a serious one. There was a need for a latrine for the high priest in the Temple as part of the ritual of his preparation for the service on Yom Kippur, and the question of whether the prostitute's hire could be used as alms for this nonholy purpose would be an entirely appropriate question within the canons of halakhic discourse.

The Christian proposes a lenient reading of the verse that prohibits the taking of the earnings of a prostitute to the Temple: although such earnings are forbidden for holy purposes, for mundane and even lowly purposes like the building of a toilet for the high priest, they are permitted. The Christian proposes a typical midrashic justification for this conclusion, as well. Rabbi Eli'ezer "enjoys" this utterance, perhaps, for two reasons. First of all, there is the sheer intellectual pleasure of a clever midrashic reading, one that, I emphasize, is in method identical to "kosher" midrash,[26] and second, the result of this midrash would be increased funding for the Temple. The Rabbi however, is punished for this enjoyment by the humiliation and fright of being arrested by the Romans for being a Christian, an outcome from which he just barely escapes.

The analogy seems clear: just as one may not take the hire of a prostitute for any purpose connected with holiness, so one may not take the "Torah" of a heretic for any purpose connected with holiness. Although the substance of the words of Torah seem identical—just as the money itself is identical—the source in "impurity" renders them unfit for holiness and renders their acceptance punishable. Sectarianism is homologous with prostitution—as it is also frequently enough in early Christian writings, as well. Moreover, the seductiveness of the heretical interpretation matches formally what its content encodes, for there, also, the temptation is to make use for holy purposes of what originates in impurity, the harlot's wage. When Rabbi Eliᶜezer indicts himself for having violated the precept "Keep her ways far away from you!" both of these moments are comprehended.

There is more that can be said about this story, however, for there is evidence that the question of the use of a harlot's hire for purposes of charity was a living question among the Christians who inhabited the Holy Land, or at any rate, its desert hinterland.[27] As Benedicta Ward writes: "The matter of alms from a prostitute's earnings had been a point of contention in the deserts of Egypt."[28] The reformed harlots whose narratives Ward presents decide to withdraw from their earnings and not to try to do good with them in any way. But there was another view:

> Abba Timothy the priest said to Abba Poemen: "There is a woman who commits fornication in Egypt and she gives her wages away in alms." Abba Poemen said, "She will not go on committing fornication, for the fruit of faith is appearing in her." Now it happened that the mother of the priest Timothy came to see him, and he asked her, "Is that woman still living in fornication?" She replied, "Yes, she has increased the number of her lovers, but also the amount of her alms." Abba Timothy told Abba Poemen. The latter said, "She will not go on committing fornication." Abba Timothy's mother came again and said to him, "You know that sinner? She wanted to come with me that you might pray over her." When he heard this, he told Abba Poemen, and he said to him, "Go and meet her." When the woman saw him and heard the word of God, she was filled with compunction and said to him weeping, "From today forward I will cling to God and I resolve not to commit fornication any more." She entered a monastery at once and was pleasing to God.[29]

Because the question of the legitimacy of alms from a harlot's hire was a live issue in eastern Christian circles in the fourth century, it is not implausible that when the rabbinical editors of this story in the fourth century put in the mouth of Jesus a midrash in which he permitted the giving of alms on the part of a prostitute, they were rendering not a first-century, but a fourth-century issue.[30] In narrating Rabbi Eliᶜezer's evident attraction to this idea, the story effectively represents the Rabbis' own willingness to learn Torah from Christians—and then their horrified panic at this willingness. It should be noted that in the Palestinian midrash version of the text, the parallel is even slightly closer, since there, it is the building of public baths and toilets for the poor that is at issue, not necessarily for the Temple, and Rabbi Eliᶜezer sees the point of the Christian's argument and "enjoys" it. Moreover, in rabbinic literature itself, Rabbi Eliᶜezer does permit the gift of a prostitute's wages for holy purposes other than actual use in the Temple, so the notion that he might be represented as following some sectarian halakha becomes very conceivable.[31]

It is fascinating to see how similar this is structurally to the problem of defining the boundaries between heresy and orthodoxy within early Christian writings. Thus, Walter Bauer writes with respect to strategies for interpretation of Scripture: "On this matter, it is scarcely possible to make any distinction between a Clement of Alexandria or an Origen and the heretical gnostics. . . . But where the 'church' was in competition with heresy, the close agreement with heresy in this respect soon became distressing."[32] Note how similar this is to the situation portrayed in the text we have been reading. It is scarcely possible to make any distinction between Rabbi Eliᶜezer and the heretical Christians, and this "close agreement" is distressing indeed. The desire to learn Torah from "them" can only be compared to the desire to have sex with a prostitute, which is doubly suitable as a metaphor for "true" Torah learned from a heretic because the sex itself is identical in substance to legitimate sex and only its "source" renders it illicit, and similarly, as yet another common coin of metaphor for Torah, of which one *could* say, but the Rabbis don't, "pecunia non olet."[33] The rabbinic ordinance forbidding the use and even denying the sacrality of a Torah scroll written by a sectarian, even if it is otherwise entirely proper, would be of a piece with this ideology.[34]

What we learn from this story, then, particularly in its highly elaborated and sophisticated later versions, is that the Rabbis themselves understood that in notably significant ways there was no difference between Christians and Jews, and the difference had to be maintained via discursive force, via the tour de force. This was the case, as well, with "the making of martyrdom."[35] At one and the same time, the Talmud story both concedes Bowersock's point and contests his model. Through its very negation— Rabbi Eli‛ezer enjoyed the Torah of Jesus, but repented that enjoyment— the Rabbis reveal their understanding that not only was there contact between rabbinic Jews and Christians throughout their period, but that this contact resulted in religious fecundity in both directions. There is Torah to be learned from them, and although we insist that we shouldn't, that their coin is "a whore's wages," nevertheless, we recognize that the coin of their Torah has value and gives us pleasure.

Such, I would suggest, can be said as well of the discourse of martyrdom as it was reconfigured in the early part of late antiquity. A discourse highly contested by some of the rabbinic tradition, it was nevertheless enthusiastically adopted by formidable parties within that very tradition, together with the early Christians for whom it became, of course, a centrally valorized practice.

Contending for the Crown

Bowersock, it might be said, reenacts an ancient contention. Already in antiquity, various religious groups had contended over the merit of their respective martyrdoms. For instance, the fact of martyrdom was used as a demonstration of religious truth. As Elizabeth Clark has phrased it, martyrs "constitute strong 'apologies' for the faith to pagan audiences."[36] The martyrs also served as counters for internal "apologies" within Christianity between groups, as for instance in the Montanist claim that the great number of Montanist martyrs demonstrated that the divine power of the living prophetic spirit resides in Montanism.[37] This claim had to be refuted by other Christians, as we find in Eusebius's *Ecclesiastical History*:

> I will also quote short passages in which he [the "Anonymous"] thus replies to those who were boasting that they too had many martyrs in their ranks.
> "So then, when worsted in all their arguments they are at a loss,

they endeavour to take refuge in the martyrs, saying that they have many martyrs, and that this is a reliable proof of the power of that which is called among them the prophetical spirit. But this, as it appears, proves to be absolutely untrue. For it is a fact that some of the other heresies have immense numbers of martyrs, yet surely we shall not for this reason give them our assent, nor acknowledge that they possess the truth. To take them first, those called Marcionites from the heresy of Marcion say that they have immense numbers of martyrs of Christ, but as regards Christ himself they do not truly acknowledge him."

And shortly afterwards he goes on to say:

"It is doubtless for this reason that, whenever those called from the Church to martyrdom for the true faith meet with any so-called martyrs from the heresy of the Phrygians [Montanism], they sever themselves from them and are perfected, without holding communion with them, for they do not wish to assent to the spirit [that spoke] through Montanus and the women" (V. xvi 20–22, 161).[38]

There are rabbinic texts that enter into the same contest—not, of course, the contest between the "orthodox" and the "heretics" in Christendom, but between the rabbinic Jews, the "orthodox," and the Christian "heretics," precisely on the question of martyrdom. Martyrdom was taken as a sign of divine grace and favor, and both rabbinic Jews and Christians contended for the martyr's crown. In rabbinic tradition, these texts seem to center on the emblematic figure of Rabbi Akiva, the first and model martyr. Here is a text that, depicting a scene of shared martyrdom, like that of the Phrygians and the orthodox in Eusebius, portrays a confrontation between Rabbi Akiva and a certain Papos ben Yehuda:[39]

Rabbi Akiva says: "With all your soul": Even if he takes your soul.

Our Rabbis have taught: Once the wicked kingdom made a decree that people should not be occupied with Torah, and anyone who occupies himself with Torah will be stabbed with a sword. Papos the son of Yehuda came and found Rabbi Akiva sitting and teaching, gathering crowds in public,[40] and a scroll of the Torah in his lap.

Papos said to him: Akiva, Aren't you afraid of this nation?

He said to him: You are Papos ben Yehuda of whom they say: "great sage"?! You are nothing but a dunce. I will say for you a parable. To what is the matter similar—to a fox who was walking on the banks of the sea, and he saw the fish gathering together. He said to them, "Why are you gathering?" They said to him, "Because of the nets and the weirs that people bring to catch us." He said to them, "Come up onto the land, and we will dwell together, I and you, just as our ancestors dwelled together!" They said to him, "You are the fox of whom they say that you are the wisest of animals? You are nothing but a dunce! If now that we stand in the place of our life it is so [that we are endangered], in the place of our death even more and more." And you also: If now we sit and study Torah about which is written, "For it is your life and the length of your days to dwell on the land" [Deut. 30:20]—and it is so [that we are endangered], if we go and become idle from it, all the more so.

They have said: Not many days passed before they arrested Rabbi Akiva and chained him in the prison. And they arrested Papos the son of Yehuda and chained him with him.

He said: Papos! What brought you to here?

He said to him: Blessed art thou, Rabbi Akiva, for you have been arrested for the words of Torah. Woe to Papos, who has been arrested for *superstitio*.[41]   Babylonian Talmud, Berakhot 61b; Oxford Opp. Add. Folio 23

The application of the parable follows in the form of the continuation of the story. Both the Jewish "fish" and the Roman "fox" end up being hunted and caught by the "men." The fox, however, now confesses to the fish that he is in worse shape than they, for his death is meaningless, while theirs is momentous.

I tentatively suggest that what we have here is a story of contention over martyrdom between rabbinic and Christian Jews—from the rabbinic perspective, of course. From this perspective, there is a great irony in the fact that Jews who have abandoned the traditional practice of the Jews by becoming Christians end up in greater danger than they were in to start with. I speculate that in the late Babylonian tradition, Papos ben Yehuda, always an ambiguously liminal figure in rabbinic texts, was supposed a Jewish Christian.

There is not a lot of evidence that this Papos is a figure for a Christian, but there is some. First, it is clear from the context of the story that Papos also has been arrested for a religious crime equated with Judaism in the eyes of the Romans. Otherwise he presumably would not be sitting in the same cell with Rabbi Akiva the Confessor. His crime was clearly not teaching Torah, as he himself admits in the story. In the talmudic version of the story of Rabbi Eliʿezer's arrest, the Hebrew term בטילים דבדים is explicitly a reference to Christian sectarianism, the crime for which the Pharisee had been arrested, and is, therefore perhaps arguably a calque on the Latin *superstitio*,[42] so it does not seem to be too far-fetched to understand it similarly here.[43]

Second, there is direct evidence from within the tradition of the Babylonian Talmud itself that Papos was understood as a Christian.[44] The following quite fantastic controversy will bring this out:

> "One who inscribes on his flesh [is punishable by death]": We have been taught, Rabbi Eliʿezer said to the sages, "But the son of Satda brought the magic books out of Egypt by inscribing them into his flesh."

In contradiction to the Mishna that indicates that writing on the body is a capital crime according to the Torah, Rabbi Eliʿezer cites an authority who actually engaged in this practice. For him, obviously, this authority is a definitive one, but his fellows disagree:

> They said to him: "But he was a fool, and we do not bring proof from fools."

As we shall see immediately, the authority whom Rabbi Eliʿezer cited was none other than Jesus of Nazareth, who is occasionally styled in rabbinic literature "the pious fool." The Talmud, however, does not understand why he is referred to here as the son of Satda:

> The son of Satda?? He was the son of Pandira!
>   Rav Hisda said: The husband was Satda; the paramour was Pandira.

The Talmud refers here to the Jewish slander tradition, known at least as early as Celsus, that Jesus was the bastard son of a Roman soldier named Panthera. However, the Talmud has a strikingly different tradition as to the identity of the cuckolded husband of Mary:

> *But the husband was Papos the son of Yehuda!*
> Rather, his mother was Satda.
> But his mother was Mary Magdalene![45]

Rather, as they say in Pumbeditha, This one strayed (*satat da*)
from her husband.[46]   Babylonian Talmud, Shabbat 104b, only in mss

We learn much from this remarkable passage.[47] First of all, once more we
find Rabbi Eliᶜezer represented as citing Torah for authoritative halakhic
purposes in the name of Jesus. Most important for our immediate purpose,
however, is that a late Babylonian tradition associates Papos the son of
Yehuda with Christianity, to the extent that he was actually a member of
the Holy Family.[48] It is possible, in fact, that "Papos" was a form of Jo-
sephos, or at any rate was so understood.[49]

I think, therefore, that it is not unjustified to see in the dialogue between Rabbi Akiva and this Papos a reflection of competition for martyrdom between rabbinic and Christian Jews as late as the third or maybe
even the fourth century. As a final suggestive point at least, if not evidence
for the line of interpretation that I am taking here, one might think that
Rabbi Akiva's parable is connected with the Christian figure of the apostles
as fishers of men (Mark 1:17, Luke 5:10).[50] Papos, the Christian "fox," proposes to the persecuted rabbinic Jewish fish that they would be safe on land
with him, out of the sea of Torah.[51] Rabbi Akiva's parable indicates precisely what the narrative enacts. Even outside of the river of Torah, the fish
are likely to be caught and killed, and in the meantime, they have abandoned what guarantees them life eternal. The rabbinic text places this view
in the mouth of the "Christian" fisher of men who confesses "Blessed art
thou, Rabbi Akiva, for you have been arrested for the words of Torah. Woe
to Papos, who has been arrested for *superstitio*."

"Whose Martyrdom is This?"
The Decian Persecutions and the Midrash

Rabbi Akiva is the Polycarp of Judaism, the ideal type of the rabbinic martyr. The extant *acta* of Rabbi Akiva, who also died in the second century,
are found only in the talmudic texts of the fourth or fifth centuries, however. These narratives would seem to be, therefore, legendary accounts that
can teach us almost nothing about the history of the Hadrianic persecutions in the second century. Studying them nevertheless will instruct us
well in the history of medieval rabbinic martyrology, for these texts,
whether fictional or not, became the dominant cultural model to be emu-

lated within the religious discourse of medieval north-European Jewry. I begin, therefore, with the continuation of the Babylonian talmudic narrative of the arrest of Rabbi Akiva that I cited above:

> They have told: In the hour that they took Rabbi Akiva out [to be executed], his disciples said to him, "Our teacher, so far" [i.e., "Is this necessary?"] He said to them, "All of my life I was troubled by this verse, 'And thou shalt love the Lord with all thy soul'—even though he takes your soul, and I said, when will it come to my hand that I may fulfill it? Now it is come to my hand, shall I not fulfill it?"
>
> They have told: "He did not manage to complete the word, until his soul went out with "One." The Ministering Angels cried out before the Holy Blessed One: "This is Torah, and this is its reward!? "[He should have been] from those who died of your hand, and not those who died [at the hands of flesh and blood]" [Psalms 17:14].[52] He said to them: "Their place is in life" [ibid.].[53]
>
> A voice came out of heaven and said: "Blessed are thou Rabbi Akiva, for you are already in the Next World!"   Babylonian Talmud, Berakhot 61b; Oxford Opp. Add. Folio 23[54]

This story about Rabbi Akiva's death dramatizes the connection between the "reading of the Shema[c] [Hear O Israel]," the declaration of God's unity and oneness, and Jewish martyrology. It also encapsulates perfectly the mystical fulfillment that is that death in order to fulfill the command to love God with all one's soul—the verse immediately following the Shema[c] and liturgically read as part of it—because Rabbi Akiva is actually killed while fulfilling the speech act of loving God.[55] All Jewish martyrs after this story was promulgated were to seek the same kind of speech at their deaths. Death as a martyr was to become an actively sought-after fulfillment in the Judaism that the Talmud and midrash of late antiquity were producing, although not in all quarters, of course.

We must also recognize the amount of ambiguity and conflict that the talmudic story continues to manifest, just under the surface, as it were.[56] This aspect appears in both "halves" of the martyrological narrative, the story of the confrontation between Rabbi Akiva and Papos and the story of Rabbi Akiva's execution. The first half of the narrative, in the form of the parable of the fish and the fox, seems to present a fairly simple theodicy, which is interrupted or even fatally disrupted by Rabbi Akiva's arrest and execution. In spite of this fish staying in the water, he, nevertheless, was killed. The second half of the narrative provides a resolution to the problem that the first half presents, but even in this more sophisticated theodicy, the conflict is represented, first in the form of Rabbi Akiva's students, who cry out: "Our teacher, so far?!" and then in the form of the protesting angels. At the same time that the text is representing almost allegorically a historical transition, the invention of martyrdom as positive command and spiritual fulfillment among the Rabbis, then, it is also representing the continuing opposition to this discourse, in much the same fashion as the rabbinic texts discussed above do, as well.

Thus, even this, arguably the text most unequivocally in favor of martyrdom in rabbinic literature and the founding text for later Jewish martyrology, records the persistence of the question "Quo vadis?" for rabbinic ethics and textuality. The students, the angels, even Papos, are indeed silenced by the dominant narrative of the text, but their voices of opposition to martyrdom continue to echo, here as in the more blatantly polyvocal narrative of the two Rabbis also discussed above. The dominant voice of the Akivan text, however, was to win the day, certainly among Ashkenazic Jews throughout the Middle Ages, making medieval Judaism, once more, look at least partially similar in ethos to late antique Christianity in its enthusiasm for martyrdom, its choosing of death.[57]

The astounding thing is that we can actually almost catch this transition happening in the texts: "When Rabbi Akiva died a martyr's death, a verse from the Song of Songs was applied to him, 'Yehoshua ben Yonathan used to say of those executed by the wicked Turnus Rufus. They have loved thee much more than the former saints, "sincerely they have loved thee."'" There were, indeed, saints in former times, that is, those who were willing to die for the faith, so why have Rabbi Akiva and his fellows "loved thee much more than the former saints"? I would claim it is because they died with joy, with a conviction not only that their deaths were necessary, but that they were the highest of spiritual experiences. Another way of saying this would be to spotlight the eroticism of these texts. They are all about love, about dying for God. What was new in martyrology was the eroticization of death for God, in the representation of martyrdom as the consummation of love, and it was new for both Christians and Jews.[58]

This transition is identifiable as well in the parallel story of Rabbi Akiva's martyrdom in the Palestinian Talmud:

> Rabbi Akiva was being judged before the wicked Tunius Rufus.[59] The time for the reading of the "Shema^c" ["Hear O Israel", which includes the verse, "Thou shalt love the Lord with all they soul!"] arrived. He began to recite it and smile. He said to him, "Old man, old man: either you are deaf, or you make light of suffering." He said, "May the soul of that man expire!"[60] Neither am I deaf, nor do I make light of suffering, but all of my life I have read the verse, "And thou shalt love the Lord, thy God with all your heart, and with all your soul, and with all your property." I have loved him with all my heart, and I have loved him with all my property, *but until now*, I wasn't sure I could *love him with all my soul.* But now that the opportunity of loving him with all my soul has come to me, and it is the time of the recital of the "Shema^c," *and I was not deterred from it, therefore, I recite, and therefore I smile.*   Palestinian Talmud Berakhot 9:5[61]

In this text, we catch Rabbi Akiva in the act of discovering that he could die to fulfill the commandment of loving God.[62] Like the nearly contemporary Sabina, Akiva smiles at the prospect of being martyred. There also, the temple warden was nonplused and asked, "You are laughing?"[63] There *is*, after all, something very "Roman" in this laugh of the martyr: "'How exalted his spirit!' Cicero exclaims at Theramenes' ability to jest while drinking the fatal poison," but how different the explanation for that laugh, the story that is told about it.

Furthermore, we find here the dramatization of the innovation, the deep connection between martyrdom and the reading of the *Shema^c*, the "Unification of God's Name," even more explicitly than we did in the Babylonian talmudic text just discussed. This is the speech act of reading the "Unification of the Name" at the moment of death, the functional equivalent of the final declaration of the Christian martyr, "I am a Christian," just before her or his death. Ekkehard Mühlenberg has written that "the public identification with the Christian name is the last word, followed by death."[64] Similarly, we could say that the public identification with the words "The Name is One" is the last word, followed by death. A transformation has taken place in which it is no longer the facts of Jewish observance, the teaching of Torah, alleged *maleficium*, and violation of the *lex*

Cornelia de sicariis that are at issue but, just as in the Christian martyrologies, "it is not special laws or the life styles of the Christian existence, but . . . the belonging to the one God, and that excludes the claims of any other powers." The crucial function of this transformation is that it is this moment that most completely serves to enable the martyrology to serve the production of "group identity and self-definition. . . . The confession 'I am a Christian' binds the martyr with all Christians everywhere,"[65] and so also the confession "Hear O Israel, the Lord, our God, the Lord is One" binds the martyr with all Jews everywhere and always.[66]

This element in the development of both Christian and Jewish martyrology is most critical in producing the moment of identification with the martyr, even, and especially for those communicants who are themselves no longer in a situation of persecution. In other words, this new component serves in the production of a "cult of martyrs" as a fundamental formative constituent in the making of the "new" religions of Christianity and rabbinic Judaism, and we observe an eminent structural and theological parallelism between the developing genres of Christian and Jewish martyrologies of the second, third, and fourth centuries.

The Talmud thus tells the story of the making of a new Jewish martyrology. However, was this cultural event earlier or later than the one that was taking place in the Christian orbit? In the following text from the late-third-century midrash on Exodus, the Mekhilta, I believe that we can discover the one of the earliest Rabbinic instances of the discourse of martyrdom:

> *This is My God, and I will beautify Him* (Exodus 15:2): Rabbi Akiva says: Before all the Nations of the World I shall hold forth on the beauties and splendor of Him Who Spake and the World Came to Be! For, lo, the Nations of the World keep asking Israel, "What is thy Beloved more than another beloved, O most beautiful of women?" (Cant. 5:9), that for His sake you die, for His sake you are slain, as it is said, We have loved you unto death, (ʿad mwt) "for thus do the maidens (ʿalmwt) love Thee" (Cant. 1:3)—and it is said, "for Your sake we have been killed all the day" (Ps. 44:23). You are beautiful, you are heroes, come merge with us!

Israel here describes the beauty of her God in response to an initial Gentile approach to the Jews to merge with them. The Gentiles cannot understand who this God is for whom the Jews are willing to be killed all day.

Israel replies in a response suffused with the eroticism of the Song of Songs:

> But Israel reply to the Nations of the World: Do you know Him? Let us tell you a little of His Glory: "My beloved is white and ruddy, braver than ten thousand. His head is purest gold; his hair is curls as black as a raven. His eyes are like doves by springs of water, bathed in milk, fitly set. His cheeks are like perfumed gardens, yielding fragrance. . . . His palate is sweetmeats and He is altogether desirable; This is my beloved and this is my friend, O daughters of Jerusalem" (Cant. 5:10–16).

At this point, hearing this praise of the beauty of the divine lover, the Gentiles wish to join Israel, instead:

> And when the Nations of the World hear all of this praise, they say to Israel, Let us go along with you, as it is said, "Whither is thy Beloved gone, O thou fairest among women? Whither hath thy Beloved turned, that we may seek Him with thee?" (Cant. 6:1).
>
> But Israel reply to the Nations of the World: You have no part of Him; on the contrary, "My beloved is mine, and I am His; I am my Beloved's, and He is mine; He feedeth among the Lilies" (Cant. 2:16 and 6:3).[67]

This text signals its connection with martyrdom in several ways. First of all, explicitly: the question that the Jews are asked is "Why are you willing to die for your God?" and the verse of the Psalm that is cited, "For your sake we are killed all the day," is a topos of Jewish martyrologies.[68] Second, intertextually: Rabbi Akiva himself is the prototypical Jewish martyr. This is brought out beautifully in an otherwise curious but nevertheless insightful scholarly comment from the previous generation: "Rabbi Akiva himself stated on the scriptural words, 'He is my God and I will praise Him (*Exod.* 15:2)': I shall speak of the splendour. . . . The biblical phrase 'my Beloved is white and red' *alludes to the ecstatic vision* which was given to the martyrs in the days of their torments, and at the hour when they gave up their ghost."[69] The oddness of this interpretation is, of course, that it positivistically attributes the text to Rabbi Akiva himself. Since, however, Rabbi Akiva, according to rabbinic discourse, was the first of the martyrs of his time, he hardly could have expounded upon the ecstatic vision that those martyrs beheld.[70] The comment nevertheless may be recuperated for its insight because it is virtually certain that it was not Rabbi Akiva himself who authored the text.[71] Instead, then, of a problematic "historical text," we have a semifictionalized representation, a pseudo-autobiography, that alludes to the ecstatic visions of dying martyrs and attributes them to Rabbi Akiva as the prototype.[72]

Given then, that this text is a portrayal of a martyrology, the similarity with the Christian martyrologies of the same period becomes striking. Rabbi Akiva is privy to a vision, indeed. This vision, moreover, renders him, and by metaphorical extension the whole martyred people of Israel, brides of God—female, desiring subjects who render their desire in graphic description of the body of the desired divine male.[73] Precisely because the desired object is male, within the normative heterosexuality of the text, the desiring subject is gendered female, whatever her sex. In other words, the martyr is the bride of God here, as in the stories of archetypical fourth-century virgin martyrs, Eulalia or Agnes.[74]

Elizabeth Castelli has presented a critical feminist description of these late female martyrologies in some detail and has uncovered certain phenomena that emblematize them. First of all, there is the explicit thematization of sight that is the center of Castelli's argument.[75] One of the striking features of both Christian and Jewish martyrologies is the visual eroticism of the experience as represented by the texts.[76] Second, there is the collapsing of time that the martyrdom text enacts. Castelli has identified "a desire to situate contemporary readers/hearers in continuous relation to events of the distant and more recent past in which divine activity has touched human existence directly. The writer promises that the text will create an intimacy between those who suffered, those who were direct witnesses to that suffering, and those who hear or read about it all later. The writing is about bringing the reader into the event, and situating that event within a continuous historical passage."[77] Peter Brown refers to this quite inimitably as time being "concertinaed" at a martyr's shrine.[78]

The midrash has powerful similarities to the martyrologies discussed by Castelli. First, there is the obvious and explicit eroticism of the experience of death projected for the martyr. In the midrashic text, this is made palpable through the use of the Song of Songs as its dominant intertext. Second, and equally striking, the midrash reproduces what Castelli remarks as the explicit intent of the writers of martyrologies: to render possible for readers to experience the erotic intimacy with God, now lost, that the martyrs once had, as well as to experience a prophetic or apocalyptic moment.[79] Third, there is the translation of Israel and its male mystics and religious adepts into desiring female virgins. Rabbi Akiva, as the alleged author of the midrash, thus reproduces the classic pattern and ideology of the martyrologies of the time when this text was redacted, the mid-third century.

Scholars of the historical-philological school of The Science of Judaism have read this Mekhiltan text as a reflection of events that took place in the time of its speaker, Rabbi Akiva, who died a martyr's death, a few decades before the martyrdom of Polycarp. Thus, the leading scholar of rabbinic thought, E. E. Urbach, argues with regard to this text, "Hadrian's decrees and the consequent facts of martyrdom as the supreme expression of the Jew's love for his Creator gave rise to interpretations that discovered in Canticles allusions to Jewish martyrology and to the uniqueness of Israel among the nations of the world. Rabbi Akiva already expounded, 'I shall hold forth.'"[80] Similarly, the historian Yizhak Baer argued in a text that I already have cited that "Rabbi Akiva himself stated on the scriptural words, 'He is my God and I will praise Him (*Exod.* 15:2)': I shall speak of the splendour. . . . The biblical phrase 'my Beloved is white and red' *alludes to the ecstatic vision* which was given to the martyrs in the days of their torments, and at the hour when they gave up their ghost."[81] Most trenchantly, the historian Gedaliah Alon remarks that "I do not think this homily can be assigned to the time of the Hadrianic persecution following the Bar Kokhba War. This was scarcely a time to arouse 'envy' of the Jews among the pagans. Apart from that, we have no quotations from Rabbi Akiva for the post-Revolt period, even though we do have a story about a communication from him in prison before his execution by the Romans. It seems more likely that the present passage echoes memories of the days following the Destruction of the Temple, or of the 'War of Quietus'. I would opt for the latter possibility here."[82]

If we were to take seriously these historical judgments, Bowersock's argument would simply, positivistically, be wrong because the martyrdom of the "real" Rabbi Akiva was earlier than that of Polycarp, the first of the new Christian martyrs. However, Alon's very embarrassment in looking for a moment in which Jews were being persecuted en masse and also in which so-called pagans wished to convert in numbers is indicative of the difficulty of this approach to reading the text. The final act of historiographical desperation was committed by Moshe David Herr, who writes of this passage: "The remarks must have been made just before the Bar Kokhba rebellion and the subsequent decrees of persecutions. After the rebellion, it would no longer have been possible for gentiles to observe: 'You are pleasing [beautiful], you are mighty [heroes]. . . . ' On the contrary . . . the failure of the rebellion was interpreted as the failure of Judaism and its God. As a result, mass proselytizing activity ceased. The mention of dying and killing does not refer to suffering the penalty of death for *Kiddush Hashem*—to sanctify God's name, but to all persons who accept the yoke of the Kingdom of Heaven."[83] Herr's need to distort the meaning of "for him you are being killed all the day" into a form of "white martyrdom" speaks as loudly as a trumpet. In my view, Alon, Herr, and all of the other historians are looking in the wrong place for a historical context for this text as long as they are looking at the lifetime of Rabbi Akiva and seeking there historical persecutions and mass conversions of pagans.

I find it much more plausible to assume that "the nations of the world" in Rabbi Akiva's midrash refers to Christians, and not to pagans at all. The context is not the early second century and the life of Rabbi Akiva, but the mid-third century, when the text probably was produced, and Rabbi Akiva is a symbol here, an icon for martyrdom. This is not to say that the matter was invented then out of whole cloth. Christian martyrology may very well have entered Jewish consciousness as early as the late second century (cf. the polemic between Justin Martyr and his fictional but realistic rabbinic opponent), but this midrash probably found its form in the third century, a time of massive persecution of Christians and of the development of Christian martyrology, the period of the persecution of Christians under Decius in 250–251 and under Valerian at the end of the decade.

In either case, this text is part of a contestation over martyrdom, not about pagans who wanted to convert in spite of martyrdom. It asks "Whose martyrdom is this, anyway?" This reading makes much more sense of the ending of the text, as well. However ambivalent rabbinic Jews have been over proselytism and conversion to Judaism, there is little evidence, if any, that at any time sincere converts were completely rejected on the grounds that God is exclusively the lover of Israel according to the flesh.[84] However, if the gentile Christians were claiming that they had a part in him, owing to their experience of martyrdom, then it makes sense—but not inevitably so (see below)—that a late antique rabbinic Jewish text might respond: "This martyrdom and the experience of divine favor and love that it brings are only for Jews—including converts who accept the commandments."[85]

Thus, while we cannot speak of any precise historical background that determines the midrash, we can grasp hold in it of a crucial cultural moment, one common to late antique rabbinic and Christian Jews, the moment of the creation of the idea of martyrdom as a positive and eroticized religious fulfillment. In the past, there also was a concept of martyrdom, but it was very different from this one. The previous model was that of the Hasmonean period, in which the martyr refused to violate his or her religious integrity and was executed for this refusal. Now we find martyrdom being actively sought as a spiritual requirement and as the only possible fulfillment of a spiritual need. To put this in more classic Jewish terminology, in the past, martyrs refused to violate a negative commandment—to worship idols. Now we find martyrs fulfilling through their deaths a positive one—to love God.[86] It is in this formulation that we find the eroticization of the martyr's death, as well. This text, then, certainly gives the lie to Frend's ratio that "the Jew might accept death rather than deny the law. The Christian gave thanks that he had been offered the chance of martyrdom."[87] Frend could make such a statement only because for him, "the Jew" was a creature that no longer existed in late antiquity.

Martrydom and Rome?

Martyrdom as a discourse was shared and fought over between rabbinic Judaism and Christianity as these two complexly intertwined religions and social formations were approaching their definitive schism in Eusebius's fourth century. As Lieberman has written of the Jewish martyrologies: "It seems that the homilists have communicated to us the acts of the government which they saw with their eyes (in the middle of the third century in the time of Decius, and in the beginning of the fourth in the era of Diocletian) with respect to the Christians, and they attributed them to the time of persecution under Hadrian and said that that is how they behaved towards Jews as well."[88] And even Bowersock admits that "the alleged martyrdom of Rabbi Akiva in the second century [is] a retrospective construction of a posterior age, an age substantially later than that of the first Christian martyrdoms."[89] Once again, the area of doubt is not as to whether the events of the martyrs' deaths were more or less as described in the texts, but the details of textualization of those deaths that are most susceptible to alteration as a discourse develops and is transfigured.[90]

Thus, for example, the martyrdom of the mother and her seven sons in 4 Maccabees, I would propose, was produced in the same religious atmosphere, the same (Asian?) religious environment, in which figures such as Ignatius and Polycarp (and perhaps even the Martyrs of Lyons) lived and breathed. And if, as Bowersock confidently presumes, "the two stories in the books of the Maccabees have nothing to do either with the authentic history of the Maccabees or with the lost original text that recounted it," but " have everything to do with the aspirations and literature of the early Christians,"[91] they have everything to do with the aspirations and literature of contemporary Jews, as well. How could they not? But this hardly constitutes an argument that Christian "martyrdom had nothing to do with Judaism or with Palestine. It had everything to do with the Greco-Roman world, its traditions, its language, and its cultural tastes."

As Bowersock himself has noted, "When it was written IV Macc. reflected Hellenistic Judaism but hardly Christianity."[92] Indeed, for the first-century (or even second-century) milieu in which 4 Maccabees was produced,[93] the whole distinction could make no sense whatever, any more than the question of whether James or Peter was a Jew or a Christian could. The prodigious similarities between the ethos and phraseology of this text and Ignatius's Letter to the Romans, the *Martyrium Polycarpi* and the Letter of the Martyrs of Lyons and Vienne have often been remarked.[94] At the same time, we must remember as well that through the third century and the early fourth, when Christians were being persecuted and killed, Jews generally were not, and in this sense, Bowersock's point holds.[95] It was most plausibly within circles in which persecutions were more current memories that martyrology developed, spreading as well to other circles and subgroups of the Judeo-Christian cultural system, including, notably the Rabbis, as a mode of interpreting their own past of persecutions and deaths for the faith.

There is, moreover, another reason why we could expect that martyrology would develop more urgently among Christians: the Christological impulse itself. There is no doubt that Ignatius conceived of his Christian duty as "being crucified with Christ," and the example of Ignatius was crucially formative for Polycarp, as well.[96] The story of Rabbi Eli'ezer escaping martyrdom by convincing the *hegemon* that he was not Christian demonstrates rabbinic recognition of this fact, and the earliest version of this story comes from a text edited apparently right in the midst of the Decian/Valerianic persecutions, or soon thereafter. The cultural materials of which martyrdom was made, however, hardly were entirely from outside the Jewish cultural context, both diachronic and synchronic.

Although it is crucial that we take seriously the notion that there have always been deaths under oppression, the interpretation and reinterpretation of these deaths as martyrdom is a specific discourse and one that (speaking conservatively) seems to belong much more to late antiquity than to the Hellenistic period. The deaths of the Maccabees, the death of Rabbi Akiva, and some early Christian deaths as well, became martyrdoms only at a later moment in discourse, and it is absolutely stunning how similar in tone the descriptions of Rabbi Akiva's and Polycarp's martyrdoms are. In both the Akiva and the Polycarp narratives, the proconsul speaks to the aged sage with respect and concern, and in both, the candidate for martyrdom is unwavering in exactly the same melody, even if the lyrics vary slightly. Being killed is an event. Martyrdom is a literary form, a genre. By this I surely do not mean that it belongs only to "high" culture or does not have significance in the lived world, but rather that it is a form of "collective story" in the sense that Michelle Rosaldo has elaborated the term: "We come to know [a culture] through collective stories that suggest the nature of coherence, probability and sense within the actor's world."[97] Such "collective stories" have enormous impact on social practice and on the molding of subjectivities. They are, in the strict sense, praxis.[98]

What were the collective stories of deaths that were being told in the rabbinic and Christian worlds of the first, second, third, and fourth centuries, and how did they vary over this time, to the extent that we can learn this? I believe that they varied, in fact, in ways that are remarkably similar. These actors shared, I suggest, a common, or at least an overlapping cultural world.

This avenue of thought would account for the patently close connections between the Maccabean texts and the Eusebian Letter of the Martyrs of Lyons, or the Letters of Ignatius, both of which Frend has demonstrated so compellingly.[99] There are also very "striking parallels [of the prayer of Polycarp] with 4 Macc 6, 27–29 (the prayer of Eleasar)."[100] Our best evidence therefore seems to suggest a complexly imbricated origin for this discourse in the second, third, and even fourth centuries in which Greek-speaking Jews, Jewish Christians, Roman Christians, and rabbinic Jews all had a hand in different ways and to different degrees. They brought with them all of their collective cultural traditions: the Roman generals' *devotio*, with its Greek analogues,[101] chaste Greek and Roman wives (and virgins) threatened with rape,[102] Maccabees, gladiators, Socrates, Jesus on the Cross, even Carthaginian child sacrifice.[103] The "invention" of martyrdom, far from being evidence for Christian influence on Judaism or the opposite, is most plausibly read as evidence for the close contact and the impossibility of drawing sharp and absolute distinctions between these communities or their discourses throughout this period.[104]

I would suggest the following tentative model for thinking about the historical processes of cultural interaction that issued in the full-fledged martyrological literature of both late antique Judaism and Christianity. The earliest "Jewish" and "Christian" sources for martyrdom, as has been pointed out, are very similar in their milieux and structure. Both 4 Maccabees and the earliest contemporary Christian martyr texts draw heavily on the earliest Jewish rudimentary martyrologies of the pre-Christian 2 Maccabees. Moreover, there are important similarities between 4 Maccabees itself and early Christian martyrologies that suggest shared innovation.[105]

Furthermore, as Judith Lieu has shown, early Jewish martyr texts and the *Martyrium Polycarpi* both make heavy use of the Sacrifice of Isaac and midrashic connections to the Passover in their imagery. As she writes: "The most cautious assessment would conclude that rather than the Christian use of the story being adopted from and used in polemic against a fully fledged earlier Jewish doctrine, the two developed in some form of interaction with each other, probably during the second century. At some stage in this development the Isaac story became associated with the Passover, an association we find in the Targums and also in Melito, but again it is a matter of debate how far this was a Jewish response to Christian understanding of the death of Jesus, whose Passover links were fixed, rather than part of its inspiration. It was a dialogue which was to continue; rabbinic elaboration of the tradition becomes increasingly detailed with surprising echoes of Christian ideas, while Christian authors also used the story in their own interests, as when Apollinarus describes Jesus as the true Pascha, 'the bound one who bound the strong' (cf. Matt. 12.29)."[106]

Other specific differanda of late antique martyrdom grew up most naturally in the Christian milieu in the third and early fourth centuries, during the Decian persecution and the and Great Persecution.[107] Since most of the persecutions in the third century, if not virtually all, were of Christians, and not of Jews, martyrology naturally transformed and evolved in that century primarily within Christian circles, adapting and adopting various cultural elements from within the worlds of the martyrs and the martyrologists, in particular tragic and gladiatorial motifs,[108] as well as the fascinating way that the Sacrifice of Isaac was somehow reconnected with child sacrifice at Carthage. In addition, another momentous element seems to have been added to the mix at some time, namely, "the authentic [sic] documentation of the legal hearing."[109]

These themes, narratological and theological, were recycled back into talmudic texts as a way of narratizing and grasping the deaths of the persecuted Jews of the second century under Hadrian, and ultimately the original Maccabean death stories were rethematized along these lines, as well.[110] Bowersock is simply wrong in his assumption that the talmudic texts manifest a "complete lack of interrogation procedures."[111] All of the talmudic texts about martyrdom, whether Rabbi Eliᶜezer's and Rabbi Elᶜazar's escapes from martyrdom or Rabbi Akiva's and Rabbi Ḥanina's martyrologies, manifest this element of the interrogation.[112] This allows for a complicated, nuanced, historical account of how Jewish, Greek, and Roman cultural elements became creatively combined into late antique martyrology. We must think of circulating and recirculating motifs, themes, and religious ideas in the making of martyrdom, a recirculation between Christians and Jews that allows for no simple litany of origins and influence.[113]

On the other hand, the question of actual chronologies is important here, too. This is a highly significant question for the problematic this book addresses, and beyond it, as well. In order to ask questions of context, we have to have some mode of establishing the relative synchronicity (or not) of given pieces of textual evidence. Not infrequently, the protocols of dating differ between the different disciplines or fields between which the comparison or contextualization is to be carried out.

For the rabbinic texts, my teacher, Professor Saul Lieberman of blesssed memory, established the principle:

> The simple rule should be followed that the Talmud may serve as a good historic document when it deals in contemporary matters within its own locality. The legendary portions of the Talmud can hardly be utilized for this purpose. The Palestinian Talmud (and some of the early midrashim) whose material was produced in the third and fourth centuries contains valuable information regarding Palestine during that period. It embodies many elements similar to those contained in the so-called documentary papyri. The evidence is all the more trustworthy since the facts are often recorded incidentally and casually. The rabbinic literature has much in common with the non-literary papyri and the inscriptions.[114]

We have accordingly learned certainly that rabbinic legends cannot be taken as historically reliable sources vis-à-vis the events that they purport to recount, and a legend, for these purposes, has to be defined as any narrative for which the only sources we have are in texts produced hundreds of years after the "events."[115]

In contrast to this position vis-à-vis rabbinic narratives, after much debate and discussion in the last century, church historians have generally resolved that some of the documents of early martyrology preserved in Eusebius (and elsewhere) can be relied upon, by and large, as virtually contemporaneous with the events that they relate, in spite of the fact that we know of them also only as they are embedded in later texts.[116]

The strategy that I have adopted in this analysis is the doubly conservative one of maximal skepticism with respect to the talmudic narratives, tending to date them at the time of the documents—following the protocols of that discipline[117]—while accepting the consensus of Christian scholarship as to the authenticity of certain of the purportedly early martyr acts. I shall try to demonstrate that my hypothesis of shared innovation and circulation back and forth between both subgroups holds even with this doubly conservative approach, with the earliest known Christian martyrologies considered as a century earlier than the earliest rabbinic ones. A fortiori, were we to accept a more skeptical position with respect to the

Christian *acta* or, alternatively, a more credulous one for the Jewish texts, either option would suggest that the Christian and Jewish martyr texts are to be treated as actually contemporaneous.

It is generally accepted among church historians today that such texts as, at least, the *Martyrium Polycarpi*,[118] the Acts of the Scillitan Martyrs (of 180), and the Letter of the Churches of Lyons and Vienne[119] were produced very close to the time of the events in question, if not by actual eyewitnesses. It is important for me to emphasize that the question that I am raising is not one of historical "authenticity," but of the histories of discourses. Another way of putting this question would be: In the second century, when Jews such as Akiva and Christians such as Polycarp were both being killed by the Romans (in this case, within approximately two decades of each other), what were the stories that Rabbis were telling of Akiva's death and that Christians were telling of Polycarp's?

We have one precious piece of evidence that Rabbis in fact were telling a very different story in the early period. Just before Rabbi Akiva's death, we read (Mekhilta Mishpatim 19), two other figures, a certain Rabbi Shimᶜon and a certain Rabbi Ishmaᶜel were executed by the Romans. The former beseeches the latter: "My heart goes out to know why I am being killed"—a question of theodicy. Lieberman argues that they must not have been being killed for teaching Torah, for if they had been, they would have known that they were performing the great mitzva of being martyred, so therefore, they must have been caught as simple revolutionaries.[120] This argument can be subtly shifted, however, if we assume that it was only through the *acta* of Rabbi Akiva himself that the concept of martyrdom as a mitzva entered the rabbinic world. These earlier martyrs (including the "real" Rabbi Akiva of the second century) might very well have been killed for the performance of Torah and still not have had a sense of the ecstatic privilege that this death conferred, or alternatively, they might all (including the "real" Rabbi Akiva) have been executed for their part in the rebellion.[121] If it is certainly not the only way, one way that this Jewish text can be read, then, is as confirming Bowersock's insight that "martyrdom was not something that the ancient world had seen from the beginning. What we can observe in the second, third, and fourth centuries of our era is something entirely new." Before the talmudic texts, Rabbi Akiva may very well have been accepted and venerated as simply a defiant revolutionary, not as a martyr at all.

The "new" constituent that is encapsulated in the declaration of the *nomen* "Christianus sum" and that played a crucial role in the development of the *martyria* would seem to be a Christian product of the second century. It is present and central in all of the martyr acts accepted by the consensus of scholars as authentic and pre-Decian. We find it in the martyrdom of Polycarp, in the Letter of Lyons and Vienne,[122] and in the North African martyrology of 180, the Martyrs of Scilli.[123] This distribution and this consistency suggest an element of martyrology that had taken root firmly in the earliest Christian traditions of martyrdom itself.

In the Jewish texts, we have no such invariability for this principle. Indeed, if the discourse of provoked martyrdom is a particularly striking innovation among the Rabbis (and "provoked martyrdom" is a better term, in my opinion, than "voluntary" martyrdom—if martyrdom is not voluntary, it is not martyrdom), it is easy to explain the irony and near mockery that we find in a martyrology parallel to that of Rabbi Akiva, the martyrology of Rabbi Ḥanina from Tractate Avoda Zara 17b.[124] When, like Rabbi Akiva, the good Rabbi engages in the provocative public teaching of Torah, Rabbi Yose ben Kisma challenges him, to which Rabbi Ḥanina replies, "From heaven they will have mercy," which occasions Rabbi Yose's sardonic: "I say logical things to you, and you answer me: 'From Heaven they will have mercy!' I will be surprised if they do not burn you and the Scroll of the Torah with you."

In this martyrdom of Rabbi Ḥanina ben Tradyon, we do not find the identification with the "Name" at all. In its stead, we find in answer to the question of the judge, "Why do you teach Torah?": "Because so my God has commanded me." Moreover, in the talmudic versions of the story of the martyrdom of the woman and her seven sons, only one of the sons quotes the verse "Hear O Israel," while all the others quote other verses entirely, and neither is the quotation of the "Hear O Israel" at a particularly marked point in the story.[125] It seems, then, reasonable to assume that the Unification of the Name, brought to the fore in the latter-day narratives of the martyrdom of Rabbi Akiva—if indeed as I have suggested, it is a functional parallel to the "Christianus sum" of the Christian martyrs—is probably to be seen as a rabbinic "answer" to that crucial declaration of the *nomen*, the "public identification with the Christian name [that] is the last word, followed by death." This becomes the definitive moment in Jewish martyrology in the post-talmudic period. There is, moreover, something peculiarly Roman in this particular enactment of a "moment of truth,"[126] peculiarly Roman, also, in these early martyrologies: the occasional theme of "being a man," found both in those of Polycarp[127] and Perpetua.[128] So far, so Bowersock.

However, when we look at the other, to my mind equally significant development of late ancient martyrologies, the eroticization and mysticization of the martyr's death, the picture shifts considerably. First of all, as has been shown, the element of the martyr's special vision at the moment of death is very likely an older Jewish motif inherited by both rabbinic and Christian late ancient martyrologies.[129] But even more pointedly, as Burrus and Castelli have shown, the powerful eroticization of Christian martyrology is a product of the fourth century. It is absent in the second century martyrdoms, even of women.[130] The fourth-century virgin martyrs are ecstatically ravished brides, not victorious combatants, at the moment of "completion." And this motif of the virgin as "bride of Christ" is generally agreed "by Patristic exegetes . . . to be referred to in the Song of Songs."[131]

The ideology of death as the necessary fulfillment of the love of God also appears often in texts contemporary with the midrashic text interpreted below.[132] Thus, we read in a halakhic text of the period (very approximately mid-third-century): "And thou shalt love the Lord with all thy soul: [This means] even when he takes your soul, and so it says, 'For your sake we have been killed all of the day.'"[133] This text is particularly significant because it brings into the textual complex the exact same verse of Psalms that seems so intrusive in the midrash of Rabbi Akiva: "For your sake, we have been killed." The motif of the ravished bride, then, is eminently present and central in martyrological texts associated with Rabbi Akiva as early as the Mekhilta at least, a text very likely contemporaneous with the Decian persecutions, and this motif is made central via the interpretation of martyrdom as fulfillment of the commandment to "love God with all one's soul." Here, then, is a central motif of late ancient Christian and rabbinic martyrology of which it can certainly *not* be said, with Bowersock, that it had "nothing to do with Judaism or with Palestine." The eroticization of martyrdom may have first appeared among the Rabbis, or perhaps it didn't, but that is in any case precisely my point. I want to emphasize the permeability, the fuzziness, of these very borderlines.

In any case, much evidence points to mid-third-century Caesarea Maritima as one possible site for such interchange.[134] Roughly contemporaneously with the "Rabbi Akiva" of our Palestinian Mekhilta, we find Origen's also Palestinian "Exhortation to Martyrdom" 1.2, already referring to the commandment to "love God with all one's soul" as an experience of ecstatic union.[135] The memory of the death of Akiva at the hands of the Romans in that place still would have been fresh a century later, and because a mystical-erotic religiosity based on readings of the Song of Songs developed, probably first among Caesarean Rabbis and then in the works of Origen, the subsequent application of this in the narratization of that execution as martyrology is a very plausible reconstruction.[136] This Caesarean preaching tradition is one early site in which the gender of the martyr shifts from masculine to feminine, a shift that (as in from *virago* to *virgo*) comes to the fore in Christian texts in the fourth century, as we have seen. That shift seems, once again, first attested in our Mekhilta text, attributed pseudepigraphically to Rabbi Akiva. The mystical interpretation of the Song itself was also attributed to Rabbi Akiva. It thus becomes almost absurd to speak of origins and influences, let alone of exclusively Jewish and exclusively Christian elements.[137]

The story of Rabbi Eliᶜezer with which we entered this inquiry itself enacts the terms I have suggested for a history of cultural interactions that produced the full-fledged martyrological literature of both late antique Judaism and Christianity. The story admits that Christian martyrdoms began earlier than those of the Jews, since Judaism was at first *religio licita*, while Christianity was *superstitio*.[138] Rabbi Eliᶜezer escapes from being martyred by establishing, however trickily, that he is not a Christian. But if my reading of this story is not pure fantasy, the text also suggests that, with reference to the third-century context of the telling of this story, Rabbi Eliᶜezer, one of the central, if problematic, heroes of the Pharisees and later of the Rabbis, could indeed legitimately have suffered martyrdom as a Christian.[139]

I don't want to be misunderstood, however, as proposing simply something that we might be tempted to call "syncretism," as if some "ingredients" of a religion can be assigned to one "source of influence" and others to another, even a bidirectional syncretism. Such a model would still assume discrete and separated sects of Rabbis and Christians. Rather, if we are talking about one complex sociocultural group with subgroups, then in addition to competition and polemic or dialogue, even the partial identification of rabbinic Jews with their Christian brothers and sisters being martyred is plausible.

Lieberman has pointed to such an occurrence in the case of the Martyrs of Lydda, where the Jews are reported to have been moved at the sight of the suffering Christians:

> But the Jews, who were always accused by the prophets for worshipping idols, stood around, seeing and hearing, while the Egyptians renounced the gods of their own fathers and confessed the God who was also the God of the Jews, and witnessed for Him whom the Jews had many times renounced. And they were the more agitated and rent in their hearts when they heard the heralds of the governor crying out and calling the Egyptians by Hebrew names and making mention of them under the names of prophets. For the herald, when he cried out to them, called saying "Elijah," "Isaiah," "Jeremiah," "Daniel," and other similar names, which their fathers had selected from among the Hebrews, that they might call their sons by the names of prophets. And it came to pass that their deeds were in harmony with their names. And at the men and at their names, at their words and at their actions, the Jews were greatly amazed, while they themselves were despised for their wickedness and apostasy.[140]

The Jews felt kinship with the martyred Egyptian Christians because the latter worshipped their God and had chosen Jewish names. According to the midrash, the Jews who went into Egyptian exile were redeemed because they did not change their names. These Egyptian Gentiles were saved precisely because they did. Through Eusebius's own triumphalist rhetoric, which implies that the presence of the Jews there was to lead to their humiliation, we can hear, as Lieberman did, another story, a story of identification between the Jews and these Gentiles willing to die for the Jewish God.[141]

The Rabbis further discussed at length the merits of gentile Christian martyrs and their guaranteed share in the future life. As Lieberman wrote, "What did the Rabbis think of the Gentile who did not avail himself of the exemption and did suffer martyrdom for His Name? All pious Gentiles were promised their share in the future life, those of them who suffered for their good deeds were especially singled out, and there can be no doubt that the pious Gentiles who suffered martyrdom for their refusal to offer sacrifices to idols were deemed deserving of one of the noblest ranks in the future world."[142] In other words, Jews shared in the discourse of martyrology and its history, even when they were not being martyred, as much, one might say, as the vast majority of Christians who also were not killed. This attitude of sharing would compete with other moods in which the rabbinic texts engage in constructing Jewish identity as separate from and against Christian identity by claiming, as does the Mekhilta, "You have no part of Him; on the contrary, 'My beloved is mine, and I am His; I am my Beloved's, and He is mine; He feedeth among the Lilies.'"

Both of these modes of shared culture can be imagined as having been in play at the same time. We need to think about the multifold dimensions of intergroup interactions, from dialogue to polemic, or perhaps, better put, from cooperative and identificatory dialogue to polemic and disidentification, in order to understand the histories of rabbinic Judaism and Christian Judaism, the children of Rebecca, as intimately and intricately enmeshed and embroiled with each other as any twins have ever been.

Coda: Rebecca's Children Revisited; or, Credo Quia Ineptum Est

At the beginning of this essay, I introduced the ancient and modern trope of Jacob and Esau as figures for authenticity and primacy in the fraught and ambiguous relation of nascent rabbinic Judaism and Christianity in late antiquity. This figure works so well precisely because it doesn't work, and indeed the "separation," the "parting of the ways," doesn't seem quite to work, either. The instability of the opposition, at both the textual and the historical-referential level, provided the ancients with a wonderful opportunity for rich contention. If it is obvious that for the "writer" of the Torah, Jacob is Israel (as both person and people), it is not at all obvious that Tertullian, Irenaeus, and those who came in their wake were wrong in reading—for their historical situation—Jacob as the younger child, Christianity. To be sure, Jacob was the person Israel—no one could deny that as the Bible's intention, but no one, too, was constrained to reading Jacob as a type of "the Jews" and not the Christians, Christians understood as an "Israel." Indeed, it is not certain to me just how and when and where the Rabbis started to read the elder as Christianity. Is it in reaction to Christian readers, a cause of their reactive readings, or perhaps, as I have suggested, only a product of the historical succession of pagan Rome by Christian Rome?

For us moderns too, the figure works I think, as a figure for the instability of the divide and identification of Judaism and Christianity, Jews and Christians.[143] Twins in a womb, tussling with each other, striving for separation, surely not separate until they're born, and even then, never sure of their sovereign identity; in this case the figure is even more fraught than ever, since there is a prophecy that of these two twins, the elder will serve the younger. Where paradoxically, then, one normally would find a struggle for primogeniture, here we find a struggle for the opposite, for each to claim that the other is the elder, owing to the verse itself and to the oft-noted principle in Genesis of the reversal of primogeniture. Indeed, the problems here double the historical complexity and tangledness of the history of the contention over martyrdom as a means of the production of separate identities that I have traced in this essay.

We have seen this complex struggle playing itself out. Each of the children of Rebecca strives to prove himself the true son by claiming the crown, while historical reflection has suggested that martyrdom was elaborated by rabbinic Jews and Christians together via a tangled process of innovation and learning, competition and sharing of themes, motifs, and practices. Where each of the "brothers" seeks to identify himself as the true son by having been born last, now each of them seeks to identify himself so by having been killed first.[144] Sibling rivalry seems indeed a very good figure for this relationship, and indeed so thought the ancients, as well. In a sense, one could say that the interpretation of the figure enacts the figure itself, for the struggles of the Rabbis and the Fathers over the name Esau and the name Jacob double the struggles of Esau and Jacob in the womb and thus instantiate the icon itself.

Sometimes, partings can seem more like encounters.

On the Methodology and Theology of W. H. C. Frend's
Martyrdom and Persecution in the Early Church

W. H. C. Frend's claim that "Judaism was itself a religion of martyrdom" completely obscures and indeed annihilates the historical specificity of the new formations that developed both within the Rabbinic community and among the Christians of late antiquity.[1] And this claim is a central assumption that guides Frend's work: somehow, whenever the Church (particularly the African Church) was most zealous for martyrdom, this was some essentially Jewish moment in Christianity. Much that follows from Frend's assumption needs correcting, as well. Of course, no practice or discourse arises entirely *de novo*, but we must be prepared to mark epistemic shifts. The ultimate discourse of martyrdom, as Rabbinic Judaism, and as Christianity (and the Christianities), is a complex product of biblical elements and prominent figures and representations that came to Rabbinic Jews and Christians from the cultural world of late antiquity, a world of which they were all an integral part.

Frend's lack of attention to historical specificity enables him to say of Onias, the victim of a political and ideological struggle for the high priesthood in Jerusalem: "The roll of martyrs for the Law had been opened."[2] With criteria this broad, virtually any genealogy is constructible. One could ask fairly: If it had gone the other way, and it had been Jason or Menelaus who was murdered by Onias, would the roll of martyrs for Hellenism have been opened? Frend defines martyrdom as "personal witness to the truth of the Law against the forces of heathenism, involving the suffering and even death of the witness,"[3] a definition that hardly accounts for the eroticism and positive appeal of the martyr's death in late antiquity in both Jewish and Christian texts. And as Glen W. Bowersock correctly maintains, the term "martyr" does not appear even as late as Ignatius. A fortiori, it was not used with respect to the Maccabees, so even the notion of personal witness to the truth of the Law is questionable. I would rather think that the Maccabean moment is simply refusal to violate the Law, even on pain of death, quite a different matter, indeed. This transfer of the refusal to violate or change even one "jot or tittle of the Law" to the discourse of martyrdom is one that Frend repeatedly makes in order to argue his thesis. How then would we distinguish, on Frend's account, between Judeo-Christian martyrdom and the death of Socrates, for instance?[4]

Another problem with Frend's thesis involves chronology. He easily slips from accounts of Maccabeans prepared to die in order to maintain the law to Zealots and Sicarii two centuries later, and then, when he wants to give evidence for the expectation of divine reward for such deaths, he cites a text, *The Assumption of Moses*, that is surely not pre-Christian.[5] It is equally impossible to follow Bowersock, however, and disallow virtually any contribution to the formation of the later discourse called martyrdom by this earlier "native" Jewish response to religious persecution. The model offered in this essay of a religious road traveled together by Pharisees/Rabbis and Christians as overlapping and intimate collectivities is intended to bridge these gaps.

I also fail to see the parallelism that Frend posits between the halakha that there are three commandments for which one must give one's life, violation of the laws of idolatry, murder, and sexual offenses, and Tertullian's statement in *On Modesty* (chapter 19) that these (and some other) sins are unforgiveable.[6] No one would have doubted that these would be included in any list of the gravest sins for virtually any Jew or Christian. Does Tertullian say that only for these should a Christian allow herself to be martyred? Certainly not. There is no significant parallel here.[7]

Frend's position, it should be remarked, is one of thoroughgoing supersessionist theology, and it affects his historiography: "As in so much of the doctrine and practice of the primitive Church, the Christian view of the martyr's role prolongs but also supersedes Judaism."[8] He also refers to the Judaism of Jesus's time as "late Judaism."[9] Supersessionism is either good or bad theology. I have nothing to say on that score, but referring to nascent Judaism as "late Judaism" is simply very bad scholarship.[10] I am not accusing Frend of anti-Judaism (still less of anti-Semitism); his work is clearly an attempt to be fair to Rabbinic Judaism in an evangelical tradition that had been (and frequently still is) anything but.[11] Nevertheless, it must be clearly stated that Frend's orientation toward Judaism is ambivalent in the extreme. He cites as one of the reasons for the centrality of martyrdom in the African Church the strong "Rabbinic Jewish" element in Carthage and the intimacy of the Jews and Christians there, but on the same page, he writes of martyrs that "in the Ancient World only the most desperate and vindictive elements among the Jews harboured similar ideals," thus contradicting the significance of his earlier point.[12] He clearly wants to have his Jews and supersede them, too.

Part of what supports Frend's methodology and conclusions is his anachronistic assumption that the reports given in later texts either present events as they actually happened or interpretations and discursive constructions of those events as they were conceived at the earlier period. The fact that later Christian representations look back to early Jewish prototypes does not mean that those prototypes were the historical source for the later representations, whether Christian or "Jewish."[13] Thus, he accepts (and builds on) a distinction between "patriotic death" and "martyrdom," but then assumes that descriptions centuries later that describe a death as a martyrdom and not as a patriotic death are evidence for the existence of the discourse at that earlier time. (On the other hand, when it serves his purposes, Frend can be highly critical in his use of sources, for instance with respect to a document that "might refer to the time of Augustus, but was edited by Dio Cassius in the 220s."[14])

With respect to the Polycarp text, Frend's method becomes actively dangerous. Thus, we see in that narrative the Jews participating with the "pagans" in crying out "This is the teacher of Asia, the destroyer of our gods, who teaches many neither to offer sacrifice nor to worship." Frend concedes that Jews hardly could have participated in this cry, but is not hesitant to conclude that "the remainder of the account shows the Jews co-operating gleefully with the pagans in having a common enemy removed."[15] Even more problematic is his claim that "in the persecutions which were to wrack Asia Minor in the reign of Marcus Aurelius the Jew was often in the background. For nearly another century he continued to stir up trouble wherever he could."[16] To this should be contrasted Judith Lieu's careful conclusion that "as study of the texts has shown, actual evidence of Jewish instigation of persecution ('stirring up trouble') is hardly to be found."[17] It seems not to have occurred to Frend that perhaps the politics of the fourth century are reflected here, and not those of the second century, or even that the whole account of the Jewish cooperation with the pagans against the Christians is tendentious propaganda and a feature of the text that is part of its Gospel imitation. The fact that Eusebius's text reports one event that is virtually impossible hardly increases one's confidence in the rest of the account. This point has been made by various Jewish scholars since the last century, work all ignored by Frend.[18] Given the philological and literary controversy regarding the various text forms of the martyrology and the significant ideological differences that they represent, as recognized by Frend himself, his positivistic reliance on details is astonishing, but it is important to emphasize that Bowersock's work is equally as positivistic and equally as dependent on assuming the "authenticity" of the documents preserved in Eusebius.[19]

In general, Frend is particularly credulous when it comes to evidence for Jews and pagans uniting against the Christians,[20] and even blandly quotes Juvenal's satirical remark about "Jews hawking proselytism and groceries from door to door," as if it simply gave us factual information about the posture of the "Dispersion Jews" of the early second century.[21] A book that set out to counter historical positions completely disregarding any Jewish input into early Christian martyrdom ends up both seeing the Jewish input as nearly entirely negative in its effect and also blaming Jews for most violence against Christians in late antiquity: "Behind this agitation stood the Jews. It is interesting how the Jews in Carthage and seemingly in Rome too, played precisely the same part against the Christians as their coreligionists had in Asia thirty or forty years before."[22] One does not have to wish to deny any Jewish role in hostility toward Christians in order to see the tendency of this comment, and we have already seen the nature of the "evidence" for the Jewish role in the Asian persecutions. Frend does not take into account the possible ideological role that such descriptions of Jewish hostility to the martyrs play in establishing Christianity via its martyrs over against Judaism. In the end, Frend most clearly reveals his hand by the repeated use of such expressions as "The Church was lifted finally out of the rut of Judaistic sectarianism."[23]

REFERENCE MATTER

Notes

INTRODUCTION

Unless otherwise noted, all translations are my own.

1. Lauterbach, "Jesus in the Talmud," 473.

2. Alexander, "'The Parting of the Ways,'" 2.

3. Georgi, "The Early Church," 35–68.

4. Yuval, "Jews and Christians in the Middle Ages," 95–96.

5. Yuval, "The Haggadah of Passover and Easter," 12.

6. Alan F. Segal, *Rebecca's Children*. And see Simon, *Verus Israel*, x–xi and especially xiii, where he already refers to the "two cults" as "brothers." Simon's work, otherwise so sophisticated, is seriously marred by a naively anachronistic reading of talmudic texts, as if stories told first in the fourth century (or at any rate reaching us only in fourth-century redactions) could in any way represent historical realities of the first. Simon, *Versus Israel*, 13–14.

7. It is a historical misnomer to speak of "the Church" and "the Synagogue" as parallel structures. There has never been an organized hierarchical structure in Judaism corresponding to the Catholic or Orthodox Church. Accordingly, we need to refer to "the Church" as counterpart to the Rabbis as the different form of organization and structure that orthodox Judaism was eventually to take. Early and later Christian writers frequently contrasted the Church to the Synagogue for their own purposes, as we shall see immediately below.

8. Gerson D. Cohen, "Esau as Symbol," 19–48, argues compellingly that Rabbi Akiva is the source of this midrashic equation.

9. I am using the term "Principate" here to approximate the Hebrew מלכות, which means something like the "kingship."

10. Palestinian Talmud, Nedarim 38a, 3:8.

11. Tertullian, "An Answer to the Jews," chapter 1. Pace Simon, Tertullian

has forgotten nothing: he has made the same move that Paul makes in Galatians 4, when Ishma^{c}el is read as the ancestor of the Jews and Isaac of the Christians. Simon, *Verus Israel*, 188. Cf. "The typological interpretation of the twins, presumed in *de Pudicitia* and explained in *adversus Ioudaeos*, was original to Tertullian or not known to Christian theology in Carthage. . . . The obvious and traditional interpretation of this passage was that Esau, the elder, was the eponym of the Edomites, or foreigners in general, and that Jacob, the younger, was the eponym of the Jews, the people of Israel. Tertullian's identification of the Jews with the elder son was to run counter to this tradition." Dunn, "Tertullian and Rebekah," 122. However, Irenaeus, Tertullian's somewhat older contemporary from quite a different part of the Christian world, already knew this tradition:

> If any one, again, will look into Jacob's actions, he shall find them not destitute of meaning, but full of import with regard to the dispensations. Thus, in the first place, at his birth, since he laid hold on his brother's heel, he was called Jacob, that is, the supplanter—one who holds, but is not held; binding the feet, but not being bound; striving and conquering; grasping in his hand his adversary's heel, that is, victory. For to this end was the Lord born, the type of whose birth he set forth beforehand, of whom also John says in the Apocalypse: "He went forth conquering, that He should conquer." In the next place, [Jacob] received the rights of the first-born, when his brother looked on them with contempt; even as also the younger nation received Him, Christ, the first-begotten, when the elder nation rejected Him, saying, "We have no king but Caesar." But in Christ every blessing [is summed up], and therefore the latter people has snatched away the blessings of the former from the Father, just as Jacob took away the blessing of this Esau. For which cause his brother suffered the plots and persecutions of a brother, just as the Church suffers this self-same thing from the Jews.

Irenaeus, *Adversus haereses* IV.xi.3. See also the discussion in Miriam S. Taylor, *Anti-Judaism*, 101; Dunn, "Tertullian and Rebekah," 138–41.

    12. It is not uncommon to find claims to the effect that at a certain point, the Christians abandoned the claim to be the true Israel. I would argue that as long as they are reading biblical Jacob as the Church, that is, at least as late as Jerome, this figure must still be at least lurking in the background.

    13. Theodor and Albeck, *Genesis Rabbah*, par. 63.

    14. Incidentally, given the fraternal relations implied by the verse and the

image, it is fascinating that sororal metaphors dominate, even in contemporary rhetoric.

15. But perhaps even then, not completely.

16. Ruether, "Judaism and Christianity," 1–10.

17. To be sure, Jacob Neusner had already begun the rectification of the regnant historical understanding from the side of scholarship in Judaism.

> Judaism and Christianity as they would live together in the West met for the first time in the fourth century. It was then that Judaism addressed the historical triumph of Christianity in a political form that would persist, and that Christianity met the Israel defined by the sages of the dual Torah, the Israel that would enjoy enduring life in the Jewish people from then until now. . . . It follows that Judaism as we have known it was born in the matrix of triumphant Christianity as the West would define that faith.

Neusner, *Judaism and Christianity*, ix. Much as I admire Neusner's boldness in identifying the fourth century as critical in Jewish/Christian self-definition, as indeed—in Ruether's words—the first century for Judaism and Christianity, I must say, however, that I find considerably less plausible his claim that "this had not happened before and it never happened again, until our own time." *Judaism and Christianity*, 1. While I shall be suggesting that these tensions became even more acute after the accession of Christianity to imperial power, or perhaps after the swallowing up of the church by the Empire, recognizing the formative significance of the events of the long fourth century and the ways that shifts in the status of Christianity and concomitant shifts in its discourse (namely, the victory of "orthodoxy") complexly and definitively affected developing rabbinic discourse does not force us to assume that before and after this time there was no significant interaction. See Hirshman, *A Rivalry of Genius*, 9.

18. Alexander, "'The Parting of the Ways,'" 2. Reuven Kimelman has suggested that the assumption that the so-called curse of the *minim* automatically denotes Christians "is behind the oft-repeated assertion that about the year 100 the breach between Judaism and Christianity became irreparable." Kimelman, "Birkat Ha-Minim," 226–44, 391–403.

Kimelman has also indicated that this assumption is practically a commonplace, observing that "it is difficult to find studies which question this assumption" and that it is to be found in such authoritative texts as Frend, *Martyrdom and Persecution*, 179 and Baron, *A Social and Religious History of the Jews*, 135. Kimelman, "Birkat Ha-Minim," 391 n. 9. The recent handbook/

textbook entitled *Christianity and Rabbinic Judaism: A Parallel History of Their Origins and Early Development*, encapsulates this commonplace perspective that Kimelman sought to displace.

19. Frend, for instance, marks the flight to Pella of the Jerusalem church, thus absenting themselves from the heroic fight against the Romans, as a "momentous step" that damaged the Palestinian church "beyond repair." Frend, *The Early Church*, 33–34. However, the "flight" of Rabbi Yoḥanan to Yavneh at precisely the same moment as the story of the Pella flight, which in talmudic legend is what founds the rabbinic movement, was structurally identical to the, after all, also legendary Christian escape, and thus neither need have constituted a break with "the Jewish Nation." According to Galit Hasan Rokem: "The story of the exit from the city [of Rabbi Yoḥanan] as rescue reflects . . . traditions which are common to the folk narrative of the Jews which appears in rabbinic literature and the folk literature of Jewish groups who were diverse from the culture which is canonized by the Rabbis. Also with respect to the ancient Jerusalem Christian church, it has been reported in later sources, that its remnants abandoned the city at the time of the destruction and found refuge in the city of Pella in Transjordan. In both cases, the story of the egress from the city took on the meaning of legitimation and authorization for the founding of a religious center outside of Jerusalem after the destruction of the city." Hasan-Rokem, *The Web of Life*, 201. In Hasan-Rokem's reading, therefore, not only is the flight to Pella not evidence for separation between the Jews and Christians, but the precise opposite. Rabbi Yoḥanan, after all, also explicitly opposed and ran away from the fight of the Zealots against the Romans and was hardly seen as a traitor by later "orthodox" Judaism. This event cannot, therefore, be cited as evidence for a break between "Christianity" and the Jewish people. See also Daniel Boyarin, "Masada or Yavneh?" 306–29.

20. Baer, "Israel" (1961), 82. Such a statement is possible only on a reading according to which "Jewish Christians," that is, for instance, almost the entire Syrian Church, were neither Jews nor Christians, rather than both. This is, I claim, a dogmatic judgment, not a historical one. See especially Charlotte Fonrobert, "The Concept of Jewish Christianity."

21. Cohen, Gerson D. "Esau as Symbol," 28.

22. For this collusion, see Alexander, "'The Parting of the Ways.'" See also the discussion in Stroumsa, "The Hidden Closeness," 170–75.

23. Alexander, "'The Parting of the Ways,'" 3.

24. I would like to acknowledge here the productive influence of Karen L. King's work on the use of "syncretism" vis-à-vis Gnosticism in the construction of "authentic Christianity" on the development of my own thinking about the

use of Christianity in the production of "authentic Judaism." See her "Gnosticism as Heresy."

25. Alexander, "'The Parting of the Ways,'" 2.

26. The best model for understanding overlapping cultural subsystems is still that of Even-Zohar, *Polysystem Studies*, whose work and conversation were an early impetus to the research and thinking incorporated in these chapters. See also Dawson, *Allegorical Readers*, 9, who writes: "At best, culture is a general, abstract label for myriad competing, partially intertwined, partially separate cultures."

27. Bhabha, *The Location of Culture*, 38.

28. Dina Stein has suggested to me that already Douglas, *Purity and Danger*, had articulated this understanding, at least implicitly.

29. A similar point has been made by Martin Goodman in his review of *Christianity and Rabbinic Judaism: A Parallel History of Their Origins and Early Development*, in which he writes: "The question is whether this disparateness is necessary, since there are of course common themes which run through Jewish and Christian history in this period, not least attitudes to a shared sacred text. But perhaps the best way to view Jews and Christians together would be a study of the world of late antiquity itself. . . . It can be argued that rabbinic Judaism and early Christianity are best understood not only on their own terms, as in this book, but also as part of the general religious change of late antiquity which accompanied the apogee and collapse of the Roman empire and the progress of Europe and the Middle East into the Middle Ages." Goodman, Review, 314.

30. In Hebrew parlance, proto-Semitic is referred to as "the Mother of Semitic."

31. I prefer "B.C." (= Before Christ) and "A.C." (= After Christ, as in the French usage) as a more honest designation than the politically correct assertions of a "Common Era," or the theologically loaded "A.D." One of the evidences that has been traditionally cited for an early separation is the Epistle of Barnabas, with its clear "us" and "them" distinctions, but as Geoffrey Dunn points out, the author never uses the terms "Jew" and "Christian," and "closer attention to the contrast in the epistle reveals that it expressed the view which Frend characterized as belonging to the earlier, first phase (A.D. 65–100) of the subapostolic period: 'All Christianity at this stage was "Jewish Christianity." But it was Israel with a difference.'" Dunn, "Tertullian and Rebekah," 127–28, citing Frend, *The Rise of Christianity*, 123. My line of thinking in this book is that such a sensibility persisted for a much longer time than even Dunn will allow.

32. Note the difference between this and Kinzig's model, in which

the doctrinal and the theological levels belong to the area of *theoretical reflection*, whereas one could group the institutional level and the level of the popular piety under the heading of *religious practice*. Turning first to the area of theoretical reflection, we may define the *doctrinal* level as the level of confessions of faith, official or quasi-official doctrines, doctrinal statements of theologians etc. These doctrinal statements on the whole aim at a definition of the way Christianity understood itself. . . . Generally, one might say that the more importance was attached to the person of Jesus the clearer the separation from Judaism was. The evidence of the New Testament suggests that at this level a separation between Church and Synagogue took place at a very early stage, certainly soon after, but perhaps even before Jesus' execution (cf. Mark 8, 29 par.) In this context it is very often overlooked that the canon adopted by the Church was not only an anti-Marcionite canon, but also an anti-Jewish canon.

Kinzig, "'Non-Separation,'" 27–28. In my opinion this statement reveals several profound misunderstandings:

1. It assumes that "the doctrinal statements of theologians" are essentially coextensive with "orthodox" Christian doctrines, the doctrines of the Great or Catholic Church.
2. It assumes a sharp distinction between "theoretical reflection" and popular piety.
3. It assumes that Christology is ipso-facto not Jewish.
4. It assumes that we can speak of separate institutions called "the Church" and the "Synagogue" in the first century, even—perhaps—before the Crucifixion.

But these are exactly the postulates that need interrogation in any query as to the nature of the contact and interplay between so-called Christianity and so-called Judaism. Kinzig's formulation here begs the question. If one defines any Christological discourse as necessarily not Jewish, then, of course, *eo ipso*, the separation has already taken place, at least at the level of doctrine. The question is precisely the varieties of Judaism that were extant in the first, second, third, and fourth centuries and to what extent they could emphasize the person of Jesus and still define themselves as Jewish.

In contrast to Kinzig, I am suggesting that the official doctrines only of *particular versions* of Judaism and Christianity (understood here as any religious group adopting a Christology) inscribe absolute difference, and not all such "official doctrines," and the question then would be: when and how did these particular official doctrines achieve hegemony, become "orthodox," and indeed whether they did so.

In other respects, it should be noted that Kinzig's general historical picture of much contact between Christians (as defined above) and Jews is similar to the position adopted herein. On the other hand, Kinzig's insistence that the practices of so-called "Judaizers" belong to "women and ignorant" people who "did not really think about the significance of the Law on a doctrinal level, but obeyed it because of popular piety, a possibility which serves to [sic] their low level of education," merely takes at face value and reproduces the theological categories of the "orthodox" sources, Chrysostom and Jerome. Moreover, his statement that "it is this kind of syncretistic *milieu* from which the Pseudo-Clementines sprang" once more reproduces and assumes the very categories that it should be questioning. Kinzig, "'Non-Separation,'" 38.

For another example of this usage, see Joan E. Taylor, "The Phenomenon of Early Jewish-Christianity," 313–34, and see Strecker, "On the Problem of Jewish Christianity," 241–85, and the critique in Fonrobert, "The Concept of Jewish Christianity." There was, in fact, never an institution called "the Synagogue," parallel in form or function to the Church. Judaism never became organized as a centralized hierarchy, and even the question of the hegemonic status of the types of Judaism called "rabbinic" and its definitions of borders, both genealogical and phenomenological, remain open. Cf. Fonrobert, who writes: "What needs to be taken into consideration as well is the point that one can really only talk about 'the Church' as a subject of history, in so far as one can talk about an institution as a subject at all, with the emergence of a unified bureaucracy, with a recognition of the bishop in Rome as the primate, with the emergence of the institution of the pope." Fonrobert, "The Concept of Jewish Christianity." While this formulation seems to be extreme (could there not be "the Church" without a single primate, for instance?), nevertheless, it points up sharply why it is never right to speak of "the Synagogue," for Jews never had centralized institutions even approaching those of the Church.

33. Hasan-Rokem, "Narratives in Dialogue," 127. For a fascinating example of such dialogical interchange, see Reiner, "From Joshua to Jesus," 248–69, who shows that many local Galilean Jewish traditions about various Joshuas are very similar to Gospel accounts about Jesus, also, of course, about Joshua. He writes specifically: "The polemical interpretation is not the only possible explanation for the existence of sources that exhibit mutual literary ties." "From Joshua to Jesus," 268. This is not, of course, to deny the possibility of "folk narratives" being polemic in their own right. The *Toledot Yeshu*[c] litera-

ture, as folk parodies of the Gospels, is a perfect example. See, inter alia, Daniel Boyarin, "A Corrected Reading," 249–52.

34. Drijvers, "Jews and Christians at Edessa," 88–102.

35. Cf. also, "But after a rapid study of Tertullian's frank indictment of the Jews, the Jewish historian would do well to commence an analysis of the inner meanings of Tertullian['s] books, where he will discover information on the relationship between the two communities immeasurably more important than that which appears from polemical exchanges." Baer, "Israel" (1961), 88. I hope to pursue this analysis in a forthcoming work. Or again, "In exploring the understanding of martyrdom we have seen how the Christian imagery of *M. Poly.* and contemporary documents betrays not only its Hellenistic Jewish roots but also a continuing pattern of competing legitimation. Such competition probably implies closer interaction and possibilities for influence than the documents would have us realize." Lieu, *Image and Reality,* 94.

36. It has been suggested that the imposition of the *fiscus Judaicus* by Nerva in 96 A.C. would have enforced a separation between Jews and Christians. There certainly were some people who were Christians and not Jews by then, and some who were Jews and not Christians, but this hardly demonstrates that there were not significant groups who paid the *fiscus* and believed in Jesus, or who didn't pay the *fiscus,* but kept the Sabbath. Cf. Goodman, "Nerva," 40–44. Thus, the conversations might very well have continued, and it would be well for us not to think in anachronistic terms of resentments owing to alleged violations of group solidarity.

37. See Lieu, *Image and Reality,* 28–35. for an exploration of the anxieties to which this fuzzy border gave rise. Ignatius already seems very actively engaged in policing the border, again suggesting both that it was clearly extant, but also very permeable and unstable. See especially his Letter to the Philadelphians, in Schoedel, *Ignatius of Antioch,* 195–215. This position is partially pace Hopkins, "Christian Number," 187, who seems to regard such fuzziness (or "porosity," in his language) as particularly characteristic of Christianity. Hopkins's paper is very important and will have to be reckoned with seriously in any future accounts of Judeo-Christian origins and genealogies. It was published near the very end of the preparation of this book. See also Shaye J. D. Cohen, "'Those Who Say They Are Jews and Are Not,'" 1–45.

38. Indeed, relations don't have to even sort themselves out into either polemic or irenic, but can occupy complex spaces between these two extremes, as well. Stein, "Folklore Elements in Late Midrash," 169.

39. Yuval, "The Haggadah of Passover and Easter," 5, and idem, "Easter and Passover."

40. These terminological problems dog all our attempts to write about these relations. Thus, in the course of two sentences, we find Frend writing that "it is in the pages of Revelation with their terrible comparison between the 'true' and the 'false' Jews and the denunciation of the 'Synagogue of Satan' whose members were enemies and persecutors of the Saints that the intensity of ill-feeling between the two groups can be seen." Which are the two groups? Obviously from this quotation, they are both Jews, even from the perspective of the author of Revelation himself, but for Frend, in the very next sentence, "the struggle between Jew and Christian was bitter and incessant." Two groups of warring Jews have now become the "Jew," and the Christian, by now, has become necessarily not a Jew. Frend, *The Early Church*, 37. This consistent distortion (on the part of most writers, certainly not only Frend) renders it nearly impossible to see the more complex sets of relations that obtained.

41. It is, to be sure, very difficult to be consistent here. We all run into these difficulties. Thus, Keith Hopkins writes: "It seems reasonable to suppose that Jewish-Christians, who awkwardly straddled both Judaism and Christianity, to the eventual indignation of both, probably for a significant period constituted the central, numerical core of Christians." Hopkins, "Christian Number," 214–15. Indeed, but if Jewish-Christians were the "central, numerical core," then why say they "awkwardly straddled" Judaism and Christianity?

42. "Interestingly, in his attempt to persuade his brethren not to be bound by 'vain bonds' anymore, the *Didascalia* chooses the terminology of conversation [Latin *conversatio*; Syriac: *devurchon*]: Do not 'remain in your former conversation that you should keep vain bonds.' He does not tell them to leave their 'former religion' or their 'former community,' not to leave the authority of the rabbi in order to submit to another authority, namely the authority of the bishop and the deacons. This rhetorical choice raises some important questions with respect to how the Didascalia understood and constructed the boundaries between Judaism and Christianity: Did the author, indeed, think in those terms, that is, in terms of the juxtaposition of two different religions, whose respective characters would be recognizable as two of the major protagonists in the cultural mappings of Late Antiquity." Fonrobert, "The Concept of Jewish Christianity."

43. Meeks and Wilken, *Jews and Christians in Antioch*, vii. See also Baer, "Israel" (1961), 79. Then see Lieu, *Image and Reality*, especially 11–12. Note that Miriam S. Taylor, *Anti-Judaism*, demonstrates that a "vital social and religious force" and an "independent religion alongside Christianity" does not imply, at all, a Jewish mission to the Gentiles, Jewish competition for converts, or Jewish aggressiveness toward Christianity.

44. Frend, *Martyrdom and Persecution*, 18. Frend's reasoning is as follows: Biblis cries out under pressure: "She directly contradicted the slanderers, saying: 'How could they eat their children, who may not eat blood even of creatures without reason?'" (V.1.26). Lawlor and Oulton, *Eusebius*, 1: 143. These Christians were still, therefore, following the apostolic levitical rule to eat only meat from which all blood had been drained, that is, meat slaughtered in the Jewish fashion. This, then, by itself does not indicate intimacy with Jews or Judaism, but Le Clerq had argued from this that, considering the conditions in Lyons, they must have been purchasing their meat from Jews, as this does indicate.

45. Susanna Elm cites a text from the *Historia Lausiaca* that describes a fourth-century Egyptian female ascetic who takes no food except on Saturday and Sunday in order to more fully devote herself to prayer. Elm, "*Virgins of God*," 315. Obviously, the reason for her to be eating on those two days is that they are *both* being observed by her as Holy Days, that is, the Sabbath and the Lord's Day. This double observance was also the case in the Palestinian *lauras* of the fourth century and in the Pachomian and Nitrian foundations, as well, Chitty, *The Desert a City*, 15, 23, 31. See Odom, *Sabbath and Sunday*. According to both the *Didache* and Ignatius, observance of the Lord's Day rather than the Sabbath was the mark of the Christian as opposed to the Jew, Joan E. Taylor, "The Phenomenon of Jewish-Christianity," 317, 319.

46. II.27.5. Lawlor and Oulton, *Eusebius*, 1: 89.

47. This point is all the more striking, since already in the third century, observing the Lord's Day rather than the Jewish Sabbath was seen in some texts as a touchstone of orthodoxy, Vööbus, *The Didascalia Apostolorum*, 233. I am grateful to Charlotte Fonrobert for calling this text to my attention in this context.

48. De Lange, *Origen and the Jews*, 188.

49. Krauss, "The Jews in the Works of the Church Fathers," 238 n. 2.

50. Robert, *Le martyre*; den Boeft and Bremmer, "Notiunculae Martyrologicae III," 110–30.

51. "Indeed, Christian preoccupation with the wickedness of the Jews, from Pharisees to High Priest, and with establishing their moral inferiority illustrates the urgency of Christian leaders' needs to differentiate themselves from their prime rivals." Hopkins, "Christian Number," 215–16.

52. The precise details of Quartodeciman practice remain complex and are beyond the scope of the present discussion. See meanwhile Lieu, *Image and Reality*, 209. For a very concise summary of the issue, see Frend, *The Early Church*, 76. See also Huber, *Passa und Ostern*.

53. There is an extraordinary irony here, for, as Israel Yuval has recently shown, the Jews began to refer to the Saturday before Passover as the "Great Sabbath" only in medieval Ashkenaz and apparently in concert (or competition) with the Christian usage of Holy Saturday. Yuval, "*Two Nations in Your Womb*;" idem, "Passover in the Middle Ages." For exegetical associations between Pesaḥ and Purim that *might* be (but probably are not) germane, see Michael G. Wechsler, "The Purim-Passover Connection," 321–27.

54. Lieu, *Image and Reality*, 74.

55. Cf. Bowersock, *Martyrdom and Rome*, 82–84, including references to other literature. See also the discussion in Lieu, *Image and Reality*, 70–79, which certainly points up the intimate relations between the dating of the Christian Pascha and the Jewish Pesaḥ, especially in the context of the traditions of Asia, as well as the density of the associations between martyrdom and Passover, particularly in these churches. Lieu, *Image and Reality*, 77. This observation is particularly cogent in the light of Schoedel's conclusion that the appendix to the text that is the basis for the dating is "an addition to the Martyrdom of Polycarp," with the only question remaining "how early an addition it may be." Schoedel, *Polycarp*, 78. For an important discussion and recent bibliography, see also Robert, *Le martyre*, 50.

56. Yuval, "The Haggadah of Passover and Easter"; idem, "Easter and Passover." On the other hand, I am somewhat mystified by Schoedel's remark that "the Great Sabbath indicated in medieval Jewry the Sabbath before Passover and in the early Church (but not before the age of Chrysostom) the Saturday before Easter (Schwartz, *Ostertafeln*, 127). In the latter sense it would be out of place in a Quartodeciman community like Smyrna (Eusebius, *H.E.* 5.24.16). This is a key point in Keim's (pp. 103–6) late dating of the Martyrdom of Polycarp. It is more likely that the phrase is an imitation of John 19:31; if so, it may represent an interpolation reflecting the same impulse that led to dating the arrest on 'the Preparation [The Eve of the Sabbath, Friday]' (7:1)." Schoedel, *Polycarp*, 61. "Keim" here is Theodor Keim, *Aus dem Urchristenthum* (Zurich, 1878). "Schwartz" is E. Schwartz, *Christliche und jüdische Ostertafeln*, Abhandlungen der königlichen Gesselschaft der Wissenschaft zu Göttingen: Philologisch-historisch Klasse, N.F. Vol. VIII/6 (Berlin, 1905). It may be that the term "Great Sabbath" is not attested before the fourth century, and this may very well indicate interpolation in MarPol, but there seems no reason at all to assume that Quartodecimani would not consider this a special Sabbath, just as the Jews, who also obviously do not celebrate Pesaḥ on Sunday (probably in imitation of the Christian usage—wheels within wheels!), refer to this Sabbath as the "Great Sabbath." In any case, the evidence from this usage for intimacy be-

tween Jews and Christians is compelling. There seems not the slightest warrant at all for ever calling Purim "the Great Sabbath."

57. L'Huillier, *The Church of the Ancient Councils*, 21 Emphasis added to point out how dependent religiously on Jewish authority these Christians were willing to be. The source is Epiphanius, quoting a text closely related to the *Didascalia*. Ibid., 87 n. 37.

58. V.24.9. Lawlor and Oulton, *Eusebius*, 1: 169.

59. L'Huillier, *The Church of the Ancient Councils*, 19–26.

60. However, much of the extant scholarship on religious interaction between Judaism and Christianity in late antiquity has, indeed, to do with shared liturgical innovation. See Schirmann, "Hebrew Liturgical Poetry," 123–61; Sigal, "Early Christian and Rabbinic Liturgical Affinities," 63–90. The advantage of the former article is that it deals with the later period that interests me here. While the latter is too ready to see influence (direction arbitrarily determined) where I would see common or shared development, it still provides a useful compendium of earlier suggested liturgical commonalities. See also the two volumes by Eric Werner, *The Sacred Bridge* (1979) and *The Sacred Bridge* (1985).

61. Peter Brown, *The Cult of the Saints*, 103. Sadly, what transpires on p. 104 is the violent destruction of this concordia. On this whole incident, see Severus of Minorca, *Letter on the Conversion of the Jews*.

62. Sozomen, *Ecclesiastical History*, 2, 4 in the translation by Kofsky, "Mamre," 24–25, and see the discussion there as well.

63. Satran, *Biblical Prophets*, 4–6 and literature cited there. Also Shaw, "Body/Power/Identity," 281 on the Testament of Job.

64. See Lieu, *Image and Reality*, 161–62.

65. I am not implying, of course, that it is impossible that this text has an earlier origin than its context.

66. Hasan-Rokem, "Narratives in Dialogue," 121.

67. Hasan-Rokem, *The Web of Life*, 165

68. Hasan-Rokem, "Narratives in Dialogue," 122.

69. Reuven Kimelman has cited impressive patristic evidence for Jewish aid to Christians in times of trial and for Jewish attempts to persuade Christians to follow the Law without necessarily "converting" to Judaism, Kimelman, "Birkat Ha-Minim," 239–40.

70. Le Boulluec, *La notion d'hérésie*; Burrus, *The Making of a Heretic*.

71. Markus, *The End of Ancient Christianity*. Averil Cameron has written: "One even gets into problematic areas with the application of the very terms 'Christian' and 'pagan,' as though there were always firm and easily detectable

boundaries between them instead of a murky overlapping area." Cameron, *Christianity and the Rhetoric of Empire*, 122. Synesius provides an elegant example of the "murky overlap."

72. Bauer, *Orthodoxy and Heresy*, 59. Strikingly, however, Bauer continues to use the term "syncretism" as the mark of an even more heretical heresy than the heresies that he is prepared to admit to Christianity. Bauer, *Orthodoxy and Heresy*, 101.

73. For the analogy, see Sigal, " Early Christian and Rabbinic Liturgical Affinities," 64. Fonrobert, "The Concept of Jewish Christianity" provides an elegant case to demonstrate such a thesis for at least one locale and community in Syria.

74. Clements, *"Peri Pascha,"* 2.

75. Simon, *Verus Israel*, 182.

76. "Usque hodie per totas orientis synagogas inter Iudaeos haeresis est, quae dicitur Minaeorum, et a pharisaeis huc usque damnatur, quos uulgo Nazaraeos nuncupant, qui credunt in Christum, filim dei natum de Maria uirgine, et eum dicunt esse, qui sub Pontio Pilato et passus est et resurrexit, in quem et nos credimus, sed, cum uolunt et Iudaei esse et Christiani, nec Iudaei sunt nec Christiani." Jerome, *Correspondence*, 55: 381–82.

77. In a very carefully argued case, Georg Strecker comes to the nearly inexorable conclusion that the third-century Syrian work the *Didascalia* evidences "an active relationship between Christians and Jews in the author's world. Even though with regard to particulars the question of the extent to which such a contact contributed significantly to the development of the outlook of the author and the practice of his community must remain open, it is quite clear that the Syrian environment of the *Didascalia* supports an intensive influence of Jewish thought and conceptual material." Strecker, "On the Problem of Jewish Christianity," 251. See also Fonrobert, "The Concept of Jewish Christianity." In a work that unaccountably only came to my attention after my book was completed, Alan Segal takes a position similar to mine here. Alan F. Segal, *The Other Judaisims of Late Antiquity*. I regret my failure to incorporate his arguments into my text.

78. But see Le Boulluec, *La notion d'hérésie*, for much earlier beginnings of this phenomenon.

79. Hopkins even points to corresponding movements within Zoroastrianism at this time: "But it is worth noting that successive Sassanian kings towards the end of the third century moved the Iranian empire towards religious (Mazdean) exclusivism and the systematic persecution of religious 'deviants,'" Hopkins, "Christian Number," 223.

80. Markus, *The End of Ancient Christianity*, 20.

81. Ibid., 28.

82. "The Talmud contains evidence for exchanges in the early fourth century between Alexandrian Jews and Palestinian rabbis, most particularly over liturgical matters such as the use of oils in the Sabbath lighting and the proper preparation of unleavened bread for the Passover. Just as Alexandrian Christians are making efforts to clarify their Christian Pasch, its date and its fasting, especially to bring into conformity with Christians elsewhere, so too their Jewish contemporaries are seeking advice from rabbinic authorities over how to celebrate their festivals in the normative fashion. Both communities are seeking to transform or adapt local traditions to emerging international standards." Brakke, "Passover and Particularity." I thank the author for generously letting me quote this paper prior to its publication.

83. Clements, "*Peri Pascha*," 133–34, 135.

84. Rajak, "The Jewish Community," 12. For the idea of a revival of Judaism in the fourth century parallel to the "pagan revival," see Wilken, *John Chrysostom and the Jews*, 55.

85. I have been using the term "late antiquity" somewhat loosely. At this point, some precision is perhaps required. Traditional among Roman historians is a division between "the Principate, the High Empire, and the world of later antiquity, the Dominate or Low/Late Empire." Simon Swain remarks that

> there is, conveniently for historians, a historical break between the two which comes in the third quarter of the third century. It is introduced by the first systematic persecutions of Christians by Decius in 250 and Valerian a few years later, pointing to Christians' growing impact on secular power, by the ending of the "epigraphic habit", the phenomenon of advertising public and private power on stone and bronze that was so important in the High Empire, in the years following 250, and by the three or four decades of imperial misrule and military insecurity before the ascendancy of Diocletian in 284/5, the institution of the Tetrarchy and the other administrative reforms that set the tone for the late Empire.

Swain, "Biography and Biographic," 3. Properly speaking, then, "late antiquity" is the period following "the making of late antiquity." In my work, I, like many others working more on religious and cultural histories, particularly of Judaism and Christianity, use the term to refer to the transitional period between the Principate and the Dominate, as well, even, sometimes, to indicate cultural continuities or genealogies that have their origins in the cultural and social (sexual, gendered) ferment of the second century (the Second Sophistic) and that come to fruition in the fourth century. The developments in martyrology with which this essay is concerned are an example of one of those genealogies. The developments to which Swain points, as well as others focused on by Peter Brown in *The Making of Late Antiquity*, are crucial in the story that these chapters have to tell.

86. This is seemingly a questionable practice, since the Palestinian texts were redacted in a society in which Christianity was dominant, while the Babylonian texts weren't, and this ought to make a big difference. In fact, however, in a recent study, Christine Hayes has shown that there were very minor differences between the two literary cultures in this respect, and especially significantly with respect to the primary texts for dealing with religious difference, the two talmudic tractates on idolatry that will figure centrally in this research. Hayes, *Between the Babylonian and Palestinian Talmuds*. Moreover, Peter Brown has written: "Northern Mesopotamia, including Edessa, though from the military point of view a frontier region, fought over by the armies of Rome and Persia, formed an undivided cultural zone. It was the clamp that held east and west together. As the center of a region of shared high culture, the horizons of the inhabitants of northern Mesopotamia reached from the Mediterranean to Central Asia." Brown, *The Rise of Western Christendom*, 7. See also Daniel Boyarin, "On the Emergence of the Aramaic Dialects," 613–49.

The ease of travel of Rabbis between the Babylonian and Palestinian centers certainly attests to this cultural connectivity. For early Babylonian rabbinic knowledge of Christianity, a passing citation in the Talmud Avoda Zara 6a is very significant. Rabbi Ishmaᶜel, an early Palestinian authority, held the opinion that one may not trade with Gentiles for three days before and three days after their festival. On this, the Talmud reports that Rav Taḥlifa bar Abdimi said that Shmuel said: "The day of the Nazarene [Sunday, "the Lord's Day"] prohibits [trade with Gentiles] forever, according to Rabbi Ishmaᶜel." The only plausible interpretation of this text is that it is a reductio ad absurdum by Shmuel of Rabbi Ishmaᶜel's claim, namely, if you indeed say that three days before and after the festival we are forbidden to deal with Gentiles as well, then Sunday would disable Jews from ever doing business with Christians at all, pace Ray A. Pritz, *Nazarene Jewish Christianity*, 98. Assuming, as we have no reason not to, in this case, that a statement from third-century Babylonia is before us, then we have probable evidence for Christian influence on the Jews then and there. In any case, even if the dating is uncertain, the documentation for a significant effect of Christians on the Babylonian Jews is certain.

87. This does not mean that I doubt the historical existence of such a figure, but only that most, if not all, of what we "know" about him is the stuff of legends told centuries after his life.

88. In addition to the third-century Tosefta 2:22, we find it in the fourth-to fifth-century Qohelet Rabbah: 1.

89. To be sure, to a certain extent, the Rabbis were in general antihistoricistic in their approach, to use a somewhat anachronistic term. However, the presence of pagan Rome is everywhere felt in the texts, and often, I think, disguises through anachronism the Christian Rome that is both context and referent for the text. Christianity was, I think, too close for comfort too often.

90. Pace Neusner, *Judaism and Christianity*, x.

91. A word about the term "discourse" as used here may be of use. The locution, as I use it (within a particular intellectual tradition, of course), indicates the multiple layerings of linguistic and other usages that make up a particular form of practice. Thus, one could speak of "the discourse of colonialism, the discourse of race," even "the discourse of fashion," to include both literary and other verbal practices, various forms of economic life, the exercise of power, and the like. In other words, the term intends to capture exactly the sense that textual practice is practice like any other and has its (often deadly) effects in the "real" world. For this essentially Foucauldian notion, see Tilley, "Michel Foucault," 290–304. Foucault's own definition is, moreover, clear in itself: "Discourses are practices that systematically form the objects of which they speak. Of course, discourses are composed of signs; but what they do is more than use these signs to designate things. It is this *more* that renders them irreducible to the language (*langue*) and to speech (*parole*)." Foucault, *The Archaeology of Knowledge* 49.

92. Hasan-Rokem, *The Web of Life*, 135. See also Fischel, "Martyr and Prophet," 269.

93. As Nicole Loraux points out, the deaths in tragedies are reported, not seen. Loraux, *Tragic Ways of Killing a Woman*, vii. She also writes that "in real life the city did not sacrifice its young girls" (33), but Christians did, in a sense, at least occasionally, even if most martyrologies are as literary as *Iphigenia in Taurus*.

94. Cf. Satran's similar case-study approach to the same issue: "Viewed in this light, the *Lives of the Prophets* can be appreciated as a testing ground for the contiguities and divergences of Judaism and Christianity in Late Antiquity." Satran, *Biblical Prophets*, 6. Satran's theoretical position is not far from the one adopted in this book.

CHAPTER 1

1. *Esxema.* Like its Greek etymon, the word in Syriac can mean either "special attire" or "practice."

2. It is perhaps in their avoidance of idol worship that "orthodox" Christians most appropriated their "Jewish" patrimony. In an important discussion, Itzhaq Baer has claimed to show how close Tertullian's *De Idololatria* is, *in detail*, to the talmudic laws of idolatry as expounded in the tractate, *Avoda Zara*. Baer concludes, "It can be recognised from the examples cited that the Christian teacher is basing his words on the decisions of the Jewish rabbis taught in our Mishna and Baraitot." Baer, "Israel" (1961), 88–93, especially 92. J. B. Rives, on the other hand, has denied the connection. Rives, *Religion and Authority*, 220–21. This topic deserves further detailed investigation.

3. Bedjan, *Histoire de Mar Jabalaha*, 211–14. The translation here is mine, with the advice of Schlomo Naeh.

4. The significance of his "Jewish" name, "Joseph who was called Moses" (Bedjan, *Histoire de Mar Jabalaha*, 211) is duly noted by Gero, "With Walter Bauer on the Tigris," 290 n. 9.

5. Bauer, *Orthodoxy and Heresy*, 23, cites this text as evidence that Marcionitism was the aboriginal form of Christianity in the area of Edessa. I believe that he is wrong in his interpretation of the text itself and will argue this in a separate paper, *deo volente*.

6. For fourth-century Christians who call themselves by the name "Jew" and Augustine's reaction to them, see Shaye J. D. Cohen, "'Those Who Say They Are Jews and Are Not,'" 2.

7. A word on the dating of rabbinic texts and historical phenomena: I tend to follow what I would call a loose and revised version of Neusner's documentary (or canonical) history-of-ideas approach. I attempt to keep the levels of rabbinic textuality broadly apart, seeing in Tannaitic works, *grosso modo*, the rabbinic discourse of the late-second to mid-third centuries, and in the Amoraic works (the Talmud and the classical midrash), the discourse of the fourth century and perhaps also the fifth, when these texts took their major shape, even when they are allegedly quoting or referring to earlier authorities. However, I do not assume that just because a given discursive moment appears only in a later text that it could not have been earlier, or certainly was not earlier, as Neusner does. Cf. Daniel Boyarin, "On the Status of the Tannaitic Midrashim," 455–65. Instead, I try to show how a given discourse actually develops from one layer to another. Or, frequently enough, I just use the presence of a given story in a later document as evidence for the continued exis-

tence of a certain way of thinking/talking at the time of that later document. The Palestinian Talmud (Ḥagiga 2:2 = 77d) preserves a parallel story in which Jesus does not figure at all, but a different master and a different disciple. As will be clear, this only enhances the historical importance of this late Babylonian version. See Gero, "Stern Master," 287–311. I am obliged to Prof. Menahem Kister for reminding me of this article.

8. Fascinatingly enough, Elchanan Reiner argues that "many of [Yehoshua the son of Peraḥya]'s traits, as featured both in the Aramaic versions of *Toledot Jeshu* [the Jewish parodic Gospels] and in the Babylonian Talmud, are actually reflections of Jesus' personality as portrayed in the Gospel according to Matthew and in *Toledot Jeshu* itself. The point of departure for this comparison, the basic reason for the use of this particular mishnaic scholar in these contexts, is, first and foremost, his name 'Joshua', whose significance in this context has already been point out." Reiner, "From Joshua to Jesus," 257–58. Reiner plausibly connects the talmudic story being discussed here with the Gospel account of the flight of the Holy Family into Egypt.

9. For the philology here, see Gero, "Stern Master," 301–2 n. 36. Gero denies the double meaning and claims that the master is also speaking of the hostess. However, the fact that Yehoshua's statement follows immediately upon the honor given him in the inn suggests that he is indeed intended to have meant the inn, and not the innkeeper's daughter. This, of course, also renders the story much stronger from a literary point of view.

10. R. Travers Herford is as puzzled as everyone else as to the exact nature of the object that Jesus is represented as having worshipped. Herford, *Christianity in Talmud and Midrash*, 54. Jacob Z. Lauterbach also, after considering various wild options and emendations, writes, "The phrase as it stands in our text makes no sense." Lauterbach, "Jesus in the Talmud," 484.

I wonder if an icon is not meant. A word meaning "tile" might very well be adopted for icon, and the word icon איקונין itself could not be used because it had quite a different meaning in Hebrew. I'm not sure of the chronological likelihood that a Babylonian talmudic text of probably the fourth or even fifth century would have referred to icons as a characteristic aspect of Christian worship. See Elsner, "The Origins of the Icon," 178–99. Gero thinks differently, arguing that a brick is sometimes a brick, Gero, "Stern Master," 290–91 n. 9. At any rate, there does seem to be some real practice referred to in this notation, since TB Avoda Zara 46a also contains notice of someone erecting a brick for idolatrous worship. See also Gero, "Stern Master," 305 n. 41, where the brick has become, somewhat improbably, in my view, a fish.

11. For this exact charge, see Justin Martyr, *Dialogue with Trypho*, 69.7,

where Justin accuses Jesus's contemporaries of rejecting him as a "worker of magic and deceiver of the people." See also Lieu, *Image and Reality*, 131. See the discussion in Kalmin, "Christians and Heretics," 156–57.

12. On this text, see Alexander, "'The Parting of the Ways,'" 16–18. The difference between our interpretations is clear. On the philological aspect, see especially Maier, *Jesus von Nazareth*, 104–29. For literature *in extenso*, see Gero, "Stern Master," 288 n. 2.

13. On the other hand, I am astonished at how Bauer undermines his own insight by making statements of the following ilk: "Rome possessed the most tightly knit, perhaps the only more or less reliable anti-heretical majority, because it was farthest removed from the oriental danger zone and in addition was by nature and custom least inclined or able to yield to seemingly fantastic oriental ways of thinking and oriental emotions that becloud clear thought. The sober sense of the Roman was not the proper seed-bed for Syrian or Egyptian syncretism." Bauer, *Orthodoxy and Heresy*, 230. Similar statements are to be found throughout. By positing that "heresy" is the product of Oriental syncretism and fantastic ways of thinking, Bauer seems to be assuming a prior, uncontaminated, and pure version of Christianity, the precise opposite of the claim that his book sets out to make. Koester, "Gnomai Diaforoi," 279, makes essentially the same point that I am making, but more delicately. For an essential remake of Bauer's work that accomplishes two main tasks, see Le Boulluec, *La notion d'hérésie*. The two tasks are demonstrating that, contra Bauer, it was not Eusebius who originated the schema of "orthodoxy" followed by "heresy," but rather Justin and Irenaeus in their anti-Gnostic struggle and demonstrating that it was these very writers who began to develop the notion of orthodoxy itself. Like heterosexuality, which came into being together with homosexuality only in the nineteenth century, orthodoxy came into being with heresy only in the second. See also, Hopkins, "Christian Number," 218, who writes:

> In the beginning, leaders of the primitive church had little (or insufficient) power to enforce their views. But the very idea that correct belief identified the true Christian and that incorrect belief pushed the believer who wanted to be a Christian beyond the pale became entrenched as a core defining characteristic of early Christianity. By the end of the second century, leaders tried to enhance their authority by claiming that the catholic church had held constant and unified beliefs since apostolic times.

Hopkins, however, also, somewhat oddly, writes that Irenaeus "celebrated Christian centripetality and diversity." Hopkins, "Christian Number," 187 n. 4.

14. Origen, *Origen, The Song of Songs*, 3.

15. Bauer, *Orthodoxy and Heresy*, xxiii–xxiv; see also 39.

16. Ibid., 128–29. For the nonce, the actual details of the history of Valentinianism and whether Bauer was correct or incorrect are beside the point. See McCue, "Orthodoxy and Heresy," 118–30. What is important for me is the literary form and the ideology that it encapsulates, and that ideology is that the historical winners in religious debates present themselves as having been always dominant and the "others" as having deviated, frequently enough for venal reasons.

17. Given the typical character of such stories, I must confess to a bit of surprise at finding Frend crediting the story of Porphyry's having been "at one time a catechumen turned away from Christianity by personal insult and injury received from Christians, and his hostility towards them increased with age." Frend, *Martyrdom and Persecution*, 483, especially 524 n. 56.

18. Pace Herford, I don't consider the implied accusation that Jesus was lustily looking at the innkeeper's wife (or daughter) to be anything other than the usual charge against heretics that they are immoral. *Christianity in Talmud and Midrash*, 53. For the ubiquity and topical character of such charges (as well as the charge of practicing magic), see e.g., Frend, *Martyrdom and Persecution*, 11.

19. Gero, "Stern Master," 292–97.

20. Ibid., 310–11.

21. Nearly two decades ago, Shaye Cohen pointed to the "ecclesiological theories held in common by rabbis and fathers." "A Virgin Defiled," 1–11. (I thank Virginia Burrus for this reference, and many others, as well). This text supports strongly the suggestion of Marcel Simon, *Verus Israel*, 183, that "the Jews, for their part, continued to apply [the term *minim* = "sectarians"] to all Christians of whatever kind. . . . In short, for the Jews themselves the term *minim* may have comprehended orthodox Christianity along with all the other dissidents." My argument is that on the evidence of this text, at least (and of course, this is not probative for all Rabbis everywhere and always), Christianity was precisely a matter of "Sinners they were, but Jews all the same" as late as the fourth century or maybe even later, pace Lawrence H. Schiffman, "At the Crossroads," 115–16, who maintains that the Rabbis considered Christianity "another religion entirely" as early as the early Tannaitic period. According to David Brakke, "Athanasius understood his Jewish opponents to be similar to all his other enemies; for him, they were, in essence, Christian heretics, or at least the model for all Christian heretics." Brakke, "'Outside the Places, Within the Truth.'" We can construct, therefore, a perfectly symmetrical system.

For the lateness of this text, see Gero, "Stern Master," 306–10. Lauterbach already had made this argument, as well. Incidentally, it is quite fascinating to observe how Lauterbach demonstrates that this text must belong to the later Amoraic period (fifth-sixth centuries) or even slightly later and then concludes that it has "no real historic value," in contrast, it must be said, to many scholars who, quite absurdly, attempt to recover the kernel of positivist historical truth in this story. (For literature see Gero, "Stern Master," 291.) On the other hand, he does get the point that "it is significant that they speak of him as a onetime disciple." Lauterbach, "Jesus in the Talmud," 490. Richard Kalmin has made the point that Jesus becomes *more* Rabbi-like in later Babylonian talmudic portraits than in earlier or Palestinian ones. Kalmin, "Christians and Heretics," 156.

22. Jerome knows that the term *mîn*, "sectarian," is a name for Jewish Christians, as we see from his famous letter to Augustine. Jerome, *Correspondence*, 55: 381–82. This letter was written about 404. Pritz, *Nazarene Jewish Christianity*, 53. See also Friedländer, *Patristische und Talmudische Studien*, 62.

23. On the use of this term in Roman legal texts and martyr acts, as well as the parallel *gradus* of the later versions, see Lieberman, "Roman Legal Institutions," 69–71.

24. In the later versions of the text, "these matters" has been revised to "these idle matters," which I believe must reflect a technical term from Roman legal practice. In any case, I believe that Frend's interpretation that the judge is ridiculing Eliᶜezer here in order to release him is wrong. Frend, *Martyrdom and Persecution*, 185. Moreover, Frend's gloss on this phrase as "the rabbi 'was an old fool to get himself mixed up in this sort of thing'" (222), is exactly upside-down. The reference to Rabbi Eliᶜezer's age is an allusion to wisdom, not to foolishness. In support of this, one can offer the *Qohelet Rabbah* version, which reads explicitly: "A great man such as you." Hirshman, "Midrash Qohelet Rabbah," part 1, 53. The conclusions that Frend wishes to draw from his palpable misreading are equally invalid, of course.

25. According to the reading of Alice Bach, the Book of Judith presents an elegant parallel "when the beautiful widow referred to her unwavering obedience to ᶜadonai, 'my lord.'" Bach, *Women, Seduction, and Betrayal*, 31. Note the similarity with John 6:42–44, where the Jews refer to Jesus's "father" and he responds by referring to having been sent by "the Father," or, according to some manuscripts, by "my Father." For the latter and discussion of other textual variants, see Ehrman, *The Orthodox Corruption of Scripture*, 57. Cf. also Numenius, who says of Plato: "If Plato had openly criticized these things, he would have given the Athenians an opportunity to show again their malice and

kill him, just as they had done with Socrates. Now it is not the case that he preferred life to speaking the truth, *but he saw an opportunity to combine life and safely speaking the truth.*" Cited in van der Horst, "Plato's Fear," 11.

26. This place, referred to in other texts in an Aramaicized form as "Kefar Sekhania" cannot, it seems, be identified with certainty. Pritz, *Nazarene Jewish Christianity*, 120.

27. "Pantiri" = Latin "Panthera," the name of a Roman soldier. There is an enormous literature by now on this name and its meanings: Herford, *Christianity in Talmud and Midrash*, 39; Krauss, "The Jews in the Works of the Church Fathers," 43–44; Lauterbach, "Jesus in the Talmud"; Strack and Billerbeck, *Kommentar zum Neuen Testament aus Talmud und Midrasch*, 1: 538. I believe that the most likely explanation was given over a hundred years ago by Paulus Cassel and has been forgotten. Origen remarks in his commentary on John 20:14 that Jesus was born εκ παρθενου, but the Jews say that he was born εκ πορνειας. Some scholars have been led, therefore, to see in Pandera a "corruption" of *porneia*. Krauss, "The Jews in the Works of the Church Fathers." This is obviously not satisfactory, but it does, I think suggest the direction to a better explanation. My guess is that there were Jews who had a better gibe at the Christian claims. The Christians claim that he was born εκ παρθενου, but he was really born εκ πανθερος. I am therefore strongly inclined to accept Cassel's conjecture in "Caricaturnamen," 334, that "Panthera" is an intentional distortion of *Parthenos*. I believe that he was wrong, however, in concluding that this was meant as "son of a Panther." Adolf Deissmann has proved that "Panthera" was a fairly well attested name in the imperial period and was attested as the name of Roman soldiers, including one of apparently Semitic origin, because his first name was Abdes. Deissmann concluded, therefore, mistakenly in my opinion, that "*Panthera* was not an invention of Jewish scoffers." Deissmann, *Light from the Ancient East*, 74. However, his correct assertion that it is an attested name hardly discredits the notion that Jews attributed this cognomen to Jesus as a taunting deformation of παρθενου. Indeed, if anything, this makes a much stronger case for this interpretation. This would be a fine example of the form of Jewish taunts against Christians and pagans that Lieberman used to call "cacophemism." This "discovery" was made once more by L. Patterson, "Origin of the Name Panthera," 79–80. It seems to me more appealing than any that has been put forth since. The practice itself is explicitly recognized within rabbinic literature. Thus, the Talmud remarks in one place: "All places which are named for idolatry are given pejorative appellations. What is named פני אלה [Face of the goddess] is called פני כלב [Face of the dog]" (Tosefta AZ 6:4)," and the medieval Jewish authority asserts that

the same must be done for apostates. Thus, calling Jesus the "Son of Pan-thera," instead of the "Son of Parthenou," would seem to be a very plausible explanation indeed. See also Chadwick, *Origen: Contra Celsum*, 31 n. 3.

The notice of the name "son of Pandera" as a slanderous cognomen for Jesus also suggests the possibility of an early polemic encounter, since Celsus (ca. 170) remarks that the Jews promulgate an aspersion that Jesus was the bas-tard son of a Roman soldier named Pandera. We also have excellent indirect evidence of this Jewish charge against Christianity from Tertullian at the end of the second century. When Christ comes again, triumphs Tertullian: "'This,' I shall say, 'this is that carpenter's or harlot's son, that Sabbath-breaker, that Samaritan and devil-possessed! This is He whom you purchased from Judas! This is He whom you struck with reed and fist, whom you contemptuously spat upon, to whom you gave gall and vinegar to drink! This is He whom His disciples secretly stole away, that it might be said He had risen again.'" *De spec-taculis* 3.30. These ringing sentences for the most part surely are simply cita-tions of the Gospels, and have no evidential value for the later period. But, on the other hand, there is one charge that is almost certainly an indirect citation of a charge of the Jews against Christ that is not found in the Gospel: that he is a whoreson. This must have been an allegation of the Jews in Tertullian's own world and thus confirms the evidence of Origen's *Contra Celsum*. (Con-tra Miriam S. Taylor, *Anti-Judaism*, 42, who in her generally convincing zeal to displace explanatory models of Christian anti-Judaism based on "competition" seems to miss the point of this text.) It follows, then, that there was discussion of Christianity by Jews by the middle of the second century.

28. Zuckermandel, *Tosephta*, 503.

29. See also Alon, *The Jews in Their Land*, 1: 292–93.

30. Pliny, *Letters and Panegyricus*, 2: 402–3.

31. Indeed, as one anonymous reader pointed out, the "whole point of Pliny's letter is to ask advice *because he doesn't know what exactly the procedure is*, not because he is outlining an established practice."

32. Schoedel, *Polycarp*, 65.

33. Lieberman, "Roman Legal Institutions," 79, and especially n. 150. Kimelman has interestingly interpreted the notice in Justin Martyr that the Jews "scoff at the King of Israel" after their prayers as owing to the Jewish need to demonstrate to the Romans *at the time of Justin*, precisely this, that they are not Christians, for the purpose of escaping martyrdom and persecution as such. Kimelman, "Birkat Ha-Minim," 235.

34. Lieberman, "Roman Legal Institutions," 78.

35. There is indeed evidence that my conjecture is correct, that is, that the

published answer offered by Lieberman was indeed evasive and intended to lead the reader to the suggestion offered here. In unpublished lectures delivered to his students, Lieberman openly proposed a partial version of the hypothesis that I tender and argue for here. According to Marc G. Hirshman, "Midrash Qohelet Rabbah," part 1, 52, Lieberman "connected the suspicions of Rabbi Eli⁽e⁾zer of sectarianism (being Christian) with his excommunication on the part of the Sages in the matter of the Akhnai Stove."

36. I have pointed to the proximity of Rabbi Eli⁽e⁾zer to Christianity in cultural/ideological matters before, particularly with respect to his attitudes toward sexuality. See Daniel Boyarin, *Carnal Israel*, 47. See also Stein, "Folklore Elements in Late Midrash," 173–81.

37. Rashi, in what I take to be yet another making of a "hidden transcript," improbably interprets the phrase to mean "arrested [in order to make him into] a sectarian," that is, that the Romans were trying to force him to become a heretic. This interpretation is so linguistically strained and so inadequate to the narrative context that it is hard to believe that Rashi intended as other than a cover-up. Cover-ups multiply upon cover-ups, but leave the marks of the covering up all over the place.

38. The division is always, obviously, a constructed one. My argument, then, is that in this period, much more active work was being done to construct it than would be necessary at later times, although in the early modern period, it would become necessary again—but that is another story. This active work was both diachronic, in that the division was being made through history, and also synchronic, in that certain discursive forces were actively trying to make it appear as a given. We are observing the effects of those forces in our texts.

39. Baumgarten, "Literary Evidence," 46–47.

40. For the dating of the Pseudo-Clementines, see Jones, *An Ancient Jewish Christian Source*, 1

41. Ibid., 100–101.

42. For another possible (if somewhat improbable) connection of this type, see Marmorstein, "Judaism and Christianity," especially 233. Marmorstein also discusses the relation between the *Didascalia* and the Pseudo-Clementine literature. See also Strecker, "On the Problem of Jewish Christianity," 251, and especially Fonrobert, *Constructing Women's Bodies*, chapter 6 n. 33; idem, "The Concept of Jewish Christianity."

43. Hopkins, "Novel Evidence for Roman Slavery," 6.

44. See Neusner, *Why No Gospels*.

45. Finkelstein, *Akiba*.

46. See Neusner, *Eliezer Ben Hyrcanus*, and Fränkel, *Readings in the Spiritual World*, just to take two examples of their prodigious writings particularly related to the subject of this book.

47. Smith, "Differential Equations," 13–14, and see King, "Gnosticism as Heresy." This process goes both ways, of course. A beautiful example is the famous passage in the *Didache* in which the author exhorts the faithful: "but do not let your fasts fall on the same day as 'the hypocrites' [i.e., the Jews; see Matt. 6:16–18], who fast on Monday and Thursday. Rather you should fast on Wednesday and Friday." Kraft, *Barnabas and the Didache*, 165.

48. See also Alon, *Jews in Their Land*, 1: 183.

49. See also Guttmann, "The Significance of Miracles," 386. I would like to thank Dina Stein for reminding me of this reference.

50. To get some sense of the uncommon extent of this punishment, it would be well to compare a similar story in which Rabbi Eliᶜezer's own colleague, Rabbi Yehoshua, violates majority agreements at least as significant as that of Rabbi Eliᶜezer's disagreement and is essentially made to go stand in the corner. "All scholars concede that R. Eliezer's disagreement with the sages alone cannot have been the reason for the ban. Such disagreements in *halakic* [sic] matters are numerous and carry no penalty for the individual sage opposing the majority or opinion." Guttmann, "The Significance of Miracles," 383. This same point has been made by Jeffrey Rubenstein for quite another purpose: "In any case the punishment is far out of proportion to the crime, a nonconformist opinion concerning an unusual type of oven." Rubenstein, "Torah, Shame, and the Oven."

51. My interpretation here is directly contra to that of most scholars, who see Rabbi Eliᶜezer as defending some hide-bound notion of "tradition," as opposed to the openness of the (other) Rabbis to change. For instance, Avi Sagi writes:

> Traditionalists do not place value on the very element that sets
> halakhic discourse in motion, namely, substantive argumentation
> and criticism. For the traditionalist, the study of Torah entails merely
> the repetition of traditions, without autonomous analysis and inter-
> pretation. The practical implication of this approach is that sages
> cannot contend with current problems because there can be no
> answers to new questions without an interpretive mechanism. The
> sages did not deny R. Eliezer the right to study and teach, but when
> R. Eliezer sought a conclusive ruling that would state "Halakha is as I
> say" and preclude dissenting views, they were forced to take extreme

measures. The freedom to teach and rule on halakhic issues was a crucial feature of the development of Halakha before the destruction of the Temple.

Sagi, *The Meaning of Halakhic Discourse.* Quite apart from the question of whether or not this text has anything to do with anything that happened "before the destruction of the Temple," I have other problems with this formulation of the issue. First of all, it is not the case here that Rabbi Eliᶜezer demands allegiance simply on the basis of "repetition of traditions." He provides legitimating proofs of his position from miracles and a form of prophecy. Consequently, there is no reason to assume that there could not be answers to new questions in accord with his view, as well. After all, the Torah itself provides at least two examples within which new questions came up and were answered via Moses's prophetic authority. Finally, there is no evidence that Rabbi Eliᶜezer was insisting on "precluding dissenting views." Indeed, if anything, the story seeks to prevent Rabbi Eliᶜezer from continuing to practice in accord with his dissenting view. Consequently, I think that a much stronger case can be made for competing models of authority (and much later than the first century).

Rabbi Eliᶜezer is perhaps conservative with respect to his halakhic positions, if we accept as relevant other traditions ascribed to him and about him, but hardly so with respect to his mechanisms for justification and proof. In a sense, he is a rabbinic Montanist. The institution and consolidation of the power of the majority of the Rabbis to impose their halakhic position as authoritative without the destabilizing effect of individual prophetic voices seems to me what is at play here. I argue instead that "on that day" is a virtual semiotic code locution for legends that are foundational of rabbinic authority and the modes of rabbinic rationality and religious authorization. See Daniel Boyarin, "On That Day" (forthcoming). At a later point in his discussion, Sagi comes closer to the position expressed here and developed there, writing: "The shift—from an argument about ways of arguing to a dispute about authority—is understandable: the kind of justification adduced by the traditionalist—establishing the reliability of tradition through supernatural elements—threatens the authority of halakhic institutions as well as the standard patterns of argumentation."

52. Unpublished lectures, cited in Hirshman, "Midrash Qohelet Rabbah," part 1, 56.

53. Guttmann, "The Significance of Miracles," 383.

54. And, in fact, Guttmann points to fairly close comparisons between the "miracles" of Rabbi Eliᶜezer and New Testament miracle stories. Guttmann, "The Significance of Miracles," 381. This stands contra Gilat, *R. Eliezer Ben Hyrcanus*, 483–85, who understands Rabbi Eliᶜezer as representing only older,

oral traditions in the halakha and ignores the "prophetic" or "magical" aspects of his mode of legitimation of his views. Nevertheless, Gilat also agrees that it was not the content of Rabbi Eliᶜezer's views that was ominous, but the very fact of his authority. *R. Eliezer Ben Hyrcanus*, 490.

55. Guttmann, "The Significance of Miracles," 386.

56. See also Stein, "Folklore Elements in Late Midrash," 175 n. 124.

57. In addition to the passage cited above, see Sanhedrin 43a and 106a–b, in which Jesus is implicitly compared to Balaam. Celsus also emphasizes particularly Jewish charges against Jesus that he was an Egyptian magician (Contra Celsum I 28), and we find as well identical indictments in the parodic Jewish antigospel known as *Toldoth Yeshu*. Daniel Boyarin, "A Corrected Reading," 249–52. And see Mark 3:22 and Matthew 12:24.

58. There is some reason to believe, in fact, that this was a virtual stock figure of a disciple of Jesus for the rabbinic story makers.

59. This is a place name unknown elsewhere and perhaps fictive and emblematic, since the word "Sama" means "Pharmakon." In other versions of the text, this disciple of Jesus is identified as being the same one and from the same place as in the story of Rabbi Eliᶜezer's brush with martyrdom. Richard Kalmin has taken the fact that nearly all the stories about *minim* provide them with the name Yaᶜkov as evidence that "it follows that overly careful attempts to determine the precise heresy described in the sources may be misguided." Kalmin, "Christians and Heretics," 169. My conclusion would be the exact opposite. Yaᶜkov, "James," seems very plausibly to have been a stereotyped (and probably very common) name among Galilean Jewish Christians, who would have seen James as the founder of their church.

60. Zuckermandel, *Tosephta*, 227.

61. Cp. "The aforesaid Papias related on the authority of the daughters of Philip that Barsabas, who was also entitled to the name Justus, was forced by unbelievers to drink the poison of a snake but in the name of Christ was preserved from harm." Schoedel, *Polycarp*, 119. In Eusebius's version of this story [*H.E.* III, 39, 9], there is a deadly poison, but snake venom is not specified. Lawlor and Oulton, *Eusebius*, 1: 100. See also Mark 16:18. Justin Martyr, *First and Second Apologies*, 78. Interestingly enough, only a century later, Chrysostom would be fulminating against Christians who went to the Jews in search of miraculous cures. See Kinzig, "'Non-Separation,'" 37.

62. Elegant support for this interpretation has been offered by Christine Hayes, who suggests Qohelet [Ecclesiastes] Rabbah 10:8 (paralleled by Bereshit Rabbah 79:6) as a pendant. In that story, a man is punished for violating a rabbinically ordained precept regarding the aftergrowth of the Sabbati-

cal year. Such rabbinically ordained additional precepts are frequently referred to as a "fence around the Torah." According to the narrative, the one who pronounces the curse of Ecclesiastes 10:8 upon the violator is none other than Rabbi Shimᶜon, who himself had disagreed with the institution of this "fence." As Hayes has elegantly put it, "Having the condemnation come from the very rabbi who is said to have opposed the majority halakhah is a perfect device for showing that rabbinic authority (rather than halakhic 'truth') is the issue" (personal communication).

63. For another tradition in which Jesus is presented as a reliable magical healer, see Palestinian Talmud Shabbat 14d.

64. Den Boeft and Bremmer, "Notiunculae martyrologicae," 44–45. The Latin equivalents are *amentia*, or the lack of a *bona mens*, *dementia*, *furor*, and Greek μανια, as pointed out in Janssen, "'Superstitio,'" 131–59, especially 137–38. These are exact equivalents of the Hebrew here. I would argue that the coincidence of meaning "out of his mind" = dementia = *superstitio* is one of the stronger pieces of evidence I have for my reading. Whether or not Rabbi Eliᶜezer is being alluded to as a Christian, then, surely these topoi of martyr acts have had their impact on our story. See also Justin Martyr's Dialogue, 39.3, in which Trypho accuses the Christian of being literally "out of his mind," the precise etymological counterpart of the Hebrew expression used here. This usage lends a certain extra force to Le Boulluec's analogy between the discourse of heresy and the discourse of madness as treated by Foucault. Le Boulluec, *La notion d'hérésie.*

65. Christine Hayes has remarked in a personal communication that phylacteries (*tefillin*) are a particularly apt emblem in this story, owing to the fact that the precise mode of observance of this ritual was a Shibboleth marking the boundary between rabbinic "orthopraxy" and sectarianism:

> M. Meg 4:9 indicates that there were various deviant practices regarding tefillin, some of which are explicitly labelled in that Mishnah as *minut* [sectarianism] or *derekh haḥiṣonim* and are forbidden by the rabbis. Also, at times the rabbis are at pains to distinguish between tefillin and mere amulets, suggesting that in fact the two were not all that distinct. Thus, Rabbi Eliᶜezer's disdain for rabbinic details as regards the wearing of tefillin may signal his preference for alternative (in the view of the rabbis, heretical or magical) tefillin practices. Further, in m. Sanh. 11:3, the paradigmatic "rebellious elder" is the elder who rebels against rabbinic halakha concerning tefillin. . . .
>
> Second, the juxtaposition of purity laws and magic as R. Eliᶜezer's

particular expertise is likewise no accident, and may also signal
R. Eli°ezer's heretical leanings. Purity laws are viewed by the rabbis as
irrational laws and in some texts they appear to be the Jewish analog
to pagan magic. For example, in Num Rab, Huqqat 19:8, a pagan
questions a rabbi concerning the purification ritual involving the
ashes of the red heifer. To him, this looks like sorcery, and indeed the
rabbi explains it as analogous to the magic or exorcistic rituals of
pagans. In an aside to his astonished disciples afterward the rabbi says
that in fact there is no efficacy in the ritual at all; it is done simply
because it was ordained by God. This fascinating text illustrates the
rabbis' self-consciousness, their sensitivity to the fact that to outsiders, Jewish purification rituals look like so much hocus-pocus. It
is indeed interesting that R. Eli°ezer is an expert in that which is
most easily confused with and taken for magic by outsiders, as well
as being accomplished in actual magical arts. In short, the R. Eli°ezer
materials contain more hints of the heretical interest of R. Eli°ezer,
and the threat to rabbinic authority that such an interest entails, than
Boyarin allows.

66. On the halakhic issue, see Gilat, *R. Eliezer Ben Hyrcanus*, 161.

67. On this passage, see discussion in Neusner, *Why No Gospels*, 52; Stein,
"Folklore Elements in Late Midrash," 166–67.

68. This is, of course, the verse that Elisha cried out upon the death of
Elijah. For Elijah as a model for Christian ascetics, see Brock and Harvey,
Holy Women of the Syrian Orient, 8 and Stein, "Folklore Elements in Late Mid-
rash," 178.

69. See Green, "Palestinian Holy Men," 619–47; Bokser, "Wonder-Working," 42–92; Kalmin, "Christians and Heretics," 158.

70. According to the Mishna Sanhedrin 7:11, "Rabbi Akiva says in the
name of Rabbi Yehoshua that [of] two who gather cucumbers [via magic],
one who gathers is guilty and the other who gathers is innocent: The one who
actually performs a deed [magically] is guilty, while the one who only performs an illusion is innocent." According to Origen, one of the charges of Celsus against Jesus was that he performed his miracles through "trickery." *Contra Celsum* 1.39; 1.68. Oddly, if this was the case, he would not be liable for
sorcery under rabbinic law. In other words, the Rabbis recognized a category
of real, but forbidden sorcery between trickery (literally "deceit of the eyes")
and miracles.

71. Cf. Guttmann, "The Significance of Miracles," 380–82.

72. According to a passage in the manuscripts of TB Sanhedrin 43a,b, Jesus was crucified by the Sanhedrin on the Eve of Passover for sorcery and for misleading Israel into idol worship.

73. Brown, *The Making of Late Antiquity*, 24.

74. Ibid., 21.

75. Ibid., 39.

76. Ibid., 60.

77. *Ecclesiastical History*, V:7; Lawlor and Oulton, *Eusebius*, 1: 152.

78. Brown, *The Making of Late Antiquity*, 17.

79. Cf. Guttmann, "The Significance of Miracles," 385. Guttmann certainly pioneered the suggestion that contact between the Rabbis and Christians is prerequisite for understanding these stories about Rabbi Eliᶜezer, but owing to the positivistic approaches current at his writing, he reaches very different sorts of conclusions from this recognition. Guttmann ascribes first-century relevance to stories not known before the third or fourth century at the earliest and in some cases to details from texts not edited before the fifth or even sixth centuries.

80. Trevett, "Gender, Authority and Church History," 14.

81. Guttmann further argues that it was precisely the fact that Rabbi Eliᶜezer was responsive in the matter of purities, an aspect of Jewish law that "Christian leaders" allegedly opposed that indicated to the Rabbis that he was no longer suspect of Christian leanings. "The Significance of Miracles," 388–89.

82. For fascinating evidence of continued cultural interaction between rabbinic Jews and Christians in an area entirely different from the one considered in this monograph, see Shaye J. D. Cohen, "Menstruants," 273–99. On the same topic, see Charlotte Fonrobert, "Women's Bodies, Women's Blood," and her *Constructing Women's Bodies*.

CHAPTER 2

The epigraph is from Brown, *The Making of Late Antiquity*, 66.

1. Of course, for Ignatius himself, it was the Christian's desire for martyrdom, the Imitation of the Cross, that distinguished him from the non-Christian Jew. But what if Rabbi Eliᶜezer were, in fact, like Ignatius (or, at any rate, like his Philadelphian correspondents)—a "Christian?"

2. Lieberman, "Roman Legal Institutions," 57–58.

3. In a very important paper published originally in Hebrew in 1956 and then in a revised English version in 1961, the Jerusalem historian Itzhaq Baer pointed out many highly significant and convincing parallels between Chris-

tian martyrologies of the Decian persecutions and the Great Persecution—including "polished" works such as those of Cyprian and Gregory of Nyssa—and talmudic and midrashic texts. For example, see his comparison of a story in the Palestinian Talmud and Gregory's biography of Gregory the Thaumaturgy. Baer, "Israel" (1961), 128. As Baer notes, this parallel originally had been pointed out in 1854. Until the generation of Talmudists trained since World War II, patristics was considered an essential part of the knowledge of a scholar of that field. Unfortunately, Baer's work is marred by a serious naiveté with respect to the reliability of "sources." Oddly, he is highly suspicious of Eusebius and highly credulous where it comes to the Talmud, almost the exact opposite of Frend and Bowersock. See Chapter 4 below and especially the Appendix.

4. Momigliano, "Popular Religious Beliefs," 18.

5. Brown, *The Cult of the Saints*, 19.

6. Cameron, *Christianity and the Rhetoric of Empire*, 112. She also argues that "even after the acceptance of the canon, and therefore, their exclusion from it, the popularity and influence of the apocryphal narratives was so enormous and so widespread at all levels that they must rank high among the contributors to the early Christian world-view" (90). For further analysis of the ways that Christian textuality blurs the boundaries between elite and popular literatures, see Cameron, 36–39, 107–13, 186–88, and the discussion in Virginia Burrus, "Reading Agnes," 27.

7. I am assuming that if the Tosefta was redacted in the mid-third century, its materials can safely be considered somewhat earlier and thus are *roughly* contemporaneous with the late second-century *Apocryphal Acts*.

8. As Frend points out, this question already was being adumbrated in Paul at Philippians 1:20–26, *Martyrdom and Persecution*, 85.

9. On the gendered aspects of this sequence, see Burrus, *Chastity as Autonomy*, 43–44.

10. See also Guha, "Dominance Without Hegemony."

11. Scott, *Domination and the Arts of Resistance*, 87.

12. Schneemelcher "The Acts of Peter," 317–18.

13. Scott, *Domination and the Arts of Resistance*, 18.

14. Jan Assmann provides us with a very excellent example from ancient Egypt: "Until the Late Period, cryptography is a very rare variant of hieroglyphic, used predominantly for aesthetic purposes, to arouse the curiosity of passers-by. But in the Greco-Roman period, an age of forcign domination, the methods of cryptography were integrated into the monumental script of hieroglyphics; this created enormous complexity and turned the whole writing

system into a kind of cryptography. Clement and Porphyry reflect this latest stage of hieroglyphics." Assmann, *Moses the Egyptian* 108.

15. This was less true in the Middle Ages, when for a variety of historical reasons, the Talmud became available to non-Jews and a violent sort of de-layed-reaction response was indeed generated, producing finally a self-directed censorship of the Talmud on the part of early modern Jews.

16. The terms "alienation" and "accommodation" are those of Virginia Burrus in *The Making of a Heretic*, 126–29, where they function as the basic oppositional terms in the Priscillianist controversy. My use of them is slightly different from hers, but they fit well enough, and the analogies are close enough to be interesting and worth evoking in their own right.

17. I use this term advisedly. I do not have to assume that these are *ipsissima verba* of the "real" Rabbi Shim‘on in order to mobilize what is said about him elsewhere in interpreting a passage attributed to him because the individual Rabbis themselves came to be personifications of particular ideological stances within the tradition, and we don't have to know how "authentic" these personality sketches are in order to read them.

18. Scott, *Domination and the Arts of Resistance*, 33; Ophir, "Victims Come First."

19. Scott, *Domination and the Arts of Resistance*, 34.

20. Ellison, *Invisible Man*, 16, quoted in Scott, *Domination and the Arts of Resistance*, 133.

21. Jonathan Boyarin, *A Storyteller's Worlds*, 10.

22. Niditch, *Underdogs and Tricksters*, 70–125.

23. The term "diasporic" here is not so much in contrast with "Palestinian" or "rabbinic" as it is a reference to the decentered national life of all Jews since the enormous growth of the Diaspora in the centuries before Christ. This thinking has been much influenced by the work of my brother, Jonathan.

Erich Gruen has reminded me of an excellent early version of a Jewish trickster tale with a hidden transcript. In 3 Maccabees 7:10–16, Jews who have remained steadfast in the faith trick their Ptolemaic masters into allowing them to execute those who have become apostates on the king's orders by "using the clever argument that those who were disloyal to their own commandments could not be trusted to be loyal to the king. Hence those who had actually resisted the royal orders triumph over collaborators by posing as protectors of royal interest." Gruen, letter to the author. This is a typically rather clever interpretation of the passage and quite a convincing one. The best edition of the text is Hadas, *The Third and Fourth Books of Maccabees*, 80–82. See also Charlesworth, *The Old Testament Pseudepigrapha* 2: 528.

24. As David Biale has written: "The rabbis built a much more durable political system than had any of the earlier leaders, whether tribal elders, kings, or priests, who were only partially successful in confronting an imperial world and in maintaining some partial semblance of Jewish sovereignty." Biale, *Power and Powerlessness*, 11.

25. The term is again drawn from a work by James C. Scott, *Weapons of the Weak*.

26. Edwards, *The Politics of Immorality*, 93; Sered and Cooper, "Sexuality and Social Control," 47–49.

27. 5.7.I. See also Bowersock, *Fiction as History*, 44.

28. Daniel Boyarin, *Unheroic Conduct*; "Jewish Masochism," 3–36; and "Homotopia," 41–71.

29. Niditch, *Underdogs and Tricksters*, 126–45; Amy-Jill Levine, "Diaspora as Metaphor," 105–18; Daniel Boyarin, "Masada or Yavneh?" 306–29. Note that the point is not only that Esther, a heroine, represents the Jewish people in the book, but also that the modes of action employed by Mordechai are also tricksterlike and thus representable as feminized.

30. Scott, *Domination and the Arts of Resistance*, 41.

31. Shaw, "Body/Power/Identity," 275.

32. In a separate Hebrew essay, I have hypothesized how different, ideologically contrary sources have been combined in the talmudic text in order to produce the ideological uncertainty that characterizes this text. Daniel Boyarin, "A Contribution." This is virtually a characteristic of the Babylonian Talmud and thus foundational for later rabbinic orthodoxy. See Stern, "Midrash and Indeterminacy," 132–62. Much remains yet to be done on this major issue in comparative Judaisms.

33. If not the enthusiasm, then why the extreme "punishment"? Pace Herr, "Persecutions and Martyrdom," 111. It is conceivable that the "truth" is the exact opposite of Herr's argument that "if the Sages conducted themselves in this manner [evading martyrdom], how much more was this behaviour prevalent among ordinary people?" Herr, 112. That is, it could just as likely have been the case that being martyred was a practice that non-rabbinic Jews approved of and that the Rabbis opposed. When Herr was writing, a generation ago, the scholarly tendency was to take as positivist "fact" any narrative that didn't contradict reason, and even some that did (cf. the *tefillin* that miraculously become pigeon's wings). It is striking how similar in methodology in some ways Herr's work is to that of Frend of the same period. (See the Appendix below.)

34. This tension or social contestation is perhaps most sharply phrased in another talmudic passage, which says: "As for one who gives himself over to

death for the sake of Words of Torah, we do not cite the halakha in his name" (Baba Qamma 61a). This passage seems to indicate both Jewish enthusiasm for martyrdom in late antiquity and at least some sharp rabbinic opposition to the practice. Schoedel, *Polycarp*, 59. Directly contradicting this position, we find the Palestinian Amora Resh Lakish quoted in Gittin 57b as saying that the words of Torah endure only for one who gives himself over to death for them.

35. Ibid., 64–65.

36. Frend, *Martyrdom and Persecution*, 246.

37. In order, however, to both preserve the sense of Rabbi Ḥanina's blame-lessness and yet justify God's actions toward him, the Talmud cites a text in-dicating that one time he was holding two types of public money and he con-fused them and thus distributed the money intended for one purpose to the poor by mistake. For that lack of care in the administration of public money, he was arrested and martyred and, moreover, it is this carelessness that justifies the judgment put in his own mouth that he had not engaged in good deeds. This interpretation runs counter to the apologetic and incoherent one of the traditional commentators, as Lieberman already pointed out in "On Persecu-tion," 220. For a somewhat similar issue having to do with the misuse of pub-lic funds in a roughly contemporaneous Christian text, see Harry O. Maier, "Purity and Danger," 229–47.

38. In the most diffident of veins, I raise the question of whether there isn't some reflex here of the Decian persecutions. Some among the confessors, ac-cording to Eusebius, were also accused of being thieves: "A certain Nemesion, he also an Egyptian, was falsely accused of consorting with robbers, and when he had cleared himself before the centurion of that charge so foreign to his character, he was informed against as being a Christian, and came bound be-fore the governor." *E.H.* VI; 41.21; Lawlor and Oulton, *Eusebius*, 1: 208; see Frend, *Martyrdom and Persecution*, 411–12. On the other hand, Ruth Clements has remarked that the thief motif was of particular importance to Eusebius be-cause of its function within *imitatio crucis*. Personal communication.

39. Daniel Boyarin, *Unheroic Conduct*, 7.

40. Following Lieberman, "The Martyrs of Caesarea," 445. See also Hadas-Lebel, "Jacob et Esau," 369–92. Gerald Blidstein reads this text quite differ-ently, arguing that just as Rabbi Elʿazar's disclaimer of studying Torah was disingenuous, so was his claim of having been a "robber," that is, a violent rebel against the Romans, and he does have a point—if not an ineluctable one. In-deed, Blidstein speculates that the "good deeds" with which the Rabbi busied himself were these acts of active rebellion. Blidstein, "Rabbis, Romans, and

Martyrdom," 56–57. I can no more disprove Blidstein's reading than I can approve it. Different assumptions produce different hermeneutics.

41. Lawlor and Oulton, *Eusebius*, 1: 229–30.

42. See also Lieberman, "The Martyrs of Caesarea," 445; den Boeft and Bremmer, "Notiunculae Martyrologicae II," 395. Incidentally, this provides us with an example in which the rabbinic text helps to understand the patristic one more exactly. Frend has read this passage as meaning that the bishop's is an act of persuasion: "Choose the Gospels rather than the centurion's vine-switch," that is, choose martyrdom rather than apostasy. *Martyrdom and Persecution*, 442. In the light of the talmudic parallel, however—from the same time and place as Eusebius himself—I think we can read it rather as an indication on the part of Theotecnus that you can't have both, the book and the sword, or if you are to be martyred as a Christian, give up first your martial bent. This provides a stronger reading to the text, for there is, in fact, no indication whatever that Marinus was wavering in his commitment.

43. For the topos of the warp as female and the weft as male and weaving as sexual intercourse, see Scheid and Svenbro, *The Craft of Zeus*, 87.

44. Perhaps the "Odeon," "a meeting place where religious controversies were held." Kimelman, "R. Yoḥanan and Origen," 571. See also Lee I. Levine, *Caesarea Under Roman Rule*, 83, and McGuckin, "Caesarea Maritima," 3–25. See also Clements, "*Peri Pascha*," 126–27. I would argue, however, that here is a classical instance where careful methodological criteria need to be employed. Whether or not "The House of Avidan" can be identified with the Caesarean Odeum in this passage or that passage of the Talmud (notably TB Shabbat 116a and 152a–b) has virtually nothing to do with what *this*—fictional!—text might have understood the term to mean. In the context of this story, it almost certainly must be a place for pagan worship and not a site for the disputations between Jews, Christians, and pagans, for if it were the latter, how would the Rabbi's attendance or absence been indicative of his religious identity?

45. It is at least worth noting that in this Jewish representation, manumission was considered a sign of adherence to Torah and disloyalty to Roman authority. It is not entirely clear to me (in fact, it is quite obscure to me) what the historical background for this judgment could be. However, issues surrounding Galatians 2:28, 1 Corinthians 7, and Philemon seem not out of place in this matter.

46. In talmudic style, detrimental predicates are nearly always put into third-person sentences in order to avoid predicating them of the speaker or his interlocutors in a situation in which the text was read out loud. So "that man" frequently has to be translated as "I" or as "you."

47. Gleason, *Making Men*, 37.

48. Frend, *Martyrdom and Persecution*, 411, citing a letter from Roman presbyters to Cyprian. For the distinction between *libellatici* and *sacrificati*, as those who had actually sacrificed, see Clarke, *Letters 1–27*, 101, 309. See also Cyprian's explicit

> It is, therefore, manifestly callous and cruelly overrigid to insist on including amongst those who did offer sacrifice those who merely obtained certificates. For in the case of a person who acquired such a certificate he may plead for himself: "I had previously read and I had learnt from my bishop's preaching that we should not offer sacrifice to idols and that a servant of God ought not to worship images. And so, in order to avoid doing this action which was forbidden, I seized an opportunity which offered itself for obtaining a certificate."

Cyprian does, however, go on to say that "even though his hands remain undefiled and his mouth unpolluted by any contact with that deadly food, his conscience has nonetheless been polluted" and prescribes certain forms of penance. Clarke, *Letters 55–66*, 41. For a discussion of this passage emphasizing the category distinction between *libellatici* and *sacrificati*, see Clarke, *Letters 55–66*, 161.

49. Bowersock, *Martyrdom and Rome*, 54. See also below the discussion of Clement of Alexandria. In the fourth century, we find Athanasius (also in Alexandria) justifying his flight before the persecuting "Arians" in chapter 18 of his Apology or "Defense of his Flight":

> *The Saints Who Fled Were No Cowards.*
>
> Of a truth no one can possibly doubt that they were well furnished with the virtue of fortitude. For the Patriarch Jacob who had before fled from Esau, feared not death when it came, but at that very time blessed the Patriarchs, each according to his deserts. And the great Moses, who previously had hid himself from Pharaoh, and had withdrawn into Midian for fear of him, when he received the commandment, "Return into Egypt," feared not to do so. And again, when he was bidden to go up into the mountain Abarim and die, he delayed not through cowardice, but even joyfully proceeded thither. And David, who had before fled from Saul, feared not to risk his life in war in defence of his people; but having the choice of death or of flight set before him, when he might have fled and lived, he wisely preferred death. And the great Elijah, who had at a former time hid

himself from Jezebel, shewed no cowardice when he was commanded
by the Spirit to meet Ahab, and to reprove Ahaziah. And Peter, who
had hid himself for fear of the Jews, and the Apostle Paul who was let
down in a basket, and fled, when they were told, "Ye must bear witness at Rome," deferred not the journey; yea, rather, they departed re-
joicing; the one as hastening to meet his friends, received his death
with exultation; and the other shrunk not from the time when it
came, but gloried in it, saying, "For I am now ready to be offered,
and the time of my departure is at hand."

Athanasius, "Defense of his Flight," 18.

50. Frend, *Martyrdom and Persecution*, 416, once more citing Cyprian's letters. And indeed, Cyprian himself left town without sacrificing.

51. For the verisimilitude of this detail, see Robert, *Le martyre* 68–69.

52. "The religious and legal foundations of American culture reinscribe this
dichotomy [law and spirit] again and again—in Augustinian and subsequent
expressions of Christianity, particularly acutely in Protestantism, and throughout the Anglo-American tradition of law. Indeed, the story becomes crisis: The
spirit is connected not just to God but to virtue ("manliness") and straight-
talking *honestia* [sic], while the law is connected to the Jew, the flesh and the
cunning but dishonest female." Michaelson, "Antilawyerism/Antisemitism," 4.

53. For the philology, see Daniel Boyarin, "A Contribution."

54. For early Jewish Christian parallels, see Frend, *Martyrdom and Persecution*, 95. These strongly suggest that the original context within which Rabbi
Ḥanina's action was interpreted was political, that is, as an open challenge to
the hegemony of Rome.

55. Laurie Davis makes the excellent point that as articulated above, Rabbi
Ḥanina's virtue, like that of his wife and daughter, was precisely about accepting God's judgment, and here, paradoxically, it is his interlocutor who claims
that he has not sufficiently submitted himself to that judgment. Davis, "Virgins in Brothels."

56. Scott, *Domination and the Arts of Resistance*, 127.

57. Lieberman, "On Persecution," 219, 226. For further discussion of
Rabbi Ḥanina's pronouncing of God's name in public and its meanings in the
context of this story, see Chapter 4. The association of sedition and *maleficium*
is to be found in Pliny's letter, discussed above, and even earlier allegedly the
basis of Nero's persecution of Christians in 64, as remarked by Suetonius
("nova et malefica"). "Nero," *The Twelve Caesars*, 38.2.

58. For a vivid recent evocation of this moment in early Christianity, see

Bowersock, *Martyrdom and Rome*, 1–5. In Chapter 4, I shall be dealing at some length with Bowersock's thesis in that book that martyrdom per se is a Christian practice and adopted by the Jews from them.

59. However, as Markus makes clear, the real efflorescence of the cult of the martyrs comes in the post-Constantinian Church, as a mode of anamnesis. *The End of Ancient Christianity*, 24.

60. One interesting marker of this difference is the contrasting evaluations of such figures as Yaᶜel or Judith in midrash and in Christian exegesis. Whereas in midrash these figures and their deception "are poetically eulogized as the most noble" of women, Sered and Cooper have pointed out, in Christian exegesis they are frequently condemned as deceivers.

61. Nearly forty years ago, Itzhaq Baer wrote of the works of Cyprian that, "these books deserve special study by Jewish historians." "Israel" (1961), 95. He meant, of course, historians of Judaism. Baer's is an excellent programmatic essay for the study of patristics for research on Roman-period Judaism. There is little evidence of his program being followed until very recently. Baer's work is replete with what he himself refers to as "cursory comparisons" that now require very careful analytical interrogation.

62. For some of the historical background as well as further bibliography, see Clarke, *Letters 1–27*, 208.

63. Cyprian's story is, of course, that he completely escaped during the Decian persecutions and only returned to Carthage when it was safe to do so. During the later persecution of Valerian, he was deported, brought back, tried, and executed in 258. This, in part, marks a shift in Christian ideology between the two persecutions, which for a lesser figure than Cyprian might have been textualized as a failure and a second chance to redeem himself. This shift is earlier paralleled in a hardening of Tertullian's own attitudes toward escape between his early text, *Scorpiace*, and his later *de fuga*. Barnes, "Tertullian's *Scorpiace*," 105–32.

64. Clarke, *Letters 1–27*, 67–68, 211.

65. Ibid., 203.

66. Again, I don't wish to introduce here the somewhat misleading taxon of voluntary versus involuntary martyrdom. Cyprian was a noted opponent of voluntary martyrdom, if by this term we refer to a seeking of death where none had been imposed from outside, as in some famous early Christian cases. But Rabbi Ḥanina, by convening groups to study Torah in public, while not seeking death as a martyr, certainly expected the possibility, as did Rabbi Akiva, whose martyrdom we shall be reading in Chapter 4. Moreover, both re-

ceived their deaths with the kind of equanimity and even joy that is characteristic of the Christian martyrs, including Cyprian himself.

67. Frend, *Martyrdom and Persecution*, 360–61.

68. Ibid., 356.

69. For this topos in Lucian, Clement's near contemporary, see Droge and
Tabor, *A Noble Death*, 25, 141.

70. Frend, *Martyrdom and Persecution*, 358.

71. See also Hopkins, "Christian Number," 19 n. 24.

72. Frend, *Martyrdom and Persecution*, 355.

73. According to Baer, at any rate, "Clement of Alexandria (d. before 215)
was the writer who showed most moderation in his polemics with the Jews. In
my view he uses books written in Greek in his own time by Jewish scholars
with whom he had contact," Baer, "Israel and the Church," 85.

74. However, oddly, at other moments, it is precisely this scholar who is
represented as having the deepest connections with Judaism. The trope of such
connections is, it seems, quite protean, and therefore needs much more careful and nuanced articulation and documentation. This is a large part of the
projected larger research project for which this case study in martyrology is intended as program, experiment, and first fruits.

75. Frend, *Martyrdom and Persecution*, 358; Schoedel, *Polycarp*, 77.

76. Rabbi Akiva's view became very problematic through the Jewish Middle Ages, wherein enthusiasm for martyrdom (at least in Ashkenaz—northern
Europe) became so great that it proved a positive danger to Jewish existence.
In response, various Rabbis articulated other interpretations of the commandment to "love the Lord with all one's soul," replicating, in effect, the interpretations of Christian Gnostics.

77. See also Droge and Tabor, *A Noble Death*, 142. But, of course, it is not
impossible that Tertullian had contact with contemporary Hebrew tradition as
well. Baer, "Israel" (1961), 85. The question of Tertullian's "Judaizing" is one
that requires much further research and reflection.

78. One is reminded once more of Cicero's "slippery ways of Greeks and
Asiatics." See Detienne and Vernant, *Cunning Intelligence*. I wish to thank
Guy Stroumsa for reminding me of this vitally important reference. Herr
points out, as well, that there were prominent Romans, such as Tacitus, who
seem opposed to the notion of death for *libertas*. "Persecutions and Martyrdom," 111 n. 85.

79. For another fascinating comparison between these two figures, see
Levinson, "Bloody Fictions."

80. TB Pesaḥim 112a, as correctly interpreted I think by Herr, "Persecutions and Martyrdom," 115.

81. Barton, *Roman Honor*. I wish to thank Prof. Barton for letting me read her manuscript prior to publication.

82. Cited Frend, *Martyrdom and Persecution*, 367.

83. This is permanent *deportatio* to an unhealthy climate, also, for instance, substituted for execution in the beginnings of the Decian persecutions of Christians. Frend, *Martyrdom and Persecution*, 390 and references cited there.

84. And see Mekhilta, Wayehi, Parasha 1.

85. "'We have nothing to do with the Jews,' [Tertullian] wrote in the *Apology*, but the prescriptions contained in the *De Idololatria* are remarkably similar to those found in the Jewish *Aboda Zara* of the same date." Frend, *Martyrdom and Persecution*, 373–74.

86. Dawson, *Allegorical Readers*. This suggestion was made to me by Virginia Burrus. Burrus has argued that in Ambrose's *On Virgins*, one of the functions of including the story of the martyred virgin of Antioch after the story of Thecla's miraculous escape from martyrdom is precisely to erase the embarrassment of that escape. Burrus, "Reading Agnes," 32. See Chapter 3 below for an extended discussion of the Ambrose text.

87. Bruns, "The Hermeneutics of Midrash," 199

88. Hopkins, "Christian Number," 217.

89. Shaye J. D. Cohen, "A Virgin Defiled," 3. Stern, "Midrash and Indeterminacy," also emphasized the functional cast of this aspect of rabbinic Judaism, contesting romanticizing accounts of midrash as protodeconstruction or the like.

90. The continued existence of so-called "Jewish Christianity" is not really an exception to this point.

91. Frend, *Martyrdom and Persecution*, 288, 537. See, too, the offhand remark of Derwas J. Chitty: "A large proportion of the monks in Antony's close neighborhood took the Meletian side in the schism which had arisen (as schisms often do) during the persecution." Chitty, *The Desert a City*, 6.

92. Frend, *The Rise of Christianity*, 489.

93. This is a point that will need much further development in future research. For the nonce, on the Christian side, see Gray, "'The Select Fathers,'" 28, who writes: "The canon of the select fathers would be set, not just by convention, but as a literary entity from which one borrowed and on the basis of which one developed one's theology, and that canon would be so detached from the historical diversity and inconsistency of the fathers themselves, so

worked-over and reconciled with itself—a process in which forgery would certainly play its part—that it could be assumed to represent, not a living and developing tradition, but the majestic unfolding of a simple and monolithic theology." See also Vessey, "The Forging of Orthodoxy," 495–513, and idem, "*Opus Imperfectum*" 177. An argument could be made that a similar process of theoretical rejection of all development, history, and heterogeneity was to take place in rabbinic Judaism with respect to halakha, but not until very late in the Middle Ages or even in the early modern period. For the moment and the current project, it is sufficient to suggest the difference between the forms of text and authority as current in the nascent Catholic Church and rabbinic orthodoxies of late antiquity. On the internal "otherness" of rabbinic texts as a product of their social location and form, see Hasan-Rokem, "Narratives in Dialogue," 109–29, and Stern, "Midrash and Indeterminacy."

CHAPTER 3

The epigraph is from Loraux, *Tragic Ways of Killing a Woman*, 29.

1. Perpetua herself was, of course, not a virgin, but, in fact a mother. One of the arguments of Burrus in "Reading Agnes," 25–46, however, is that the relevance of the figure of the virgin was coming to the fore in the fourth century. See also, however, Burrus, "Word and Flesh," 30 n. 8: "the distinction between virginal and nonvirginal ascetic women is of relatively little use for understanding women's asceticism from a female point of view." The relevant distinction from "the female point of view" was sexual domination by a man or not, and in that sense, Perpetua is as relevant as a virgin.

2. Note that this is the same distance the Rabbis took from the "heretic" Rabbi Eliᶜezer on his death bed, as discussed Chapter 1, creating one more resonance between heresy and whores.

3. Marcel Simon makes the interesting point that by the time of this text, in fact, "sectarianism," that is, Christianity, and the Roman government were themselves "twins," indeed, according to a sequel in this same talmudic passage, the twin daughters of Gehenna:

> "The leech has two daughters: Give! and Give!" [Proverbs 30:15]: Said Rav Ḥisda, said Mar Uqba, "The voice of two daughters cries out from Hell and says in this world 'Give! Give!' And what are they?— heresy and the government." There is another version: Said Rav Ḥisda, said Mar Uqba, "The voice of Hell cries out and says, 'Bring me two daughters that say in this world, 'Give! Give!' [And what are they?—heresy and the government.]"

See Simon, *Verus Israel*, 187. Cf. Athanasius's representation of Arianism as "the daughter of the devil." Burrus, "Word and Flesh," 37.

4. An important source for this image is, to be sure, to be found in the Bible, for in Ezekiel 16 there is an explicit figure of Israel as female infant, then nubile maiden, and God as her lover. The transfer of this image of the nation as virgin to each individual male Israelite as female virgin is accomplished via the liturgy of the circumcision, in which the verse "I said to you when you were in your blood, Live; I said to you when you were in your blood, Live" (Ez. 16:6) is applied to the newly circumcised male infant. See also Pardes, *The Biography of Ancient Israel*, Chapter 2.

5. Naturally, Christians at this time were gendering "Judaism" as feminine in almost exactly the same way, especially via the associations between Arianism and "Judaizing." Burrus, *Begotten, Not Made*, chapter 2. And, in general, "heresy" is gendered in the same way. Burrus, "'Equipped for Victory,'" 461–75.

6. In the rabbinic text, the "foreign woman" of Proverbs, almost a perennial source of sexual excitement in many human cultures, becomes the primary metaphor for all that is exotic and thus alluring to Jews, whether as political power or seductive foreign cults. Jews are faced with the dual temptations of collaboration with oppressors or of assimilation into the dominant cultural forms. Either of those seductive options provide an escape from the sometimes unbearable tensions of difference. They provide two means of being like all of the other nations. On my reading, it is precisely the allure of these two avenues of flight from the tensions of diasporized Jewish existence that is central to the text, and it is these diversions that are thematized as being similar to the forms of escape that sexual pleasure provides, as well.

7. Daniel Boyarin, *Unheroic Conduct*.

8. Gospel, 176, quoted in Roy, *Indian Traffic*. As Parama Roy remarks, "This feminine identification was quite compatible with a marked gynophobia." Alice Jardine also reminds us that Daniel Schreber's desire to become a woman was an attempt to transcend sexual desire. Schreber wrote: "when I speak of my duty to go deeper into voluptuous pleasures, I never mean by that sexual desires towards other human beings (women) and even less sexual commerce, but I imagine myself man and woman in one person in the process of making love to myself," upon which Jardine comments: "The desire to be both woman and spirit . . . may be the only way to avoid becoming the *object* of the *Other's* (female's) desire." Jardine, *Gynesis*, 98–99.

9. In addition, however, to the question of gender and power vis-à-vis Rome that is most actively mobilized by this text, there is perhaps another subtheme of public and private that is also lurking under its surface, one that has

to do with internal power relations within Jewish society between different sects or competing elites. The "people of the land" certainly represent such competing groups. Oppenheimer, *The Am Ha-ʾAretz*; Rajak, "The Jewish Community," 13. Cynthia Baker has argued persuasively that for the Rabbis, the Bet-Hamidrash, Study House, functioned as private space in another sense, a sense internal to Jews and not only in the conflict between Jews and Romans, for the Study House was the quintessential place for the formation of rabbinic identity over against these Others who are Jews, the ʿAm Haʾaretz. Baker, "Neighbor at the Door." See also Urman, "The House of Assembly," 236–57. Since one who studies Torah in the presence of these Jewish Others is compared to one who has sexual intercourse with his fiancee in their presence, this continues a commonplace rabbinic metaphor of Torah study as the act of love, the Torah as bride for the Rabbis, and the *privacy* that such a relationship connotes—as well, of course, as marking clearly once again the gender of those who have exclusive access to Torah. In addition, then, to provoking Rome, Rabbi Ḥanina may have been inviting the wrath of the other Rabbis by convening congregations and teaching Torah in public spaces analogous to the Synagogues ("congregations"), which were still, at this early time, in the control of the nonrabbinic parties among the Jews, or even worse, in the virtual equivalent of the marketplace, that site of "social intercourse at its most chaotic and uncertain, and therefore most dangerous." Baker, "Bodies, Boundaries," 405. This interpretation of Torah as virtually esoteric knowledge, almost as a mystery, is strongly supported by the doubling in the text, whereby convening of public congregations for the teaching of Torah is made analogous to the revealing of God's Holy Name in public.

10. Bowersock, *Martyrdom and Rome*, 63–64. See Chapter 4 below.

11. See Brown, *Power and Persuasion*, 65, on Ammianus's admiration of Christian martyrs because "they had put their bodies 'on the line' by facing suffering and death." And see also Barton, *Roman Honor*: "[The Roman] looked for the contest when one proclaimed one's *Nomen* or identity. The Romans, for instance, recognized that the man or woman who proclaimed *Christianus sum* or *Judaios eimi* were doing so as challenges." Rabbinic texts, on the other hand, counseled Jews to disguise themselves as non-Jews in order to avoid being martyred. Theodor and Albeck, *Genesis Rabbah*, 984. See also Lieberman, "The Martyrs of Caesarea," 416 and especially 423. On the other hand, in a compelling reading, using both Scott's notion of the "hidden transcript" and Bhabha's "colonial mimicry," Joshua Levinson shows how the adoption of the gladiatorial model for the martyrs constitutes a fundamental subversion of Roman values—precisely, that is, what it claims to be. Levinson,

"Bloody Fictions." This results in quite a different reading of the gendering of martyrdom, as well. For Levinson, the subversiveness of the martyr is most exquisitely encapsulated in the transformation of feminine submissiveness, including the death blow to the neck for the defeated gladiator, into a moment of triumph according to a hidden transcript. See however Barton, "Savage Miracles," 41–71, who reads this as a moment of triumph, of recovered honor, for the gladiator himself. This has interesting implications for the reading of Burrus, "Reading Agnes," as well, I think.

12. Baker, "Bodies, Boundaries."

13. Carlin Barton has written: "It is important to understand that, in ancient Rome, looking was not passive but active. To look was a challenge. The *spectator* was inspector, judge, and connoisseur," Barton, *Roman Honor*.

14. Ruth Clements has suggested to me a riveting parallel here. Psalm 22 has been read, of course, as a virtual allegory of the Crucifixion, or better, the Passion narratives are a midrash on the Psalm. One of the few verses in that text that has not been given a paschological reading, is 21: "Deliver my life from the sword; my soul from the power of the dog." Given the Crucifixion motif further on in the story, and the miraculous delivery of the soldier from the cross, contrasting—perhaps parodying—Elijah's "failure" to remove Jesus from the cross in Mark, the possibility becomes very seductive that this text is a sort of anti-Gospel or folktale dialogue with a Gospel or with anti-Jewish polemics based on a paschological midrash on this psalm. Fascinatingly, the talmudic story might even preserve a bit of Christian lore, a bit of Gospel tradition in the form of a midrash on Psalms 22:21 otherwise unknown, to the best of my knowledge. Koltun-Fromm, "Psalm 22's Christological Interpretive Tradition," 37–57. Clements suggests to me a slightly different possibility, writing:

> I think there is another way of reading the significance of the presence of the biting dogs (and I freely admit that this comes partially of my unease with pushing it to be a "lost Gospel" tradition). You are postulating a situation in which Rabbis and Christians have a good deal of intimacy with each other (with which I concur). The notion of a Gospel parody testifies to intimate Jewish knowledge of Christian texts and prooftexts, and what we know from Origen's witness implies that Jews and Christians argued about these most important texts all the time. Palms. 21/22, unlike Isaiah 53, must have been even a greater stumper for the Rabbis, precisely because so many of the narrative features of the psalm are worked into the earliest versions of

the Passion narrative itself. What neater way to expose the literarily contrived nature of the actual Passion narratives than to take one of the few details of the psalm which is absolutely unable to be fit into the passion narrative as a "true fact" and use it as the pivot to show the miraculous power of God when invoked by R. Meir. In other words, in this reading, it is precisely because this detail in the psalm was an embarrassment for Christian prophecy that it shows up here in the rabbinic parody.

Clements, personal letter to the author. There is another possible echo of Christian midrash on Psalms 22, as well, namely, the fact that its opening verse is read in the Palestinian Talmud as a reference to the slow unfolding of the redemption.

15. This is plausibly read as a parody of Jesus's "My God, my God, why hast thou forsaken me," itself a midrash on Psalm 22:2, for which there are other parodic parallels in this narrative.

16. This continuation contains a whole series of Gospel parallels, including the *answered* call from the cross, the inscription on the cross, and a virtual *ecce homo*.

17. See also Amy-Jill Levine, "Diaspora as Metaphor," 105–18.

18. It has been suggested to me that Rabbi Meʾir is not approbated in this story, but condemned, and that his flight to Babylonia is a sort of punishment. This seems to me not the case because of the intervention of Elijah the Prophet as divine intercessor and miracle maker for him, just as in the case of Elʿazar ben Perata discussed in the previous chapter. Divine intervention on behalf of someone can be reliably read, I suggest, as evidence of the narrator's approval of the character and his other actions. Cf. Sered and Cooper, "Sexuality and Social Control," 45.

19. Davis, "Virgins in Brothels."

20. See also Cameron, *Christianity and the Rhetoric of Empire*, 147, on Thecla as a model in the writings of Methodius, Gregory of Nyssa, and Jerome. It is ambiguous in Cameron's context, however, whether Thecla was being held up as a model for men or only for women.

21. Burrus, "Word and Flesh," 36–45.

22. Burrus, "Reading Agnes," 44. See also her concise description of the relevant political conditions for the shifts in Christian representations of virginity. "Reading Agnes," 44.

23. Ibid., 32.

24. Interestingly enough, the Rabbis also used the lion as a symbol for a

violent male sexuality, saying that "the ignorant man is like the lion who tramples and then devours its prey," while they used the courting routine of the rooster as a positive example of the husband who plays, dallies with, and arouses his wife before intercourse. For the lion as an image of violent male sexuality in Roman literature, see the text of Martial cited in Richlin, *The Garden of Priapus*, 137. For the persistence of the lion in this guise, see James Joyce's *Ulysses*, in which Bloom remarks "the lion reek of all the male brutes that have possessed [a prostitute]." *Ulysses*, 409.

25. Gillian Clark, "Bodies and Blood," 107. I part company, however, from her statement that "this fitted very neatly with the story of the Fall in the book of Genesis, in which sexual awareness was the first sign that humans had acquired knowledge of evil." It has been adequately demonstrated by now that is neither the "original" nor an ineluctable construction of the Genesis narrative. See Pardes, "Beyond Genesis 3," 161–87, and Anderson, "Celibacy or Consummation," 121–48.

26. Castelli, "'I Will Make Mary Male,'" 29–49. While in earlier work, scholars read these representations as manifesting "genuine" spaces of autonomy for women in early Christian culture, (e.g. Burrus, *Chastity as Autonomy*), more recently, these same scholars are inclined to see male representations of self via complex and contradictory identifications with female figures. See Burrus, "Reading Agnes," and "'Equipped for Victory.'"

27. Meyer, "Making Mary Male," 554–70.

28. Burrus, *Chastity as Autonomy*. Joyce Salisbury effectively contrasts the martyrdom in the first-century or second-century century Jewish 4 Maccabees with that of Perpetua. In 4 Maccabees, the martyred woman is martyred as a mother, and "this martyrdom was about preserving family identity and piety in the face of oppression." In the martyrdom of Perpetua, after some ambivalence, the milk in Perpetua's breasts dries up, and "the baby had no further desire for the breast." Salisbury remarks: "This seeming evidence of divine approval in the text reinforced the notion that martyrdom was incompatible with maternity. The time of the Maccabean mothers was over; martyrdom was a matter of private conscience, not family ties." *Perpetua's Passion*, 88 and 91.

29. Shaw, "The Passion of Perpetua," 4.

30. Ibid., 19. In that same text, we note the transformation of the female slave, Biblis, first thought "unmanly and easily broken," who then "comes to her senses" and is martyred. For a discussion, see Burrus, "Torture and Travail." For a subtly and interestingly different take on Perpetua's gaze, see Salisbury, *Perpetua's Passion*, 138. For Salisbury, this represents the "pride of a Roman matron." On the whole, Shaw's interpretation of this seems to me more

convincing. Barton, *Roman Honor*, refers to her dismissal of her father's entreaties as exemplary of Roman *virtus*, a *virtus*, that, as Barton makes clear, was available in the early Roman culture to both men and women.

31. Burrus, "Reading Agnes," 41. According to Barton's argument, the shift is part and parcel of a shift in Roman culture, even apart from its Christianization, as Burrus's work also indicates. Burrus shows how martyrdom itself is rather slippery with respect to its complicated dialectics of defiance and passivity. But, in a sense, this is the intertextual transformation of a much earlier textual practice, for Loraux marks also that "women in tragedy died violently. More precisely, it was in this violence that a woman mastered her death, a death that was not simply the end of an exemplary life as a spouse. It was a death that belonged to her totally." Loraux, *Tragic Ways of Killing a Woman*, 3. Indeed, but we should not forget that this is a death that robs her of a life that would belong to her, if only partially. It is the constant transformation of the intertext, the transgression and remaking of the signifying practices, that constitutes cultural history, and Burrus's work here equips us with an exemplary case of such processes. One could say, perhaps, that the most strikingly new thing about the signifying practice called "Christianity" was that within it, virgins were more autonomous than wives, while in "classical" culture, and rabbinic Judaism within that, "[virgins] have less autonomy than wives." Loraux, *Tragic Ways of Killing a Woman*, 31.

32. Burrus, *Chastity as Autonomy*, 59.

33. See Burrus, "Word and Flesh," 48 for a further discussion.

34. Reading Burrus (and the other scholars whom she cites, as well), one realizes that "*the* fourth-century virgin martyr" is a nearly exact designation, since we have really one story that is split, recombined, doubled. Burrus's, "it was a favorite story in the post-Constantinian church" is thus a precise formulation. Thecla is supplemented by the virgin of Antioch, who then becomes merged in part with Agnes, who is then split into Agnes and Eulalia, and so on. The point of this is to emphasize that this figure is an ideologically charged symbol of this particular moment, a symbol of a very tensely poised balance between an assertion of female audacity ("not much" remarks Burrus—but that's still some) and its "firm restraint." Burrus, "Reading Agnes," 25.

35. Ibid., 26.

36. Strictly speaking, it is death by piercing or slashing the throat that is marked as "feminine." Loraux, *Tragic Ways of Killing a Woman*, 49–65, and see Shaw, "Body/Power/Identity," 273 n. 10. But surely, in the contrast between the manly death place of the breast and the womanly death place of the throat, this distinction would hardly have been determinative. Although, if Shaw's in-

terpretation that this piercing of the throat is a symbolic oral rape, a forced *irrumatio*, is accepted, then the distinction would make more of a difference. Shaw, "Body/Power/Identity," 305. It is not clear, however, that his interpretation is ineluctable, particularly given the antecedents in tragedy, Loraux, *Tragic Ways of Killing a Woman*, 41.

37. Loraux, *Tragic Ways of Killing a Woman*, 56–61.

38. Burrus, "Reading Agnes," 38–41.

39. I am grateful to an anonymous reader for Stanford Press for pointing out this distinction to me. See Barton, "Savage Miracles," and also Burrus, "Torture and Travail."

40. Burrus, "Reading Agnes," 42–43.

41. Ibid., 46–47.

42. Ibid.; Burrus, "Word and Flesh," 48.

43. Burrus, *Chastity as Autonomy*, 53–57; MacDonald, *The Legend and the Apostle*, 34–53; Burrus, "Word and Flesh," 45.

44. "Several factors seem crucial to understanding the fourth-century sexualized textualization of female bodies: first, the introduction of a decisively male-dominated political model for Christian community." Burrus, "Word and Flesh," 44. "But Ambrose's voice was not the only voice of his time. We can well imagine that some of the ascetic women he addressed were telling versions of Thecla's story which remained disturbingly close to the second-century 'original.'" Ibid., 48.

45. Burrus, "Reading Agnes," 32. This female lion in the earlier text, I would argue, supports the earlier readings of the *Apocryphal Acts* as narratives of female autonomy and perhaps as even female-authored narratives. Stevan Davies, *The Revolt of the Widows*. See especially Burrus, *Chastity as Autonomy*, in this regard. In my opinion, the retreat from this position has been too precipitous. Cf. for instance, Cooper, "Apostles, Ascetic Women, and Questions of Audience."

46. Burrus, "Reading Agnes," 33.

47. Richlin, *The Garden of Priapus*.

48. Daniel Boyarin, *Unheroic Conduct*, 151–85. Burrus has remarked on this similarity." Reading Agnes," 44 n. 54. See also Sered and Cooper, "Sexuality and Social Control," 54–55, on the way in which the feminized figure of Daniel in the Book of Susanna serves to reinforce male control of female sexuality by robbing women of the trickster role.

49. Condemned, of course (for clerics), at Nicaea, in the very first of the canons, as Willis Johnson has reminded me. L'Huillier, *The Church of the Ancient Councils*, 31–32.

50. Burrus, *The Making of a Heretic*, 14.

51. Burrus, "The Male Ascetic." It should be noted for clarity that the quotation marks around "become female" are not meant to indicate a quotation of Sulpicius, but rather precisely the appropriation of another culture's terms to interpret his practice. The admiration of both Sulpicius and Ambrose for Paulinus of Nora, a wealthy and cultivated poet—and disciple of Ausonius—who renounced his wealth, together with his wife, and retired to rural Italy, is emblematic of this position. Markus, *The End of Ancient Christianity*, 36.

52. Daniel Boyarin, *Unheroic Conduct*, 81–126.

53. Burrus, "Reading Agnes," 34.

54. Brown, *The Cult of the Saints*, 63–64.

55. This lack of univocity is very important to the conclusion of my argument. Cooper, *The Virgin and the Bride*, has been very important for the development of my thinking here. Her book is another extended exploration of the ways that figures of idealized women are used within late antique culture in the rhetorical struggles *between men* for prestige and power.

56. In a text that I have discussed elsewhere, such collaboration is explicitly marked as becoming leonine. Daniel Boyarin, *Unheroic Conduct*, 88, and "feminine" stealth is recommended as the antidote.

57. Burrus, "Reading Agnes," 44 n. 55.

58. This locution was originally applied to the talmudic story by Adler, "The Virgin in the Brothel." For other parallels, see Malamud, *A Poetics of Transformation*, 157, 166–67.

59. The story of Miriam bat Tanḥum and the martyrdom of the wife of Rabbi Ḥanina here demonstrate this rule, since in both cases, the martyrdom is simply an appendix to the martyrdom of the men in their lives, and in neither case do we have much more than a mere mention of the death of the woman. Moreover, both are certainly not virgin martyrs. Indeed, they are martyred mothers. "Eroticized self-sacrificial death" (Burrus, "Reading Agnes," 32), remained only for men. In part, this is simply a reflection of different gender/body politics in the two religious communities. The female roles of wife and mother were so highly honored in the rabbinic world, in which sexuality and procreation were central values, that women were practically excluded from all other possibilities, including those, notably the teaching of Torah, that would lead to martyrdom. The emblem of saintly womanhood for traditional Judaism has been Rachel, the wife of Rabbi Akiva, whose martyrdom consisted of waiting for him in poverty and chastity for twenty-four years while he was off studying in the Yeshiva. Amy-Jill Levine has remarked to me in a letter that the intertextual models for women heroes in Judeo-Greek liter-

ature are always chaste wives or widows, the only virgin being Sarah in the Book of Tobit. This acute observation only sharpens the question of why this *should* be so. To get a sense of the significance of this difference between rabbinic Judaism and Christianity in the third and fourth centuries, one need only pay close attention to the struggles Christian writers had in valorizing married female martyrs in the fifth century, as documented recently in Cooper, *The Virgin and the Bride*, 119–27. This, then, provides a direct contrast with the intertextual models mobilized in non-Christian Jewish circles.

In medieval Jewish female martyrology, the two instances of public and dangerous female heroism that are usually focused upon are attendance at the ritual bath (following menstruation and prior to the resumption of sexual relations) and attending to the circumcision of sons, exemplary practices, of course, of the married woman. For the former, see Fonrobert, *Constructing Women's Bodies*.

60. Cooper, "Insinuations of Womanly Influence."

61. For a extended exploration of the idea that rabbinic Judaism and Christianity are two different systems of sex/gender, see Daniel Boyarin, "Gender," 117–35.

62. Ambrose, in *On Virgins*, book 1, chapter 4 (15), explicitly distinguishes between the permanent virginity espoused by the Church and temporary chastity, such as that of the Vestals, a fortiori also that of Jewish girls or the heroines of Greek novels. Note that even in Ambrose's version of "virgin in the brothel" story, the virgin ends up in the arena, a martyr.

63. Virginia Burrus both called my attention to this text and its significance as a parallel to the talmudic story and suggested the direction of interpretation of it as a cross-gendering narrative that I adumbrate below and that will be much more fully developed in her own work on this. I am grateful to her, also, for sharing with me her work in progress, which has taught me so much about these texts. As long ago as 1987, Burrus had pointed out the relevance of the talmudic Rabbi Me'ir story for the Ambrose text, and had pointed to several other Christian and at least one non-Christian Roman version (Seneca) of the tale type. Burrus, *Chastity as Autonomy*, 65 n. 29. Revealingly, in Seneca's story, the virgin preserves her chastity by killing a man with his own sword, which is quite different from both our Jewish and Christian female and male tricksters, for all their internal differences, as well.

64. That is, someone who will kill her, not take her chastity.

65. One wonders at the Ambrose who is so sophisticated a folklorist that he can refer to the parallel tale of the virgin turned into a hind (in the next paragraph), not being aware that here also he is dealing with a virtual tale type.

His insistence on the uniqueness of this event could be seen, therefore, as a bit of highly effective rhetorical flourish. Alternatively, it could be seen as a very part of the topos itself, as Virginia Burrus has commented to me.

66. For this tale type, see Aarne and Thomson, *The Types of the Folktale*, 131. I am grateful to Galit Hasan-Rokem for this information. Ramsey, *Ambrose*, 222 n. 21, suggests that this is an allusion to the story of Iphigenia. She, however, was translated into a goat, not a hind, so I think rather that we have here a very ancient form of a folk tale otherwise attested only in much later sources. Another shared theme between Christian and Jewish legends in this period is the topos of the robber or the prostitute reformed. For the Christian texts, see inter alia, Ward, *Harlots of the Desert*; Elm, *"Virgins of God,"* 258, 318. Chitty, *The Desert a City*, 53. For Jewish parallels, see Daniel Boyarin, "Homotopia," 41–71.

67. Ramsey notes here: "The 'pledge' (*vadimonium*) refers to the fact that as the following paragraph explains, the soldier is a bondsman or guarantee for the virgin. The man in whose mouth these words has been placed has inexplicably grasped the situation." Ramsey, *Ambrose*, 222 n. 22.

68. Ibid., 96–101.

69. I have substituted "circumvented" from the NPNF translation for Ramsey's "defrauded."

70. Ambrose, *On Virgins*, 2, 19–20. Ramsey, *Ambrose*, 96–101.

71. Burrus, "Reading Agnes," 31.

72. Chrysostom, *On Virginity*, 1, 1.

73. For a slightly different interpretation of the meaning of "virginity" in Alexander and Athanasius of Alexandria, namely, as a Douglas-like symbolic representation of the "definition and enforcement of communal and doctrinal boundaries," see Burrus, "Word and Flesh," 35–45. This is more like the symbolic functioning of female chastity in some earlier Jewish texts such as the Book of Tobit. Amy-Jill Levine, "Diaspora as Metaphor."

74. Burrus, *Chastity as Autonomy*, 43–44.

75. Castelli, *Visions and Voyeurism*, 10.

76. In the discussion of Castelli's *Visions and Voyeurism at the Center for Hermeneutical Studies*, Steven Knapp remarked, "One could have the impression reading both the paper and the responses that the prospective women martyrs were mainly concerned on the eve of their martyrdom with the question of whether to accept or to resist the male gaze, rather than with the fact that they were about to be tortured to death in the name of their religious beliefs," thus missing the point that the resistance to the male gaze (and even more) was precisely the significant content of their belief. Ibid., 51.

77. Of course, we do not literally have the sequel to the story of Rabbi

Ḥanina's daughter, and therefore my claim that she will end up married has something of the flavor of "How many children had Lady Macbeth?" about it, I think that I can make the case stronger by referring to a parallel instance. Both rabbinic and Christian cultures in the fourth and fifth centuries told tales of reformed and converted prostitutes. It seems highly significant to me that in the Christian versions, these women end up ascetic, nuns, and even cross-dressed monks (see Ward, *Harlots of the Desert*). In the rabbinic versions, however, otherwise very closely parallel to the Christian ones, the erstwhile harlot ends up the wife of a Rabbi. Sifre to Numbers 15:37, TB Menaḥot 44a. The point that I am making about the ideological difference between the two cultures therefore seems well taken. For Christian family martyrdoms, see Clarke, *Letters 1–27*, 195.

78. Sered and Cooper, "Sexuality and Social Control," 54.

79. TB Gittin 57b. Similarly, already in the Bible, the girls gather yearly to cry over the virginity of the Daughter of Jephta, that is, to mourn the fact that she died a virgin. Chrysostom knew what he was talking about. The theme, of mass suicide to avoid sexual humiliation goes back at least to the Danaids in Aeschylus, who sought death to avoid marriage. Loraux, *Tragic Ways of Killing a Woman*, 10. Once again, the contrasts, as well as the comparisons between various forms of the motif are what make cultural difference and cultural history.

80. I thank my friends Menaham Hirshman and Galit Hasan-Rokem for reminding me of these texts from the Palestinian midrash on the Book of Lamentations.

81. In a similar thematic vein, Christian stories of reformed prostitutes all end with the repentant a nun (or sometimes a monk, as Pelagia/Pelagius), while such stories among the Rabbis end in a marriage. Ward, *Harlots of the Desert*.

82. As Ambrose emphasizes over and over in the letter to his sister Marcellina that constitutes his tractate *On Virgins*, he is not condemning marriage. "From the time of Jovinian Catholic writers had to acknowledge the good of marriage or face a charge of heresy." Cooper, *The Virgin and the Bride*, 116 and see her p. 97 as well.

83. Elm, "*Virgins of God*," 337–38.

84. Cooper, *The Virgin and the Bride*, 44.

85. Ibid., See also Perkins, *The Suffering Self*, 26, and Konstan, "Acts of Love," 15–36. Not all, to be sure, read the novels in quite this way. One recent scholar would see in these works precisely what would praise "the idea of young people—teenagers—standing up for what they wanted" and even sug-

gests that "this was not Roman, but it was what the young Perpetua did when she defied her family to follow Christ." Salisbury, *Perpetua's Passion*, 47.

86. Judith Lieu, *Image and Reality*, 17.

87. Elizabeth A. Clark, "Ascetic Renunciation," 175–208; Burrus, *Chastity as Autonomy*; Castelli, "Virginity and Its Meaning," 61–88.

88. Castelli, *Visions and Voyeurism*, 19. Cf. the point made by Loraux about the tragic deaths of women: "With its solid bolts that have to be forced back for the dead woman to be reached—or rather the dead body from which the woman has already fled—this room reveals the narrow space that tragedy grants to women for the exercise of their freedom. They are free enough to kill themselves, but they are not free enough to escape from the space to which they belong." Loraux, *Tragic Ways of Killing a Woman*, 23. Blake Leyerle has pointed out to me that the topos continues even unto Thelma and Louise [Reader's report]. Of these too, it could be said, that "women's glory in tragedy was an ambiguous glory." Loraux, *Tragic Ways of Killing a Woman*, 28.

89. Prudentius, *Poems*, 277. I have used here the far more beautiful translation found in Elizabeth A. Clark, *Women in the Early Church*, 112. See also Burrus, "Reading Agnes," 36–38 for a discussion. The "wild man" is, as Burrus notes, both executioner and Christ bridegroom, but the last lines of the speech add yet another wrinkle, for now the virgin soul identifies herself with Christ as a sacrifice to the Father. The plays of identification and desire are as complex as any neo-Freudian could possibly want.

90. Petruccione, "The Portrait of St. Eulalia," 86; Castelli, "Imperial Re-imaginings," 173–84; Markus, *The End of Ancient Christianity*, 24.

91. Cooper's chapter "The Imprisoned Heroine" comprises a study of how this tension between virginal ideal and a valorization of marriage was textualized and to a certain degree resolved in the *Gesta* of the Roman martyrs, a genre of fictional martyrology roughly contemporaneous with Prudentius, *The Virgin and the Bride*, 116–43. This was done in part by "encouraging married women to imagine themselves as the spiritual heirs of the pre-Constantinian martyrs." Ibid., 139. I will be forgiven seeming cynical, however, if I suggest that the example of Agnes or Eulalia (especially Eulalia) was more likely to encourage young women to be nuns than wives. Even Anastasia's exemplum, as discussed at length by Cooper, would hardly inspire women to marriage. Nevertheless, it is clear that the Catholic Church was powerfully engaged in a struggle to validate the spirituality of both the virgin and the bride by the fifth century. It is important to note that Cooper's thesis is that an ancient Christian tradition of validation of the chastity of the *matrona* was threatened by the rise of the ascetic movement in the fourth century, while my instinct, not nearly as

educated as Cooper's of course, suggests that the needs of the post-Constantinian Church would require a greater emphasis on the spiritual vocations of those who were the pillars of everyday society. Thus, I would be inclined to lean a priori to the option that the "emphasis on the spirituality of the *matrona* in the *Liber* and the *Passio* [of St. Anastasia]" finds its "context in the battle between orthodoxy and Manichaeism of fifth-century Rome," as opposed to the option that they "represent a last flicker of the traditionalism of late fourth-century senatorial Christians" Ibid., 140. I would argue that Cooper's own argument with respect to the contrast between "the frenzied craving for continence of the heroines of the *Apocryphal Acts*" and the "*pudor* of the honorable wife Anastasia" strongly leads in the direction of the first option. Cooper herself, it seems, leans in this direction. Ibid., 142–43, if I have read her correctly.

92. Burrus, "Reading Agnes," 37–38.

93. Sered and Cooper, "Sexuality and Social Control," 53–44.

94. Burrus, "Reading Agnes," 42.

95. For the extent to which choice of the virginal option was or was not a free-will decision in at least one fourth-century Christian environment, see Elm, "*Virgins of God*," 139–40.

96. Von Kellenbach, *Anti-Judaism in Feminist Religious Writings*.

97. Corley, "Feminist Myths of Christian Origins," 51–67; von Kellenbach, *Anti-Judaism*.

98. Fonrobert, "Women's Bodies, Women's Blood."

99. Ibid.

100. Fonrobert, "The Concept of Jewish Christianity."

101. I am grateful to Amy-Jill Levine for calling this last point to my attention, although I have "processed" it somewhat differently than her formulation. Note the highly charged concatenation of the menstruation as a space for some female autonomy and the trickster role as well.

102. Daniel Boyarin, *Carnal Israel*, 180–81.

103. Sigal, "Early Christian and Rabbinic Liturgical Affinities," 66.

104. On this point, see also the discussion in Elm, "*Virgins of God*," 160–61 n. 71 and 171–83.

105. Daniel Boyarin, *Unheroic Conduct*, 158–62.

106. Castelli, "Virginity and Its Meaning," 82. See also Salisbury, *Church Fathers, Independent Virgins*; Salisbury, *Perpetua's Passion*.

107. In my previous work, I referred to spiritual coverture in medieval and early modern Judaism, in contrast to the economic and sexual coverture of the general European culture.

108. Bal, *Murder and Difference*, 9.

CHAPTER 4

1. Frend, *Martyrdom and Persecution.*

2. Bowersock, *Martyrdom and Rome.*

3. For discussion and further literature on this question, see Rajak, "Dying for the Law," 41–43.

4. Bowersock, *Martyrdom and Rome,* 5.

5. Van Henten, *The Maccabean Martyrs,* 7.

6. This point has been made, in re Bowersock, by Rajak, "Dying for the Law," 44. Although, to be sure, 2 Maccabees is dated anywhere from the middle of the second century B.C. to the middle of the first century A.C., the current consensus is to date it before Christ. Van Henten, *The Maccabean Martyrs,* 51. There is an enormous literature on the Maccabean texts and their relations to martyrology, voluminously cited in the notes to van Henten. I will treat here only what is directly related to my own arguments. My strategy is very different from that of Bowersock, who considers the martyrologies within 2 Maccabees of later provenance than the main text. Bowersock, *Martyrdom and Rome,* 10. This argument seems less than convincing in the light of the analysis of van Henten, and see Rajak, "Dying for the Law," 44. I prefer to suggest that a nascent notion of martyrdom is already present in the very likely "pre-Christian" 2 Maccabees and that it undergoes very similar development among Jews and Christians in 4 Maccabees, Polycarp, the Martyrs of Lyons, eventually Pionius, Akiva, Ḥanina, and so on.

7. Bowersock, *Martyrdom and Rome,* 26–27.

8. Daniel Boyarin, "Language Inscribed by History," 139–51.

9. For the virtual ubiquity of this theme in early Jewish martyrologies, see Kellermann, "Das Danielbuch," 75; Rajak, "Dying for the Law," 40; van Henten, *The Maccabean Martyrs,* 298. Indeed, Brent Shaw emphasizes: "The conceptions of life after death and of the resurrection of the body are also precisely concurrent with the Maccabean rebellion." "Body/Power/Identity," 280.

10. Mühlenberg, "The Martyr's Death," 87.

11. There is a slight possibility of a form of this element as early as 2 Maccabees, but there is a great deal of doubt as to the proper interpretation of this text. Van Henten, *The Maccabean Martyrs,* 88–89.

In 2 Maccabees 6:6 we read: "No one was allowed to observe the Sabbath or to keep the traditional festivals or even to confess that he was a Jew." This verse has been much discussed in the literature. It obviously cannot mean what it seems to mean on the face of it, that one was forbidden to call oneself by the name "Jew," as later on it would be forbidden to call oneself by the name

"Christian," since "Jew" in this period was primarily an ethnic and not a religious identity, and it would be absurd to expect someone not to admit to being a "Ioudaios." Cf. Shaye J. D. Cohen, "Ioudaios," 1: 211–20. Cohen himself considers this the only exceptional passage in the entire work in which "Ioudaios" means "Jew" and not "Judean." Moreover, even in the later Roman period, it was not forbidden to call oneself "Jew," as it was to call oneself "Christian." This is why the non-Christian, Jewish parallel to "Christianus sum" is the declaration of the *Shema^c* and not the cognate "Ioudaios eimi," since even then it would have made as much sense to forbid someone to be a Jew as it would to forbid her to be a Greek.

In his commentary on this verse, Jonathan Goldstein has written:

> The prohibition of the observance of Sabbaths and festivals is easy to understand (cf. 1.45), but what is the meaning of "no one was allowed to . . . confess he was a Jew"? There is no parallel in the contemporary apocalypses or in the accounts of First Maccabees and Josephus. Later the mere acknowledgment of the name "Christian" was to be a crime, but did Antiochus forbid Jews to call themselves Jews? Surely our studies have shown that in the imposed cult Antiochus was trying to force Jews to return to what he thought was the original "wholesome" Jewish pattern. The words may be hyperbole: Jews went on practicing Judaism in secret, but for a practicing Jew to admit he was Jewish was suicidal.
>
> However, in speaking of "confessing that one is Jewish," Jason may be alluding to a ritual. Josephus (AJ iv 8.13.212) seems to call the recitation twice daily of the Shema^c (Deut. 6:4) or of some other such formula "bearing witness" (martyrein). . . . Jason could have called the same ritual "confessing that one is Jewish."

Goldstein, *II Maccabees*, 275–76. This seems to me an alluring suggestion, and one that, if correct, bears further implications. The Josephus passage reads: "Twice each day, at the dawn thereof and when the hour comes for turning to repose, let all acknowledge [martyrein] before God the bounties which He has bestowed on them through their deliverance from the land of Egypt." In spite of H. J. St. John Thackeray's bemusement at this passage, almost certainly it is simply a midrashic rendering of the commandment to recite the words of the "hear O Israel" twice a day, in the morning and evening, the recitation of which includes mention of the Exodus. If the normal term for this was *martyrein*, and if it was indeed this practice that was forbidden on pain of death, according to Jason of Cyrene, an alternative (if somewhat obscured) genealogy for the term "martyr" as one who dies confessing could be constructed, suggesting that the term has roots that go deeper than late antiquity. (This suggestion was made to me by Erich Gruen.)

Once more, the notion that we can hardly, if at all, separate "Jewish" from "Christian" elements and innovations in discourse and practice is strongly borne out. Furthermore, if this is the practice that Jason refers to, we would have a common early source for both the Christian version of the nomen as the central act of the martyr and the later non-Christian Jewish version of the confession of the *Shema*^c in this role. It must be emphasized that in 2 Maccabees it certainly does not play the liturgical, narrative, or ideological role that it plays in both later Christian and rabbinic martyrology. The confession is not the final and definitive act of the martyr's like, so at best we perhaps find here the nearly inchoate beginning of an idea that was to become the crux of martyrology later on, when the confession of identity, "Christianus sum" or "Hear O Israel," respectively (Polycarp and after, and Akiva and after), would be the central and crucial moment of the martyr act. Indeed, as van Henten points out, the prohibition on confessing the name is not connected with the actual martyrdoms of the 2 Maccabees narrative at all. It is not mentioned as an element in the martyrology of Eleazar or of the woman's seven sons in chapter 7. He glosses it, therefore, as meaning simply that "Jewish culture was completely forbidden." Van Henten, *The Maccabean Martyrs*, 90. I continue to find Goldstein's explanation intriguing, if not proven.

In his aforementioned essay, Shaye Cohen has argued that "'People could not confess themselves to be Jews' means that they could not declare themselves to be practitioners of the ancestral laws, the laws of God." Pointing to *Assumption of Moses* 8:1, "which describes how the king will 'hang on the cross those who confess circumcision,'" Cohen accordingly suggests that "oute haplôs Ioudaion homologein eina" also means to circumcise openly. "Antiochus proscribed circumcision, thus preventing people from 'confessing themselves to be Jews.'" He supports his argument from the literary structure of the passage. In verse 6, three points are mentioned: the prohibition on observing the Sabbath, the prohibition on observing festivals, and the prohibition on "confessing" Jewishness. The first is exemplified in verse 11, where Jews die observing the Sabbath, and the second in verses 7 through 9, where the Jews are compelled to observe the Dionysian and other Greek festivals. So the third would be exemplified in verse 10. There, the two women are executed for circumcising their sons. In any case, Cohen writes: "Are we to understand that the mere name 'Jew' aroused the ire of the Seleucid state just as centuries later the mere name 'Christian' aroused the ire of the Roman? I assume not." Shaye J. D. Cohen, "Ioudaios," 1: 217.

In another context, Cohen has perhaps inadvertently suggested another solution to this problem. In Justin's *Dialogue*, there is a reference to Jews who "confess God with their lips = *cheilesin homologountas*." So the same verb is used here, and Cohen remarks that "'confessing God with their lips' is probably a pun on the name Jew, which was commonly taken to mean 'confessor.' For this etymology in Philo, see the passages listed by J. W. Earp in volume 10 of the Loeb *Philo* 357 note a." Shaye J. D. Cohen, "The Significance of Yavneh," 35. If this etymology was as early as the 2 Maccabees text, we could see why a practice such as the reading of the *Shema*^c text or even circumcision would have been a "confession," using the same verb that we have in the (much later, of course) Justin text.

Prof. Daniel Schwartz of Jerusalem contributes the following from the draft of a forthcoming commentary on 2 Maccabees:

> My commentary on II Macc has: ref. to Assumption of Moses 6:2, which, apparently in connection with Antiochus's decrees, refers to Jews who "confess" that they are circumcised. For this regular Greek meaning of the verb homologein, in contrast to the LXX meaning, which includes gratitude, see E. Tov, in *Melbourne Symposium on Septuagint Lexicography*, edited by T. Muraoka (Atlanta, 1990), p. 108. For the importance of the Christian version of this ("Christianus sum"), see e.g. Mart. Polyk 12:1, where the Greek is just like that here (except it says "Christian" instead of "Jew"). See G. Buschmann, *Das Martyrium des Polycarp* (Göttingen, 1998), pp. 193–98.
>
> I am not at all certain that this was an element of persecution under Antiochus, especially since it is hard to find—in II Macc or in any other early texts—usage of "Ioudaios" in the sense of "Jew by religion," which is the sense required here. I could imagine it being an anachronism added by someone late, whether Christian or Jewish—but although it is true that II Macc 6–7 was often cited in early Christian literature, I know of no evidence that this passage was interpolated by such readers. Less relevant to your question is that the imposition of the Dionysiac cult and of monthly celebrations of royal birthdays (II Macc 6:7) seem to have virtually no precedent in the Seleucid world, but both are paralleled in the Ptolemaic world. So I imagine that they are part of the way our Jewish author, in the Ptolemaic world (Cyrene? Alexandria?),

imagined royal persecutions. But I don't know of any evidence for prohibiting self-identification as Jews in the Ptolemaic world, either.

Personal letter, October 28, 1998. I am very grateful to Prof. Schwartz for sharing his reflections on this difficult passage prior to their publication.

That criminalization of the name "Christian" itself was an innovation of the approximate period of the earliest Christian martyrologies can be inferred, at any rate, from Justin's Second Apology, where we read:

> And at last when the man came to Urbicus, he was asked only this question—whether he was a Christian. . . . And when Urbicus ordered him to be led away to punishment, a certain Lucius, who was himself a Christian, seeing the unreasonable judgment which had thus been given, said to Urbicus: "What is the basis of this judgment? Why have you punished this man, not as an adulterer, nor fornicator, nor murderer, nor thief, nor robber, nor convicted of any crime at all, but as one who has only confessed that he is called by the name of Christian?"

Justin Martyr, *First and Second Apologies*, 74–75. This text is to be dated in the later 150's, or within a decade or so of the martyrdom of Polycarp. As I have suggested above, somewhat later, rather than arguing against the criminalization of the name "Christian," Christian martyrs would glory in it. If this had been a given of martyrology since the Maccabean period (or at least since the composition of 2 Maccabees), Justin's point would entirely lose its force.

12. This does not, of course, deny the elements of spirituality in the former practice as it is manifested in the Books of Maccabees.

13. Christian martyr texts, such as the letters of Ignatius and the *Martyrium Polycarpi* add the Christological motif. Cf. Surkau, *Martyrien*, 126–34. The Quartodeciman affiliations of MPol also point in the direction of a "Jewish connection." On this question, see Dehandschutter, "*The Martyrium Polycarpi*," 504; Lieu, *Image and Reality*, 79.

14. Castelli, *Visions and Voyeurism*; Fischel, "Martyr and Prophet," 383.

15. Van Henten shows that this expression in 2 Maccabees "belong[s] to a well established tradition of Israelite wisdom literature." Van Henten, *The Maccabean Martyrs*, 130. Compare also Philo's *Embassy to Gaius*, in which it is said that "the Jews would willing endure to die not once but a thousand times . . . rather than allow any of the prohibited actions to be committed" (*Leg.* 209). See also Rajak, "Dying for the Law," 62.

16. Rajak, "Dying for the Law," 51. This Jewish Stoicism, in fact, seems to

be the main burden of meaning for the text as a whole, following in part Shaw, "Body/Power/Identity," 277; Moore and Anderson, "Taking It Like a Man," 249–73. According to my argument, it is not that the text is a polemic defense of Jewish (and Christian?) martyrdom against Stoic charges that it is not considered and judged in a proper philosophical manner (pace Rajak, "Dying for the Law," 52), but that, by the time of Marcus Aurelius, a new form of martyr praxis had developed among Christians and Jews, very different from the older Stoicizing forms. Samuel Sandmel understood the crucial difference between the ideology of suffering promulgated by 4 Maccabees and that of the later talmudic (and I would add, fourth-century Christian) martyrologies, although he did not name it in quite the same way that I do here. See Sandmel, *Judaism and Christian Beginnings*, 279. See also the fascinating discussion by Glen Bowersock of the changing evaluation of the suffering Philoctetes. A hero in the tragedy of Sophocles, by the time of Cicero, the passion-filled, suffering Philoctetes "had become a symbol of masculine weakness, of effeminacy, of the failure of a man to endure with courage as a man," Bowersock, *Fiction as History*, 64. I would argue that a Marcus Aurelius would find nothing startling about the ideology of 4 Maccabees, while texts like the midrash of Rabbi Akiva, to say nothing of Ambrose's or Prudentius's Agnes, would have shocked him deeply.

17. For the older formation, see also the *Assumption of Moses*, in which a group of Jews enter a cave, prepared to die, "rather than transgress the commands of the Lord of Lords." Licht, "Taxo on the Apocalyptic Doctrine," 95–103. Robert Doran discusses the difference between this passage and martyrology. Doran, "The Martyr," 189–221, but on other grounds than the distinctions being made here.

18. There are crucial elements that are lost in the later traditions, as well. Dehandschutter points out that "one observes that the essential ideas of the Maccabeans are lacking: the atoning power of martyrdom and its substitutional character." Dehandschutter, "*The Martyrium Polycarpi*," 513.

19. Bowersock, *Martyrdom and Rome*, 28.

20. It is quite astonishing that Bowersock nowhere makes reference to the two vital works of Saul Lieberman on these themes: Lieberman, "The Martyrs of Caesarea," 395–446 and "Roman Legal Institutions," 57–111. Bowersock maintains this model in the face of his own recognition that the Smyrna martyr Pionius's statement that he has been hearing the story of the Witch of Endor discussed by Jews since childhood constitutes "remarkable testimony to the interaction of Jews and Christians in third-century Asia and to the signif-

icance of the Jewish population that knew Pionios." *Martyrdom and Rome*, 48. See also Gero, "Jewish Polemic," 164–68.

21. In the midrash version, we find here, as in the Tosefta: "and he said a word of sectarianism in the name of Yeshu^c the son of Pantiri, and it caused me pleasure," and then the addition, "and this is what the matter was." As David Rokeah has noted, we have a clear sign of a later addition in the text, which the Talmud's version has smoothed over. Rokeah, "Ben Stara is Ben Pantera," 9, and see also Hirshman, "Midrash Qohelet Rabbah," part 1, 55.

22. Even according to David Flusser, the relevant parallels appear only in the Gospel of John and thus hardly constitute evidence that such a conversation could actually have taken place between a direct disciple of Jesus and a Pharisee. As Flusser brilliantly remarks, "This formulation testifies apparently to parallel linguistic/conceptual development in the understanding of Christianity on the part of the Sages, on the one hand, and that of the Gospel of John's understanding of the relation of Christianity to Judaism, on the other." Flusser, *Judaism and the Sources of Christianity*, 60–61. I quite agree with Marc G. Hirshman, "Midrash Qohelet Rabbah," part 1, 56, that the group that produced that Gospel might very well have put such a midrash in the mouth of their Jesus, pace Rokeah, "Ben Stara is Ben Pantera," 12.

23. See above, n. 21.

24. Kalmin, "Christians and Heretics," 156. This is patently the case, because in the earlier Tosefta version, which is otherwise identical in every respect with the version in the Babylonian Talmud, the specifics of the conversation between Rabbi Eli^cezer and the Christian are not given, but only that "he said something heretical to me and I enjoyed it." The point that the only flaw in Jesus's Torah is its origin (the only thing wrong with Christianity is that it is not Judaism—to mime E. P. Sanders's famous pronouncement on Paul) is exclusive to the later texts and not to the early Palestinian source, Tosefta Ḥullin 2:24. It is not necessarily Babylonian in origin, however, since it is found in the (relatively) late (fourth-century) Palestinian midrash on Ecclesiastes. Hirshman, "Midrash Qohelet Rabbah," part 2, 52–58. See Setzer, *Jewish Responses to Early Christians*, 159, who clearly gets the point that the Torah of the Christian is very similar to rabbinic Torah, and the only thing wrong with it is its origin. Cf. Culbertson, *A Word Fitly Spoken*, 55–61, who goes so far as to consider this a possible lost teaching of Jesus. Lieberman, "Roman Legal Institutions," 76–80 certainly demonstrates the "authenticity" of the details of the trial as portrayed in the Tosefta, but nothing that he says would indicate the ascription of any historicality to the midrashic dialogue between Rabbi Eli^cezer and Ya^cqov,

or to the midrash of Jesus as a "lost saying." I fail to understand why Culbertson claims that Neusner, *Eliezer Ben Hyrcanus*, 199 and 366, "repeatedly misses the point." Neusner's reading seems to me very close to being on target. Cf. also Bauckham, *Jude and the Relatives of Jesus*, 106–21.

25. Rokeah, "Ben Stara is Ben Pantera," 12, is of this opinion as well.

26. "It is difficult to see why this 'halakhic midrash' is referred to as a 'sectarian saying.'" Ibid.

27. These were men and women who spoke Coptic and Aramaic, just like the Rabbis and their "flocks," not Greek: "It is essential to remember, moreover, that Christianity in Byzantine Palestine, despite its heavy Greek patina, remained a Semitic culture: the language of the towns and villages was Aramaic." Satran, *Biblical Prophets*, 108. See also Rubin, "Porphyrius of Gaza," 49. And it should be emphasized that Gaza itself was apparently the center of the collection and editing of the *Apophthegmeta Patrum* literature. The use of the term "Abba" for the desert fathers, which surprises Chitty, suggests early connections between Palestinian Aramaic ascetics and Copts. Chitty, *The Desert a City*, 9. For other links between Palestinian and Egyptian monasticism at a very early date, see Chitty, *The Desert a City*, 14. Specifically for the Apophthegmeta in Palestine, see Regnault, "Les Apotegemes des pères," 320–30. For contacts between the monks of Gaza and of Palestine, see also Binns, *Ascetics and Ambassadors of Christ*, 93, and especially 158–59. These connections involved monks in Scythopolis, within easy walking distance from the main centers of rabbinic activity in Tiberias and Sepphoris in the critical period. It is thus entirely possible, as well as plausible, that themes found in the apothegms were being discussed in the Christian environs of the Palestinian Rabbis, as well.

28. Ward, *Harlots of the Desert*, 105.

29. Ward, *The Sayings of the Desert Fathers*, Timothy, 1.

30. One could also suggest, in addition, however, that Abba Poemen's forbearance and confidence in repentance was more typical of his affect and character than indicative of particular "halakhic" views. See the story cited in Chitty, *The Desert a City*, 70, from the Alphabetical Collection, Poemen 173, in which he is certain that warring brothers will make peace "because they are brothers." Nevertheless, the *question*, at least, of the legitimacy of a prostitute's almsgiving was in the air at the time. For another example of this topos, see Ward, *Harlots of the Desert*, 99, in which Maria the harlot asks her uncle Abraham "'I have this small amount of gold and these clothes, what do you want me to do with them?' And Abraham said, 'Leave it all here, Maria, for it came from evil.'"

31. Tosefta Parah 2, 2. Cf. Hirshman, "Midrash Qohelet Rabbah," part 1, 56.

32. Bauer, *Orthodoxy and Heresy*, 204.

33. A very important intertext for our story can be found toward the end of the chapter on Vespasian in Suetonius. We find there the following report: "Titus complained of the tax which Vespasian had imposed on the contents of the city urinals. Vespasian handed him a coin which had been part of the first day's proceeds: "Does it smell bad?" he asked. And when Titus said 'No,' he went on: 'Yet it comes from urine.'" Suetonius, *The Twelve Caesars*, 251. I wish to thank Chava Boyarin for pointing this parallel to me.

34. See the discussion in Alexander, "'The Parting of the Ways,'" 13–14.

35. It is not beside the point to invoke Brownian particles of language here, since as in so much else, it was indeed Peter Brown who seemingly first caught this moment: "The martyrs . . . were not particularly noteworthy as men and women who faced execution with unusual courage: as the notables of Smyrna told a later bishop: they were too used to professional stars of violence—to gladiators and beast hunters—to be impressed by those who made a performance of making light of death. Rather the martyrs stood for a particular style of religious experience." Brown, *The Making of Late Antiquity*, 55.

36. Elizabeth A. Clark, "Response," 18.

37. Bauer, *Orthodoxy and Heresy*, 135.

38. For an excellent actual example of a dual martyrdom of an "orthodox" Christian and a Marcionite, see *Martyrs of Palestine*, 10, 3: "Now on one and the same pyre was yoked with him a certain person of the Marcionite error, who called himself a bishop. And he gave himself up to this as though forsooth in his zeal for righteousness—but he was not in the knowledge of the truth—and suffered martyrdom by fire along with this martyr of God." Interestingly, the short (Greek) recension of the same text is slightly less grudging in tone: "With Peter too, Asclepius (accounted a bishop of the Marcionite error), in his zeal, as he thought, for piety, but not that piety which is according to knowledge, nevertheless departed this life on the one and self-same pyre." Eusebius, *The Ecclesiastical History*, 378.

39. In an unpublished paper, Shamma Boyarin has demonstrated convincingly that although Rabbi Akiva objects strenuously to certain midrashic interpretations of this figure, there seem to be no doctrinal or even hermeneutical reasons for his objections. Indeed, from version to version of the stories, the stances are sometimes reversed, suggesting that the only objection to Papos's arguments were that he was some sort of heretical figure, rendering his midrash as suspect, *eo ipso*, as that of the disciple of Jesus who met Rabbi Eliᶜezer. This conclusion, independently reached, supports the interpretation of this figure that I suggest here. Shamma Boyarin, "No Horseplay Allowed!?"

40. This detail may help suggest further a dating for our narrative. Ac-

cording to de Ste. Croix, it was only after 300 that public assemblies were prohibited. De Ste. Croix, *The Class Struggle*, 313–14.

41. The Hebrew is דברים בטלים, "idle matters." It is used here and in
the Babylonian talmudic version of the story of the arrest of Rabbi Eliᶜezer as
the name of a charge of which the Romans would accuse one. There, the
charge clearly consists of Christianity.

42. For "superstitio" as the crime of the Christian already at the time of
the first recorded persecutions under Trajan, see Sherwin-White, *The Letters of
Pliny*, 691.

43. According to Lieberman, the Hebrew translates instead the Latin *ina-
nia*. Tending slightly to favor my conjecture—and it is no more than that—is
the fact that the judge would be expected to make a statement that incrimi-
nates the defendant at this point in the trial, as pointed out by Lieberman
himself, "Roman Legal Institutions," 80–81, but not in connection with this
text. On the other hand, in a document roughly contemporaneous with the
midrashic and talmudic forms of this story, the *Palinode of Calerius*, Christianity is referred to as *stultitia*, "folly." See also Markus, *The End of Ancient
Christianity*, 32. דברים בטלים could conceivably reflect such a terminology,
as well. In any case, it must be remembered that the earliest form of the text in
the Tosefta (if the textual tradition is to be believed) has only "these matters,"
and whatever דברים בטלים refers to would seemingly indicate a later Latin
usage, and not an earlier one. See Janssen, "'Superstitio,'" 131–59.

44. Could this represent a dim memory of the apostolic father, Papias,
who certainly lived and was apparently martyred at about the right time? Interestingly enough, Papias's writings do "show contact with Rabbinic exegesis."
Schoedel, *Polycarp*, 90, so there is a temptation here. This notion has been anticipated by Gry, "Le Papias des belles promesses," 112–24 and "Hénoch X, 19
et les belles promesses," 197–206, although Gry did not see that the Talmud
hints that Papos was a Christian, which would strengthen his case considerably. See also the discussion in Schoedel, *Polycarp*, 94–96. My own best guess
that this is on about the same order of likelihood as that the Trypho in Justin
is Rabbi Tarphon.

45. The usual Syriac and Aramaic term for Mary Magdalene was מרים
מגדלא שערא דנשיא, Miriam the plaiter of women's hair, a sort of pun or folk
etymology of "Magdalene." This "error" in the tradition is not necessarily evidence for lack of contact between the producers of this narrative and living
Christian usage because by the fifth century, popular Christian traditions also
were confounding the two Marys, as I have learned from Karen King.

46. Cf. "Let us return, however, to the words put into the mouth of the

Jew, where *the mother of Jesus* is described as having been *turned out by the carpenter who was betrothed to her, as she had been convicted of adultery and had a child by a certain soldier named Panthera.*" Chadwick, *Origen: Contra Celsum*, 31.

47. Rokeah, "Ben Stara is Ben Pantera."

48. This is clearly a late tradition. Earlier rabbinic texts have Papos as a somewhat extreme, perhaps deviant ("Gnostic?") rabbinic figure. His association with Christianity and indeed with the Holy Family has been variously explained. For one typical, if not very convincing attempt, see Herford, *Christianity in Talmud and Midrash*, 40. This narrative itself, as we have it, seems ruptured precisely at the point of Papos's arrest. If he was opposed to Rabbi Akiva's provocation of the Romans and presumably discreet about his own religious practices, then why was he arrested? The gap in the story may reflect the historical shift in the tradition about him from deviant Rabbi to Christian heretic, which the "Holy Family" story reflects. In the earlier version, he was perhaps a conservative, somewhat pro-Roman figure opposed to this new-fangled invention of martyrdom. In the later, he is a sectarian martyr who has to "confess" to Rabbi Akiva that the latter's martyrdom is worthier than his own. For an early report that says "Gnostics" keep their views secretive and don't believe in martyrdom, see Frend, *Martyrdom and Persecution*, 11. It would be foolhardy to see in this any but the most tenuous of similarities, but, insofar as the seeking of martyrdom through public confession is indeed a religious innovation, it is not surprising that religious conservatives, whether Christian or Jewish sectarians, would be in opposition to it. It was Jesus's apparent desire for death, as described in the Gospels, that granted him the title "The Pious Fool" in rabbinic texts, a title reflected in our talmudic passage. It is fascinating that the evident fact that this is a late Babylonian tradition indicated to an earlier generation of scholars that it has "no historical value." See Rokeah, "Ben Stara is Ben Pantera," 15. For me, this is precisely its historical value. "Papos" is apparently a short form of "Josephus," as argued originally by Cassel, "Caricaturnamen," 341, who points to modern Italian, "Pepi."

49. Cassel, "Caricaturnamen," 341.

50. This nexus was suggested to me by my friend Galit Hasan-Rokem. For another Christian version of the topos of fish out of water, see Antony 10 in Ward's alphabetical *Sayings of the Desert Fathers*. See also Chitty, *The Desert a City*, 6.

51. One is reminded with some amusement of Celsus's comparison of Jews and Christians to "worms and frogs disagreeing with each other." Chadwick, *Origen: Contra Celsum*, 199.

52. The verse itself is rather difficult. It seems generally to express in con-

text a prayer for a death in bed of old age, and not a violent death. I am following Rashi's commentary here, which involves several typical midrashic
puns, for the Hebrew word ממתים "human beings" can also mean "kills," and
both senses are being mobilized.

53. Again, in the original context, the verse seems to mean that the place
of the righteous is to remain alive until a "natural" death. Here, the meaning
has been ironized, so that it is taken to mean that the place of the martyr is "in
[eternal] life," thus resolving the theodical problem that Rabbi Akiva's martyrdom is taken to raise.

54. For a further and much more detailed literary analysis of this text, see
Goldberg, "Das Martyrium des Rabbi Aqiva," 1–82.

55. For a theological reflection on this nexus as it becomes a "timeless"
structure of Jewish spirituality, see Fishbane, *The Kiss of God.*

56. This point was rendered clear to me by Dr. Dina Stein.

57. The phrase was a gift of Carlin Barton's in a letter. Interestingly
enough, medieval Sefardic Jewry was much more likely to choose life in continuing and developing the trickster mode, so that the great Maimonides himself had pretended to convert to Islam, and the story of the Iberian *conversos* is
well known, too. In at least some of these instances, the Qurʾanic suggestion
that believers hide their identity from oppressors certainly played a role. For
other examples of "assimilation" of Ashkenazic Judaism to medieval Christian
forms of spirituality and practice, see Marcus, *Rituals of Childhood,* and Yuval,
"Passover in the Middle Ages."

58. Contra Rajak, "Dying for the Law," 67 who identifies this as a particularly Christian feature.

59. Another version of the name of "the wicked Turnus Rufus" in the text
quoted in the preceding paragraph.

60. The third person is used in curses in the Talmud in order to avoid using the second person, which, when the Talmud is read aloud, could cause a
curse to fall on the hearer.

61. On this text, see Lieberman, "On Persecution," 222–23. Compare also
the following:

Abba Moses the Ethiopian himself would say, "If we keep the commandments of our fathers, I stand your surety before God that no
barbarians come here. But if we do not keep them, this place must
be laid desolate." The day came when the brethren were sitting with
him, and he said, "To-day barbarians are coming to Scetis: but rise
up and flee." They say, "Then are you not fleeing Abba?" He

answered, "For so many years have I been looking forward to this day, that the words of the Master Christ might be fulfilled which he spake, "All who take the sword shall die by the sword.""

Alphabetical Collection, Moses 10; cited in Chitty, *The Desert a City*, 60–61. I hardly deny, of course, the significant differences between the stories, but I find compelling the parallel of a reference to many years of waiting to see a Scripture fulfilled and then accepting danger and suffering with pleasure because of this completion.

I am grateful to Dr. Avram Gross, who helped me see and correct an error in my previous interpretations of this passage.

62. See Fischel, "Martyr and Prophet," 366.

63. Bowersock, *Martyrdom and Rome*, 59–60.

64. Mühlenberg, "The Martyr's Death," 89.

65. Lieu, *Image and Reality*, 82–83.

66. Right up to the Nazi persecutions of our own century.

67. I have generally followed here the elegant translation of Judah Goldin: *The Song at the Sea*, 115–17, modifying it only where my manuscripts have a better reading.

68. In addition to the texts cited here, see TB Gittin 57b, where the account of the mother and her seven sons is introduced by this verse and, in addition, where it provides the link to a previous martyr story in the same passage in which the same verse was quoted. The verse is also cited in Eikha Rabbah 1:16. For a discussion, see Doran, "The Martyr," 193. See also Romans 8:36:

> Who shall separate us from the love of God? Shall tribulation, or distress, or famine, or nakedness, or peril, or sword? (As it is written: For Thy sake we are killed all the day long; we have been counted as sheep for the slaughter,) Nay, in all these things we are more than conquerors, through Him who loved us. For we are persuaded, that neither death, nor life, nor power, nor height, nor depth, nor any other creature, shall be able to separate us from the love of God, which is in Christ Jesus our Lord.

This verse is cited in martyrological contexts from Irenaeus on, thus further belying Bowersock's thesis.

69. Baer, "Israel" (1961), 82.

70. "And when Rabbi Akiva was executed in Caesarea, the news reached Rabbi Yehuda ben Baba and Rabbi Ḥanina ben Teradyon. They rose and girded their loins with sackcloth. . . . In a short time from now, no place will

be found in Palestine where bodies of the slain will not be thrown." Semaḥot, VIII, 9. This is obviously a very late text, and I am citing it only as evidence for the *traditional* status of Rabbi Akiva's being the first of the martyrs.

71. Daniel Boyarin, "A Contribution."

72. We are, of course, immediately reminded of the vision of the about-to-die Stephen in Acts 7:58.

73. For discussions of gender shift in the direction of male to female in antiquity, see Elizabeth A. Clark, "Sex, Shame, and Rhetoric," 221–45; Harrison, "Receptacle Imagery," 23–27 and "A Gender Reversal," 34–38; Daniel Boyarin, "'This We Know to Be the Carnal Israel,'" 474–506. Note that even in the "original" Song of Songs, itself, that is, not as midrashically or allegorically read, this passage is an eloquent representation of female, ocular desire. To be sure, the desiring female is caught and beaten by the guardians of the city, but the text seems to be "on her side," and thus to be protesting the denial of desiring eyes to women, just as it is at the end of the Song, when her brothers punish her. For a reading of the representation of female desire in the Song of Songs, see Pardes, *Countertraditions in the Bible*, 118–43.

74. Burrus, "Reading Agnes," 25–46.

75. Castelli, *Visions and Voyeurism*, 2.

76. Amat, *Songes et visions*, 67; Holl, "Die Vorstellung vom Märtyrer un die Märtyrer-Akte," 68–102.

77. Castelli, *Visions and Voyeurism*, 9.

78. Brown, *The Cult of the Saints*, 81: "The hagiographer was recording the moments when the seemingly extinct past and the unimaginably distant future had pressed into the present." See also Daniel Boyarin, "Language Inscribed by History," which explicitly treats the collapse of time in the martyrology and in the midrash.

79. Castelli, *Visions and Voyeurism*, 11, 14. In my earlier discussion of this text, I had made this argument for the Jewish martyrologies without knowing anything at the time about the Christian texts. Daniel Boyarin, *Intertextuality and the Reading of Midrash*, 119–24, especially 124. In the *Passion of Perpetua and Felicitas*, the author writes: "that which we have heard and have touched without hands we proclaim also to you so those of you that were witnesses may recall the glory of the Lord and those that now learn of it through hearing may have fellowship with the holy martyrs and, through them, with the Lord Christ Jesus." Musurillo, *Acts of the Christian Martyrs*, 107–9. As Castelli so tellingly sums it up, "The recounting of Perpetua's (and Saturus's) visions, and the eventual martyrdoms of all in their party, are framed by a desire to situate contemporary readers/hearers in continuous relation to events

of the distant and more recent past in which divine activity has touched human existence directly." Castelli, *Visions and Voyeurism*, 9. This is an exact parallel to the strategies of the midrashic martyrology, which are to perform a collapse of time enabling the hearers of the text to see and experience what the martyr experienced of erotic connection with God. In the midrashic text, this is thematized via the verse of Psalms, "that which we have heard, we have seen." Psalms 48:9.

80. Urbach, "The Homiletical Interpretations of the Sages," 250.

81. Baer, "Israel" (1961), 82.

82. Alon, *The Jews in Their Land*, 2: 523–24. The "War of Quietus," or "Qitus" in rabbinic sources, refers to a minor Jewish revolt under Trajan. Smallwood, *The Jews Under Roman Rule*, 421–27. See also Lawlor and Oulton, *Eusebius*, 1: 105.

83. Herr, "Persecutions and Martyrdom," 92.

84. Goodman, *Mission and Conversion*. Thus also, Gary G. Porton, for all his exhaustive documentation of rabbinic ambivalence toward converts, finds no suggestions of a complete rejection of converts anywhere in the texts. Porton, *The Stranger Within Your Gates*, 211–20.

85. This picture is considerably less irenic than the one painted by Lieberman, for which, see below. There is no contradiction necessary, of course, because different texts may have different positions. This explanation is, to my mind, a much more plausible one also to explain the other texts that Baer cites in his paper than his highly questionable hypothesis that Jews were included in the Decian persecutions. For the weakness of the latter, see Lieberman, "On Persecution," 235. Herr also understands that "the Sages living at the end of the third and beginning of the fourth century C.E. gave a deeper justification to the ideological basis of the concept of martyrology," but doesn't seem to be able to explain why, in spite of the fact that Lieberman had suggested the answer many years previously.

86. For the differences, see Herr, "Persecutions and Martyrdom," 104–5. As Herr makes clear, in 1 Maccabees we find "the diametric opposite of a martyr-consciousness." n. 66. Even in 2 and to a lesser extent in 4 Maccabees, the models are more of the noble death, like that of Socrates or Antigone (n. 69), certainly one of the tributaries of the river that became late antique martyrdom, rather than the truly theologized and eroticized forms that we find later among both Christians and rabbinic Jews. Cf. Droge and Tabor, *A Noble Death*. This is entirely consistent with the picture that I am drawing here of a common history of cultural development. Herr, one of the most established Hebrew University historians of the old school, is not too far from Bowersock

in some respects. Thus, he writes, "The martyr consciousness evoked no real echo among Jews in Palestine. . . . On the other hand, a martyr-consciousness became increasingly prevalent among the gentile nations, and was especially frequent both as a phenomenon in real life and as a conscious attitude and ideal among the philosophers and seekers of *libertas* at Rome and the provinces." "Persecutions and Martyrdom," 105–6. Brent Shaw effectively captures this moment vis-à-vis the earlier texts, 2 and 4 Maccabees, via his characterization of them as being about saying "no" and as being "protocols of refusal." "Body/Power/Identity," 275–76. I am suggesting that the late antique texts, both rabbinic and Christian, are something else than protocols of refusal. They are about saying "yes," not "no," and it is the shared nature of this historical shift that most clearly indicates the close communion of these ostensibly (and actually) bitterly rivalrous "Judaisms."

87. Frend, *Martyrdom and Persecution*, 99. Our text is more likely to suggest support for Bowersock's chronological reconstructions with respect to this aspect of the discourse of martyrdom. But for Frend, who considers Maccabees an example of "late Judaism," anything that Jews were doing by the fourth century just doesn't exist.

88. Lieberman, "On Persecution," 230.

89. Bowersock, *Martyrdom and Rome*, 9–10. Cf. also Safrai, "Martyrdom in the Teachings of the Tannaim," 145–64, and van Henten, *Die Entstehung der jüdischen Martyrologie*.

An anonymous reader for Stanford Press has written: "The fact that so many commentators and generations of scholars cannot for the life of them figure out whether or not a text like, say, IV Maccabees, is 'Jewish' or 'Christian' speaks volumes in itself; they have similar problems in identifying the status of 'Godfearers' and a host of other persons and groups of the same time; on some tombstone epitaphs of the period, even ones that recount fairly lengthy 'theological views' (the famous Regina stone), it is also impossible to tell—there is plenty of evidence for a not inconsiderable middle ground. The author should develop more of this historical background to his thesis." This formulation is almost precisely a prospectus for the ambitions of the larger project of which this work is the first part.

90. Here the comparison between 2 Maccabees and 4 Maccabees can be taken as exemplary. As van Henten remarks: "Differences like these can best be understood as adaptations of the source material from 2 Maccabees by the author of 4 Maccabees to adjust it to the discourse and the socio-cultural context of the primary readers." *The Maccabean Martyrs*, 72.

91. Bowersock, *Martyrdom and Rome*, 13.

92. Ibid., 79.

93. Van Henten, *The Maccabean Martyrs*, 75–78.

94. Ibid., 77, 302. See also Schoedel, *Ignatius of Antioch*, 53, 64; Frend, *Martyrdom and Persecution*, 198–99; Perler, "Das vierter Makkabäerbuch," 47–72.

95. This is the whole point of Lieberman, "On Persecution," strongly countering the very hypothetical and ideologically driven arguments of Baer, "Israel" (1961).

96. As emphasized to me by Harry Maier. Ruth Clements remarks that Ignatius's interpretation of Paul's "being crucified with Christ" is a literalizing reading.

97. Rosaldo, "Toward an Anthropology of Self ," 140.

98. For a similar formulation, see Rajak, "Dying for the Law," 40, who writes:

> Martyrology is idealized representation and the characterization of martyrs is portraiture, to a lesser or greater extent stereotyped. It is as well to recognize from the outset that martyrdoms, while presented as fact, are not mere historical events—that is, if they are history at all. As it happens, the episodes [in 4 Maccabees] are also most certainly unhistorical; but to those concerned, as we are here, with the representation of the would-be historical, this makes little difference. Martyrdom is description, since in its very nature it demands a public, a response and a record. In the Christian tradition, the terminology itself is a clue, for the deaths of martyrs bear witness (μαρτυρεῖσθαι) to their faith, in front of an assumed audience immeasurably greater than the immediate one at the scene. And, already, the martyr's manner of dying may well have been influenced by literature. The event is then shaped for the future in the telling, to serve, in due course, as a model for others.

Rajak unfortunately seems to retreat from her own perspective when she writes later in the essay as if "martyrdom" is a real event to which there could be different cultural responses, rather than itself a cultural response and form of "portraiture." Thus, she writes,

> In such texts, the *portrait* of the martyr can rarely be clearly discerned. . . . There are many ways of snatching meaning out of the deaths of martyrs, of turning physical disaster into psychic (and perhaps ultimately physical) victory. The diverse Jewish literature of

the period, which incorporated a highly diversified religious world, generated varied reactions. Our concern here is with responses manifested by way of the evocation and depiction of individual martyrs and expressed in extended narratives.

"Dying for the Law," 46. Since, however, she has defined martyrdom as portraiture, a martyrology in which the *"portrait* can rarely be clearly discerned" (emphasis in the original) seems a contradiction in terms.

99. For the former, see Frend, *Martyrdom and Persecution*, 19–20. For the latter, see ibid., 198–99. See also Perler, "Das vierter Makkabäerbuch"; van Henten, "Datierung und Herkunft des vierten Makkabäerbuches," 136–49. Bowersock, *Martyrdom and Rome*, 77–81, considers 4 Maccabees a later text, and following van Henten, denies the Ignatian affiliations, but does argue for a common source in Asia-Minor for the language of both texts.

100. Dehandschutter, "*The Martyrium Polycarpi*," 507–8.

101. Van Henten, *The Maccabean Martyrs*, 299.

102. Burrus, "Reading Agnes," 38–43. This is an elegant example of the extreme care and delicacy required for working out the details of the intertextual production of such a complex cultural practice as martyrology, for, as Burrus shows, following Loraux, the place of death, the neck rather than the breast, is determined by Greek tragedy as a subjugating, female death. On the other hand, for defeated gladiators, death by the neck was an honorable death, through which the feminized, defeated gladiator recovered his masculine honor. Barton, "Savage Miracles," 41–71. So one could conceivably read the death of the female martyrs as a paradoxically virilizing death, in that it afforded them the stature of the honorable (and thus paradoxically victorious) gladiator. However, as Burrus shows, it is in the details of the intertextual allusions that the interpretation lies, and in this case, it is the fact of the choice offered of the breast or the neck and the chosen neck that mark the death as belonging to the tragic Polyxena and not Roman gladiator topos. But this is also a case study in the overdetermination of this most complex, nuanced, and fascinating of cultural praxes. (The word is chosen advisedly.)

103. Salisbury, *Perpetua's Passion*, 50–55. "Imbricated" here seems precisely the right word. Like the tiles on a roof, these discourses and practices were overlayed on each other in a partly overlapping manner.

104. Truth to tell, Bowersock seems to involve himself in virtual self-contradiction on occasion. Thus, in the space of one paragraph, he writes: "In these early years of the second century, in both the polytheist and Christian contexts and also, I suspect (on the basis of my interpretation of Second Mac-

cabees), the Palestinian Jewish context, the concept of martyrdom as we know it gradually took shape," and then, "One cannot help wondering therefore whether or not this invention of martyrdom had some kind of root in western Asia Minor, that is to say Anatolia." *Martyrdom and Rome*, 17. I far prefer, for obvious reasons, his first suggestion. Bowersock, in contrast, seems intensely committed to his second one. On the other hand, I could not disagree more with Frend's conclusion that "the problem which the Christians posed to the Empire was fundamentally the same as that posed by Judaism." *Martyrdom and Persecution*, 22. Judaism was assimilable to the system of ancestral cults, while Christianity was not. As Lieberman demonstrated brilliantly in his Hebrew essay "On Persecution," 234–45, there is no evidence whatsoever for persecution of the Jewish religion at the time of the Decian or Diocletian persecutions of Christians, and even the persecutions of the time of Hadrian, which provided the Rabbis with some claims on the crown of martyrdom, had more to do with politics than religion.

105. Lieu, *Image and Reality*, 80, following in part Kellermann, "Das Danielbuch."

106. Lieu, *Image and Reality*, 78–79. Lieu goes on to remark: "Chilton and Davies, whose position is here in part adopted, see this interaction as polemical, a stance inevitably conveyed by the literature. Other evidence of continuing influence on Christians of Jewish exegetical traditions—and why should not the process have also been reversed?—suggests that it may sometimes have been less explicitly so." The reference is to Davies and Chilton, "The Aqedah," 514–46. Similarly, Israel Yuval, in "The Haggadah of Passover and Easter," 5–29, his excellent article on very similar themes, tends to lean exclusively on the model of a polemical interaction, rather than considering the possibility of shared and diffused exegetical traditions, as well. See also Yuval, "Easter and Passover." Cf. Hasan-Rokem, *The Web of Life*, 165.

107. Thus, J. Partout Burns writes: "In contrast, the interpretation of suffering as a following of Christ to glory, which had been developing since the end of the Decian persecution, broke into full blossom under Valerian's assault on the church. Cyprian informed the confessors that their enslavement and approaching deaths were actually the crowning of a virtuous and faithful life." Burns, "Cyprian's Eschatology," 70.

108. This element is already present in the earliest form of Christian-era Jewish martyr texts, 4 Maccabees, as well as in Polycarp, and Lieu has read it as manifesting "a shared thought-world perhaps in the same geographical area" Lieu, *Image and Reality*, 81. Lieu's work is remarkable for its sensitivity and the complexity and nuance of the historical models of Jewish-Christian cultural

interaction that it develops. On this theme in Jewish literature, see also Levinson, "Bloody Fictions."

109. Bowersock, *Martyrdom and Rome*, 27, citing den Boeft, who wrote (or rather said): "In den christlichen Martyrien bildet trotz aller Verschiedenheit der Formen bei den authentischen Dokumenten das Prozessverfahren den Kern. Vielleicht liegt darin der Unterschied zu den jüdischen Martyrien, sodass dadurch auch der Begriff μαρτυρ als typisch christlicher Titel zu verstehen wäre." Van der Klaauw, "Diskussion," 221. Bowersock makes much of this vaunted "authenticity," accepting even the highly contested acts of Pionius as if they were straightforward documentation of "the society of second and third-century Smyrna." *Martyrdom and Rome*, 30.

110. Doran, "The Martyr."

111. Bowersock, *Martyrdom and Rome*, 37.

112. Lieberman, "Roman Legal Institutions."

113. Ibid., Cf. also Fischel, "Martyr and Prophet," 269, who writes: "The political and spiritual situation in the Roman Empire made it thus possible that literary and legendary motifs and theological or philosophical beliefs could travel from one religion to the other. The identification of the prophet with the martyr, found in Jewish, Christian and, to a lesser degree in Hellenistic sources would seem to bear this out."

114. Lieberman, "The Martyrs of Caesarea," 395.

115. In spite of the presumptions of the Neusner school to have introduced this caveat into rabbinic historiography, we see that it was articulated by Saul Lieberman decades earlier. Lieberman's principle is not substantially different from that articulated by Neusner, who held that documents are to be taken as evidence for their own chronotope, and not for the one(s) reported on within them.

116. This remains, however, a highly ambiguous conclusion. The example of the *acta* of Polycarp is instructive. As Timothy D. Barnes has put it with respect to another martyrology, "Even if nothing calls into question the basic facts, it is uncertain how far the narrative has been altered in retelling through the third century." Barnes, "Pre-Decian *Acta Martyrum*," 525. The same would appear to be the case for Polycarp. The earliest source for Polycarp's martyrology, according to many, is apparently none other than Eusebius, once more a close contemporary of the time of the writing of this midrash and of the Palestinian Talmud. Much current opinion, even now, holds that the form of the text in Eusebius is less interfered with, and thus "earlier," than the form of the text in Pseudo-Pionius. Von Campenhausen, "Bearbeitungen und Interpolationen des Polykarpmartyriums," 253–301, and see the discussion in Bisbee,

Pre-Decian Acts, 122ff, with a review of the critical literature. In point of fact, Bisbee sharply asks:

> We must ask ourselves. What have scholars meant by an authentic account? By what criteria are the labels "authentic" and "inauthentic" affixed? It is extremely doubtful whether any of the "canonized" acts is completely "authentic," if by "authentic" is meant "the original, unedited account." It is also doubtful that we possess the original text of any letter written by an eyewitness, or the text of an initially edited *commentarius*. In transmitting *acta Christianorum*, martyrologists, from the earliest times it would appear, often, perhaps even usually, did not resist the temptation to edit. Perhaps the community of scholars defines an "authentic account" as a text that is not necessarily the historical original but is demonstrably derived from a historical original. If so, authenticity is a matter of degree. . . . It is only a matter of degree whether the community of scholars calls such a text "a fifth-century text containing readings from the second century" or "a second-century text that has been edited in the fifth century." If texts are treated as "wholes," without regard for editorial layers and the dating thereof, the danger of incorrectly reconstructing history from anachronistic data is great. . . . This is especially true when discussions of origins are involved.

Pre-Decian Acts, 83–84. Dehandschutter writes that "in the past decades the interpolation theory of H. von Campenhausen has been most influential," Dehandschutter, "*The Martyrium Polycarpi*," 493. As venerable a scholar as Hans Conzelmann also held that "the original text has again been thoroughly interpolated further in order to concentrate on the one hero, Polycarp, who has to serve as a *model-martyr*." Cited in Dehandschutter, "*The Martyrium Polycarpi*," 496. Dehandschutter himself disagrees with the general opinion summarized by Theodor Keim who "places the text of MPol in the third century, followed by J. Réville, who is, like Keim, disturbed by the warning against an exaggerated cult of the martyrs, presumably present in MPol, which could only date from the third, not the second century." Dehandschutter, "*The Martyrium Polycarpi*," 492. Given these uncertainties, I could have adopted (and was tempted to adopt) a different "conservative" strategy, namely, to treat the rabbinic materials and the Christian *acta* as similarly ambiguous as to dating. The point of common Christian and rabbinic development then would have been easily made: both Polycarp and Akiva are only known from texts of the fourth century, and what is sauce for the *Martyrium Polycarpi* is sauce for what we could call the *Acta Akivae*, as well. This would have served my argument too neatly, however, and following the prodding of Virginia Burrus, I have changed to the current strategy, which is less conservative with respect to the authenticity of the Christian texts, but more conservative with respect to the thesis of this book.

For a recent demonstration of the significance of the revisions (or at the least, the heavily "Gospelized" stylization) in the *Polycarp*, see Miriam S. Taylor, *Anti-Judaism*, 102–4.

117. I exaggerate, of course. One frequently enough finds scholars of the Rabbis from various disciplinary formations still treating rabbinic statements and stories as if they are to be ascribed to their protagonists. Cf. the positivistic approach of Ray A. Pritz, who argues that "The *terminus ad quem* [of the text!], given the appearance of Eliezer b. Hyrkanos, must be about 130." Pritz, *Nazarene Jewish Christianity*, 96. Pritz, writing in the 1980's, was still using the methods of R. Travers Herford, who wrote in 1903, or those of Guttmann in "The Significance of Miracles," 363–406, who also treated this story as if it "reflected" historical reality of the first or early second century. I would not even mention such a position were it not, unfortunately, still all too characteristic of certain scholars and scholarship, although not nearly as prevalent as Neusner would have us believe.

118. Dehandschutter, "Le Martyre de Polycarpe," 659–68.

119. See on this, inter alia, Grant, *Greek Apologists*, 112.

120. Lieberman, "On Persecution," 227–28.

121. Schäfer, "R. Aqiva und Bar Kokhba," 65–121.

122. Lawlor and Oulton, *Eusebius*, 1: 142.

123. Stevenson, *A New Eusebius*, 42.

124. In a very stimulating, but finally (to me) not entirely convincing reading of TB Sanhedrin 74a–75b and parallels, Aryeh Cohen has argued that

> the sanctification of God's name, as constructed in this *sugya*, is only passive. Not engaging in adultery (= idolatry) is *kiddush hashem*. There is no way of active *kiddush hashem* since the sanctifier is constructed as Esther is—if he has no pleasure he has sanctified God's name. If he is like "natural soil" he resists the impurity of idolatry/adultery. The idea of an active sanctification of God's name is foreign, since that pleasure (of actively sanctifying God's name), like the pleasure of sexual intercourse, is given only to transgressors.

Aryeh Cohen, "Towards an Erotics of Martyrdom," 249. If Cohen is right in his reading, the talmudic text TB Sanhedrin 74a–75b would stand in direct opposition to the line of thought that is developed in the Rabbi Akiva texts, an opposition much more implacable and univocal than that in our *Avoda Zara* intertext. This, by itself, of course, would be an entirely plausible result. Cohen's reading hangs, however, on the assumption that according to one voice there, Esther managed to resist successfully Aḥašueroš's attempts to have intercourse with her, and it is this crucial moment in his reading that fails to produce conviction.

125. Lamentations Rabbah, 1 and Babylonian Talmud Gittin 57b. Each of the martyred children cites a verse, and the "Hear O Israel," later the sine qua non of martyrdom right up until the Nazi genocide, is the fifth out of the seven, suggesting that the particular usage of the Unification of the Name had not yet formed at the time of the midrash. This point was made to me by Galit Hasan-Rokem.

126. Barton, *Roman Honor.*

127. Schoedel, *Polycarp,* 63.

128. Barton, *Roman Honor.* Barton makes clear, as well, that "virtus," being a man, was as much for women as for men. For the ways that this theme of manliness *is* reflected in rabbinic literature, see Satlow, "'Try to Be a Man,'" 19–40. I am not arguing for its absence, but rather that it was a highly contested motif in rabbinic literature, particularly at certain crucial junctures like this one, a motif of standing up and being killed "like a man," which Polycarp is urged to do by a heavenly voice. Rajak, to be sure, relates this motif to the Hellenic element of *andreia* in "Greco-Roman" society, rather than seeing it as something particularly Roman. Rajak, "Dying for the Law," 55–56. See also Moore and Anderson, "Taking It Like a Man," 255. See also Burrus, "Torture and Travail," and Shaw, "The Passion of Perpetua," 3–45.

129. Fischel, "Martyr and Prophet"; Satran, *Biblical Prophets,* 25–29, however, see the important qualifications at 54–57.

130. Burrus, "Word and Flesh," 27–51, and "Reading Agnes"; Castelli, "Imperial Reimaginings," 173–84.

131. Burrus, "Word and Flesh," 34.

132. Some of the material in the following paragraphs has been adopted (and significantly adapted) from Daniel Boyarin, *Intertextuality and the Reading of Midrash,* 125–28, and "Midrash and Martyrdom."

133. Finkelstein, *Sifre on Deuteronomy,* 6:5.

134. "The Pseudo-Clementine literature, which took shape in its various forms between the mid-third and mid-fourth centuries, locates Peter in Caesarea as the leader of the Christian community and champion of an anti-Pauline Christianity very sympathetic to Jewish practices," Clements, "*Peri Pascha,*" 123 n. 238. For background, see Baumgarten, "Literary Evidence," 39–50.

135. O'Meara, *Prayer*, 142–43. Brent Shaw has marked the shift in the meaning of *passio* from only enduring suffering to its "positive valuation to refer to the 'passionate' experience of sexual intercourse" and finds such a shift being exploited by Tertullian. Shaw, "Body/Power/Identity," 296–97. But it does not yet issue in the eroticization of the martyr's death as it would later. See also Perkins, *The Suffering Self*. A generation before Origen, we find Tertullian referring to "loving God with all its strength (by which in the endurance of martyrdom it maintains the fight), with all its life (which it lays down for God), it makes of man a martyr." Scorpiace 6. This is quite a different matter, particularly in the context of his discourse, where the dominant metaphors are the strength and triumph of the "pugilist" and his pleasure at winning in spite of his wounds and pain. Even for the mid-third-century Cyprian, as Shaw emphasizes, "patience, endurance," is the experience and virtue of a martyr. Shaw, "Body/Power/Identity," 298–99. But see Cyprian's encouragement to confessors: "Such is the faith we too must preserve and contemplate night and day, with our whole hearts prepared for God, scorning things of the moment and with our thoughts directed entirely on the future— the delights of the everlasting kingdom, *the embrace and kiss of the Lord*, the sight of God." Clarke, *Letters 1–27*, 66. Shaw tends to meld third-century and fourth-century moments in his analysis, not marking the chronological distance between Prudentius's late-fourth-century Eulalia and earlier martyrological types, precisely the distance that my text, following Burrus, emphasizes. Shaw, "Body/Power/Identity," 306. Eulalia, the virgin bride of God, and Blandina, the defiant rebel, are treated in almost the same breath in his text. In any case, the use of this verse in third-century Christian exhortations to martyrdom is also evidence for joint Jewish-Christian religious life. I am grateful to Joshua Levinson for pointing out the parallels from Tertullian and Origen.

136. Kimelman, "R. Yoḥanan and Origen," 567–95.

137. Cf. Hasan-Rokem, "Narratives in Dialogue," 127.

138. Lieberman explained the persecutions of the Jewish religion under Hadrian in the following convincing manner. First, the Jews were forbidden to circumcise, not as an attack on Judaism, but as part of the general Roman law against genital mutilation, the *lex Cornelia de Sicariis*. This led to Jewish revolt, which led, in turn, to a harsh Roman response, but according to him, there was never a concerted attack on the Jewish religion by the Roman government. Lieberman, "On Persecution," 214. And see his classic "Palestine in the Third and Fourth Centuries," in which he demonstrates that the notion of persecution of the Jewish religion in the third and fourth centuries in Palestine is nothing other than a pure scholarly myth. Indeed, there is evidence that Jews invited

Gentile Christians to become Jews in order to avoid persecution. Lieberman argues compellingly that the Romans never forbade the practice of Judaism per se, but always only interdicted particular practices that otherwise interfered with Roman legal institutions. There was, therefore, never a crime involved in simply being a Jew, as there was in being a Christian. In both of the cases of Jewish martyrdom that we have read here, it was provocative teaching of Torah in public, understood as a potentially seditious activity (the production of the site for a "hidden transcript") that brought on the wrath of the Romans, and this even according to our half-legendary sources. Lieberman, "On Persecution," 217. This interpretation is echoed in Frend's clear definition that "Roman religion was a therefore less a matter of personal devotion than of national cult. Rome judged the religion of others from the same standpoint. 'Every people, Laelius, has its religion, and we have ours.' A *religio* was *licita* for a particular group on the basis of tribe or nationality and traditional practices, coupled with the proviso that its rites were not offensive to the Roman people or its gods." Frend, *Martyrdom and Persecution*, 106. That last proviso is, of course, vitally significant, and it is the particular offensiveness of individual practices that explains the Hadrianic persecution, which was not, as Lieberman has demonstrated, an attempt at extirpation of the Jewish religion, contra Frend, *Martyrdom and Persecution*, 227. This, then, does not imply the theory, discredited by G. E. M. de Ste. Croix in a celebrated paper, that Christians were persecuted for belonging to *collegia illicita*. De Ste. Croix, "Why Were the Early Christians Persecuted?" 17. It rather constitutes another version of the same author's positive claim, citing Gibbon, that "the Jews were a people which followed, the Christians a sect which deserted, the religion of their fathers." Ibid., 25.

139. And this text even fits the technical definition of a martyr act in that "the kernel is the authentic documentation of the legal hearing." Bowersock, *Martyrdom and Rome*, 27, referring to den Boeft in van Henten, *Die Entstehung der jüdischen Martyrologie*, 221. Pace Bowersock, *Martyrdom and Rome*, 37.

140. Lawlor and Oulton, *Eusebius*, 1: 365.

141. For a somewhat different evaluation of this passage, see Simon, *Verus Israel* 408. See also Baer, "Israel" (1961), 129–30 n. 133, and Satran, *Biblical Prophets*, 103–4.

142. Lieberman, "The Martyrs of Caesarea," 411. Lieberman even maintains that when Rabbi Aḥa, a Lyddan Rabbi, refers to the "martyrs of Lydda" who removed the "shame of Julian," that is, the shame of Jewish collaboration with a pagan, he means these very same Eusebian Christian martyrs. Ibid., 412–16.

143. Jan Assmann remarks the figure of Egypt in the Bible as the site of the original production of the binary opposition between true and false religion in

antiquity and as the site of the deconstruction of that opposition in modernity. Assmann, *Moses the Egyptian*. This double function of a memory (not a false memory and its true reconstruction) is precisely what I gesture toward here.

144. Dina Stein contributed this insight.

APPENDIX

1. Frend, *Martyrdom and Persecution*, 31.

2. Ibid., 41.

3. Ibid., 44.

4. Two caveats are in order. I use the term "Judeo-Christian" advisedly and specifically for those religious ideas and practices that Jews and Christians have developed in conversation with each other and not for a supposed common Judaic tradition superseded by Christianity.

I also would have no problem, in principle, accepting an identity between Socrates and Rabbi Akiva or Polycarp. My objection grows from what seems to me to be the palpable differences between the discourse about the Judeo-Christian martyrs and the discourse about Socrates, and our descriptions must capture these differences. This, Bowersock does well.

5. Frend, *Martyrdom and Persecution*, 55.

6. Pace ibid., 56.

7. In a future work tentatively entitled "Tertullian's Torah," I hope to test fairly persistent notions that Tertullian was heavily influenced by rabbinic texts, particularly in the production of his tractate on Idolatry.

8. Frend, *Martyrdom and Persecution*, 80.

9. Ibid., 83.

10. Of course, this is not peculiar to Frend, but in fact startlingly persistent even in very recent scholarship, for example Dehandschutter, "*The Martyrium Polycarpi*," 508. Dehandschutter blissfully, heedlessly, refers to "the precarious question of the relation between late Jewish and early Christian martyrology."

11. See, for example, his remarks about Jesus on 94, or his very positive description of the "tradition of social action inherited from Judaism," which, according to Frend, "was now contributing powerfully to the victory of the Church." Frend, *Martyrdom and Persecution*, 457.

12. Ibid., 362.

13. Pace ibid., 67.

14. Ibid., 332.

15. Ibid., 271–72.

16. Ibid., 259.

17. Lieu, *Image and Reality*, 91. See also Lieu, "Accusations of Jewish Persecution," 279–95.

18. See Baer, "Israel" (1961), 102–4 n. 80, for a discussion and earlier literature.

19. Frend, *Martyrdom and Persecution*, 295 n. 21.

20. Ibid., 323.

21. Ibid., 189.

22. Ibid., 334.

23. Ibid., 396. Frend's *The Rise of Christianity* can almost be read as a narrative of the gradual escape of the True Church from the Judaism in which it was unfortunately mired. Frend returns and returns to this theme in his massive and in many ways exemplary work.

Bibliography

Aarne, Antti, and Stith Thomson. *The Types of the Folktale: A Classification and Bibliography.* 2d ed. Folklore Fellows Communications, no. 3. Helsinki: Suomalainen Tiedeakatamia, 1987.

Adler, Rachel. "The Virgin in the Brothel and Other Anomalies: Character and Context in the Legend of Beruriah." *Tikkun* 3, no. 6 (1988).

Alexander, Philip S. "'The Parting of the Ways' from the Perspective of Rabbinic Judaism." In *Jews and Christians: The Parting of the Ways A.D. 70 to 135,* edited by James D. G. Dunn, 1–25. The Second Durham-Tübingen Research Symposium on Earliest Christianity and Judaism, Durham, September, 1989. Tübingen: J. C. B. Mohr (Paul Siebeck), 1991.

Alon, Gedaliah. *The Jews in Their Land in the Talmudic Age (70–640 C.E.).* Edited and translated by Gershon Levi. 2 vols. Jerusalem: Magnes Press, 1984.

Amat, Jacqueline. *Songes et visions: L'au-delà dans la littérature latine tardive.* Paris: Études Augustiniennes, 1985.

Anderson, Gary. "Celibacy or Consummation in the Garden? Reflections on Early Jewish and Christian Interpretations of the Garden of Eden." *Harvard Theological Review* 82, no. 2 (1989): 121–48.

Assmann, Jan. *Moses the Egyptian: The Memory of Egypt in Western Monotheism.* Cambridge, Mass.: Harvard University Press, 1997.

Athanasius. "Defense of His Flight." In *Nicene and Post-Nicene Fathers,* second series. Vol. 4. Edited by Alexander Roberts and James Donaldson. Oak Harbor, Wash.: Logos Research Systems, 1997.

Bach, Alice. *Women, Seduction, and Betrayal in Biblical Narrative.* Cambridge: Cambridge University Press, 1997.

Baer, Itzhaq [Yitzhaq]. "Israel, the Christian Church, and the Roman Empire" (in Hebrew). *Zion* 21 (1956): 1–49.

———. "Israel, the Christian Church, and the Roman Empire from the Time of Septimius Severus to the Edict of Toleration of A.D. 313." In *Studies in History*, edited by Alexander Fuks and Israel Halpern. Scripta Hierosolymitana 7, 79–147. Jerusalem: Magnes Press, 1961.

Baker, Cynthia. "Bodies, Boundaries, and Domestic Politics in a Late Ancient Marketplace." *Journal of Medieval and Early Modern Studies* 26, no. 3 (fall 1996): 391–418.

———. "Neighbor at the Door or Enemy at the Gate? Notes Toward a Rabbinic Topography of Self and Other." Paper presented at American Academy of Religion. New Orleans, 1996.

Bal, Mieke. *Murder and Difference: Gender, Genre, and Scholarship on Sisera's Death*. Indiana Studies in Biblical Literature. Bloomington: Indiana University Press, 1988.

Barnes, Timothy D. "Pre-Decian *Acta Martyrum*." *Journal of Theological Studies* 19 (1968): 509–31.

———. "Tertullian's *Scorpiace*." *Journal of Theological Studies*, n.s., 20, no. 1 (April 1969): 105–32.

Baron, Salo. *A Social and Religious History of the Jews*. Philadelphia: Jewish Publication Society, 1952.

Barton, Carlin. *Roman Honor: The Fire in the Bones*. Forthcoming. Berkeley: University of California Press.

———. "Savage Miracles: The Redemption of Lost Honor in Roman Society and the Sacrament of the Gladiator and the Martyr." *Representations*, no. 45 (winter 1994): 41–71.

Bauckham, R. J. *Jude and the Relatives of Jesus in the Early Church*. Edinburgh: T. & T. Clark, 1990.

Bauer, Walter. *Orthodoxy and Heresy in Earliest Christianity*. Edited by Robert A. Kraft and Gerhard Krodel. Translated by the Philadelphia Seminar on Christian Origins, with appendices by Georg Strecker. Philadelphia: Fortress Press, 1971.

Baumgarten, Albert I. "Literary Evidence for Jewish Christianity in the Galilee." In *The Galilee in Late Antiquity*, edited by Lee I. Levine, 39–50. New York: Jewish Theological Seminary of America, 1992.

Bedjan, Paul, ed. *Histoire de Mar Jabalaha, de trois autres patriarches, d'un prêtre et deux laïques, nestoriens*. Leipzig: Otto Harrassowitz, 1895.

Bhabha, Homi K. *The Location of Culture*. London: Routledge, 1994.

Biale, David. *Power and Powerlessness in Jewish History*. New York: Schocken, 1986.

Binns, John. *Ascetics and Ambassadors of Christ: The Monasteries of Palestine,*

314–631. Oxford Early Christian Studies. Oxford: Oxford University Press, Clarendon, 1994.

Bisbee, Gary A. *Pre-Decian Acts of Martyrs and Comentarii.* Harvard Dissertations in Religion, no. 22. Philadelphia: Fortress Press, 1988.

Blidstein, Gerald J. "Rabbis, Romans, and Martyrdom—Three Views." *Tradition* 21, no. 3 (fall 1984): 54–62.

Bokser, Baruch. "Wonder-Working and the Rabbinic Tradition: The Case of Hanina Ben Dosa." *Journal of Jewish Studies* 14 (1985): 42–92.

Bowersock, Glen W. *Fiction as History: Nero to Julian.* Sather Classical Lectures, 58. Berkeley: University of California Press, 1994.

———. *Martyrdom and Rome.* The Wiles Lectures Given at the Queen's University of Belfast. Cambridge: Cambridge University Press, 1995.

Boyarin, Daniel. *Carnal Israel: Reading Sex in Talmudic Culture.* The New Historicism: Studies in Cultural Poetics, vol. 25. Berkeley: University of California Press, 1993.

———. "A Contribution to the History of Martyrdom in Israel." In *Festschrift for Prof. H. Z. Dimitrovsky* (in Hebrew), edited by Menahem Hirshman, et al. Jerusalem: Magnes Press, 1999.

———. "A Corrected Reading of the New 'History of Jesus' Fragment" (in Hebrew). *Tarbiz* (1978).

———. "Gender." In *Critical Terms for the Study of Religion,* edited by Mark C. Taylor, 117–35. Chicago: University of Chicago Press, 1998.

———. "Homotopia: The Feminized Jewish Man and the Lives of Women in Late Antiquity." *differences* 7, no. 2 (summer 1995): 41–71.

———. *Intertextuality and the Reading of Midrash.* Bloomington: Indiana University Press, 1990.

———. "Jewish Masochism: Couvade, Castration, and Rabbis in Pain." *American Imago* 51, no. 1 (spring 1994): 3–36.

———. "Language Inscribed by History on the Bodies of Living Beings: Midrash and Martyrdom." *Representations,* no. 25 (winter 1989): 139–51.

———. "Masada or Yavneh?: Gender and the Arts of Jewish Resistance." In *Jews and Other Differences: The New Jewish Cultural Studies,* edited by Daniel Boyarin and Jonathan Boyarin, 306–29. Minneapolis: University of Minnesota Press, 1997.

———. "On the Emergence of the Aramaic Dialects." In *Essays in Historical Linguistics in Memory of J. Alexander Kerns,* edited by Yoël Arbeitman, 613–49. Amsterdam: Mouton, 1982.

———. "On the Status of the Tannaitic Midrashim." *Journal of the American Oriental Society* (1993).

———. "'This We Know to Be the Carnal Israel': Circumcision and the Erotic Life of God and Israel." *Critical Inquiry* 18, no. 2 (spring 1992): 474–506.

———. *Unheroic Conduct: The Rise of Heterosexuality and the Invention of the Jewish Man.* Berkeley: University of California Press, 1997.

Boyarin, Jonathan. *A Storyteller's Worlds: The Education of Shlomo Noble in Europe and America.* With a foreword by Sander L. Gilman. New York: Holmes & Meier, 1994.

Boyarin, Shamma. "No Horseplay Allowed!?" Unpublished paper. Berkeley, 1998. Photocopy.

Brakke, David. "'Outside the Places, Within the Truth': Athanasius of Alexandria and the Localization of the Holy." In *Pilgrimage and Holy Space in Late Antique Egypt (and Its Mediterranean Neighbors)*, edited by David Frankfurter. In press. Leiden: E. J. Brill.

———. "Passover and Particularity: Athanasius of Alexandria and the Jews." Paper presented at AAR Annual Meeting 1997. San Francisco, 1997. Photocopy.

Brock, Sebastian P., and Susan Ashbrook Harvey, trans. and eds. *Holy Women of the Syrian Orient.* 2d ed., updated with new preface. 1987. Transformations of the Classical Heritage 13. Berkeley: University of California Press, 1998.

Brown, Peter. *The Cult of the Saints: Its Rise and Function in Latin Christianity.* The Haskell Lectures on History of Religions. Chicago: University of Chicago Press, 1981.

———. *The Making of Late Antiquity.* The Carl Newell Jackson Lectures, 1976. Cambridge, Mass.: Harvard University Press, 1978.

———. *Power and Persuasion in Late Antiquity: Towards a Christian Empire.* Madison: University of Wisconsin Press, 1992.

———. *The Rise of Western Christendom.* The Making of Europe. Oxford: Blackwell, 1996.

Bruns, Gerald. "The Hermeneutics of Midrash." In *The Book and the Text: The Bible and Literary Theory*, edited by Regina Schwartz, 189–213. Oxford: Basil Blackwell, 1990.

Burns, J. Partout. "Cyprian's Eschatology: Explaining Divine Purpose." In *The Early Church in Its Context: Essays in Honor of Everett Ferguson*, edited by Abraham J. Malherbe, Frederick W. Norris, and James W. Thompson. Supplements to Novum Testamentum 90, 59–73. Leiden: E. J. Brill, 1998.

Burrus, Virginia. *Begotten, Not Made: Conceiving Manhood in Late Antiquity.* Forthcoming. Stanford: Stanford University Press, 2000.

———. *Chastity as Autonomy: Women in the Stories of the Apocryphal Acts.* Studies in Women and Religion. New York: Edwin Mellen Press, 1987.

———. "'Equipped for Victory': Ambrose and the Gendering of Orthodoxy." *Journal of Early Christian Studies* 4, no. 4 (winter 1996): 461–75.

———. *The Making of a Heretic: Gender, Authority, and the Priscillianist Controversy.* Transformations of the Ancient World. Berkeley: University of California Press, 1995.

———. "The Male Ascetic in Female Space: Alienated Strategies of Self-Definition in the Writings of Sulpicius Severus." Paper presented at the Society for Biblical Literature / American Academy of Religion, 1992.

———. "Reading Agnes: The Rhetoric of Gender in Ambrose and Prudentius." *Journal of Early Christian Studies* 3, no. 1 (spring 1995): 25–46.

———. "Torture and Travail: Producing the Christian Martyr." In *Feminist Companion to the Patristic Period*, edited by A. J. Levine. Forthcoming. Feminist Companions to Biblical Studies. Sheffield: Sheffield University Press.

———. "Word and Flesh: The Bodies and Sexuality of Ascetic Women in Christian Antiquity." *Journal of Feminist Studies in Religion* 10, no. 1 (spring 1994): 27–51.

Cameron, Averil. *Christianity and the Rhetoric of Empire: The Development of Christian Discourse.* Berkeley: University of California Press, 1991.

Cassel, Paulus. "Caricaturnamen." In *Aus Literatur und Geschichte*, 323–47. Berlin: Verlag von Wilhelm Friedrich, 1885.

Castelli, Elizabeth A. "Imperial Reimaginings of Christian Origins: Epic in Prudentius's Poem." In *Reimagining Christian Origins: A Colloquium Honoring Burton L. Mack*, edited by Elizabeth A. Castelli and Hal Taussig, 173–84. Valley Forge, Pa.: Trinity Press International, 1996.

———. "'I Will Make Mary Male': Pieties of the Body and Gender Transformation of Christian Women in Late Antiquity." In *Body Guards: The Cultural Politics of Ambiguity*, edited by Julia Epstein and Kristina Straub, 29–49. New York: Routledge, 1991.

———. "Virginity and Its Meaning for Women's Sexuality in Early Christianity." *Journal of Feminist Studies in Religion* 2 (1986): 61–88.

———. *Visions and Voyeurism: Holy Women and the Politics of Sight in Early Christianity.* Vol. 2 of *Protocol of the Colloquy of the Center for Hermeneutical Studies, New Series*. Edited by Christopher Ocker. Berkeley, Ca.: Center for Hermeneutical Studies, 1995.

Chadwick, Henry, trans. and ed. *Origen: Contra Celsum.* Cambridge: Cambridge University Press, 1965.

Charlesworth, James H. *The Old Testament Pseudepigrapha.* 2 vols. Garden City, N.J.: Doubleday, 1985.

Chitty, Derwas J. *The Desert a City: An Introduction to the Study of Egyptian and Palestinian Monasticism Under the Christian Empire.* 1966. Crestwood, N.Y.: St. Validimir's Seminary Press, 1995.

Clark, Elizabeth A. "Ascetic Renunciation and Feminine Advancement: A Paradox of Late Ancient Christianity." In *Ascetic Piety and Women's Faith: Essays in Late Ancient Christianity,* 175–208. New York: Edwin Mellen Press, 1986.

———. "Response." In *Visions and Voyeurism: Holy Women and the Politics of Sight in Early Christianity.* Vol. 2 of *Protocol of the Colloquy of the Center for Hermeneutical Studies, New Series,* by Elizabeth Castelli. Berkeley, Ca.: Center for Hermeneutical Studies, 1995.

———. "Sex, Shame, and Rhetoric; en-Gendering Early Christian Ethics." *Journal of the American Academy of Religion* 59 (1991): 221–45.

———. *Women in the Early Church.* Message of the Fathers of the Church, vol. 13. Wilmington, Delaware: Michael Glazier, 1983.

Clark, Gillian. "Bodies and Blood: Late Antique Debate on Martyrdom, Virginity and Resurrection." In *Changing Bodies, Changing Meanings: Studies on the Human Body in Antiquity,* edited by Dominic Montserrat, 99–115. London: Routledge, 1998.

Clarke, G. W., trans. and ed. *Letters 1–27.* Vol. 1 of *The Letters of St. Cyprian of Carthage.* Ancient Christian Writers: The Works of the Fathers in Translation, no. 43. New York: Newman Press, 1984.

———, trans. and ed. *Letters 55–66.* Vol. 3 of *The Letters of St. Cyprian of Carthage.* Ancient Christian Writers: The Works of the Fathers in Translation, no. 46. New York: Newman Press, 1986.

Clements, Ruth Anne. "*Peri Pascha*: Passover and the Displacement of Jewish Interpretation Within Origen's Exegesis." Dissertation, Harvard Divinity School, 1997. Photocopy.

Cohen, Aryeh. "Towards an Erotics of Martyrdom." *The Journal of Jewish Thought and Philosophy* 7 (1998): 227–56.

Cohen, Gerson D. "Esau as Symbol in Early Medieval Thought." In *Jewish Medieval and Renaissance Studies,* edited by Alexander Altmann, 19–48. Cambridge, Mass.: Harvard University Press, 1967.

Cohen, Shaye J. D. "Ioudaios: 'Judean' and 'Jew' in Susanna, First Macabees, and Seccond Macabees." In *Geschicte—Tradition—Reflexion: Festschrift für Martin Hengel zum 70. Geburtstag,* edited by H. Cancik, H. Lichtenberger, and P. Schäfer, 1: 211–20. Tübingen: Mohr Siebeck, 1996.

———. "Menstruants and the Sacred in Judaism and Christianity." In *Ancient History, Women's History*, edited by Sarah Pomeroy, 273–99. Chapel Hill: University of North Carolina Press, 1991.

———. "The Significance of Yavneh: Pharisees, Rabbis, and the End of Jewish Sectarianism. *Hebrew Union College Annual* 55 (1984): 27–53

———. "'Those Who Say They Are Jews and Are Not': How Do You Know a Jew in Antiquity When You See One?" In *Diasporas in Antiquity*, edited by Shaye J. D. Cohen and Ernest S. Frerichs, 1–45. Brown Judaic Studies 288. Atlanta: Scholars Press, 1993.

———. "A Virgin Defiled: Some Rabbinic and Christian Views on the Origins of Heresy." *Union Seminary Quarterly Review* 36, no. 1 (fall 1980): 1–11.

Cooper, Kate. "Apostles, Ascetic Women, and Questions of Audience: New Reflections on the Rhetoric of Gender in the *Apocryphal Acts*." Paper presented at the Society for Biblical Literature / American Aacademy of Religion. Atlanta, 1992.

———. "Insinuations of Womanly Influence: An Aspect of the Christianization of the Roman Aristocracy." *Journal of Roman Studies* 82 (1992): 150–64.

———. *The Virgin and the Bride*. Cambridge, Mass.: Harvard University Press, 1996.

Corley, Kathleen E. "Feminist Myths of Christian Origins." In *Reimagining Christian Origins: A Colloquium Honoring Burton L. Mack*, edited by Elizabeth A. Castelli and Hal Taussig, 51–67. Valley Forge, Pa.: Trinity Press International, 1996.

Culbertson, Philip L. *A Word Fitly Spoken: Contest, Transmission, and Adoption of the Parables of Jesus*. SUNY Series in Religious Studies. Albany: SUNY Press, 1995.

Davies, P. R., and Bruce Chilton. "The Aqedah: A Revised Tradition History." *Catholic Biblical Quarterly* 40 (1978): 514–46.

Davies, Stevan. *The Revolt of the Widows: The Social World of the Apocryphal Acts*. Carbondale: University of Illinois Press, 1980.

Davis, Laurie. "Virgins in Brothels: A Different Feminist Reading of Beruriah." Paper presented at the Graduate Theological Union. Berkeley, 1994.

Dawson, David. *Allegorical Readers and Cultural Revision in Ancient Alexandria*. Berkeley: University of California Press, 1992.

———. "Why Were the Early Christians Persecuted?" *Past and Present* 26 (1963): 6–38.

Dehandschutter, Boudewijn. "Le Martyre de Polycarpe et le développement de la conception du martyr au deuxième siècle." *Studia Patristica* 17 (1982): 659–68.

———. "*The Martyrium Polycarpi*: A Century of Research." In *Aufstieg und Niedergang der Römischen Welt.* Part 2: Principate. Volume 27.1, 485–522. Berlin: Walter de Gruyter, 1993.

Deissmann, Adolf. *Light from the Ancient East: The New Testament Illustrated by Recently Discovered Texts of the Graeco-Roman World.* 4th ed. Translated by Lionel R. M. Strachan. London: Houlder and Stoughton, 1927.

de Lange, Nicholas. *Origen and the Jews: Studies in Jewish-Christian Relations in Third-Century Palestine.* Cambridge: Cambridge University Press, 1976.

den Boeft, Jan, and Jan Bremmer. "Notiunculae martyrologicae." *Vigiliae Christianae* 35 (1981): 43–56.

———. "Notiunculae Martyrologicae II." *Vigiliae Christianae* 36 (1982): 383–402.

———. "Notiunculae Martyrologicae III. Some Observations on the Martyria of Polycarp and Pionius." *Vigiliae Christianae* 39 (1985): 110–30.

de Ste. Croix, G. E. M. *The Class Struggle in the Ancient Greek World: From the Archaic Age to the Arab Conquests.* Ithaca: Cornell University Press, 1981.

Detienne, Marcel, and Jean-Pierre Vernant. *Cunning Intelligence in Greek Culture and Society.* Translated by Janet Lloyd. European Philosophy and the Human Sciences. Sussex: Harvester Press, 1978.

Doran, Robert. "The Martyr: A Synoptic of the Mother and Her Seven Sons." In *Ideal Figures in Ancient Judaism: Profiles and Paradigms,* edited by John J. Collins and George W. E. Nickelsburg, 189–221. Septuagint and Cognate Studies 12. Chico, Ca.: Scholars Press, 1980.

Douglas, Mary. *Purity and Danger: An Analysis of Concepts of Pollution and Taboo.* 1969. London: Routledge and Kegan Paul, 1978.

Drijvers, H. J. W. "Jews and Christians at Edessa." *Journal of Jewish Studies* 36, no. 1 (1985): 88–102.

Droge, Arthur J., and James D. Tabor. *A Noble Death: Suicide and Martyrdom Among Christians and Jews in Antiquity.* San Francisco: Harper, 1992.

Dunn, Geoffrey D. "Tertullian and Rebekah: A Re-Reading of an 'Anti-Jewish' Argument in Early Christian Literature." *Vigiliae Christianae* 52, no. 2 (May 1998): 119–45.

Edwards, Catherine. *The Politics of Immorality in Ancient Rome.* Cambridge: Cambridge University Press, 1993.

Ehrman, Bart D. *The Orthodox Corruption of Scripture: The Effect of Early Christological Controversies on the Text of the New Testament.* Oxford: Oxford University Press, 1993.

Elm, Susanna. *"Virgins of God": The Making of Asceticism in Late Antiquity.* Oxford Classical Monographs. Oxford: Oxford University Press, Clarendon, 1994.

Elsner, Jas. "The Origins of the Icon: Pilgrimage, Religion and Visual Culture in the Roman East as 'Resistance' to the Centre." In *The Early Roman Empire in the East,* edited by Susan E. Alcock. Oxbow Monograph 95, 178–99. Oxford: Oxbow Books, 1997.

Eusebius. *The Ecclesiastical History.* Translated by Kirsopp Lake. 2 vols. 1925. Loeb Classical Library. Cambridge, Mass.: Harvard University Press, 1965.

Even-Zohar, Itamar. *Polysystem Studies* (special issue). *Poetics Today* 11, no.1 (1990).

Finkelstein, Louis, ed. *Akiba: Scholar, Saint and Martyr.* 1936. New York: Macmillan, Atheneum, 1964.

———. *Sifre on Deuteronomy.* 1939. New York: The Jewish Theological Seminary of America, 1969.

Fischel, H. A. "Martyr and Prophet." *Jewish Quarterly Review* 37 (1947): 265–80, 363–86.

Fishbane, Michael. *The Kiss of God: Spiritual and Mystical Death in Judaism.* The Samuel and Althea Stroum Lectures in Jewish Studies. Seattle: University of Washington Press, 1994.

Flusser, David. *Judaism and the Sources of Christianity.* Jerusalem: Magnes Press, 1988.

Fonrobert, Charlotte. "The Concept of Jewish Christianity as Retrospective Fallacy: The Case of the Didascalia." *Journal of Early Christian Studies.* Forthcoming.

———. *Menstrual Purity: Reconstructing Biblical Gender in Christianity and Rabbinic Judaism.* Stanford: Stanford University Press, 2000.

———. "Women's Bodies, Women's Blood: Politics of Gender in Rabbinic Literature." Dissertation, Graduate Theological Union, 1995. Microfilm.

Foucault, Michel. *The Archaeology of Knowledge and the Discourse on Language.* Translated by A. M. Sheridan Smith. New York: Harper & Row, 1972.

Fränkel, Yonah. *Readings in the Spiritual World of the Stories of the Aggada* (in Hebrew). Tel-Aviv: United Kibbutz Press, 1981.

Frend, W. H. C. *The Early Church.* Minneapolis: Fortress Press, 1965.

———. *Martyrdom and Persecution in the Early Church: A Study of a Conflict from the Maccabees to Donatus.* Garden City, N.Y.: Doubleday, 1967.

———. *The Rise of Christianity.* Philadelphia: Fortress Press, 1984.

Friedländer, M. *Patristische und Talmudische Studien.* 1868. Farnborough, England: Gregg International, 1972.

Georgi, Dieter. "The Early Church: Internal Migration or New Religion." *Harvard Theological Review* 88 (1995): 35–68.

Gero, Stephen. "Jewish Polemic in the Martyrium Pionii and a 'Jesus' Passage from the Talmud." *Journal of Jewish Studies* 29 (1978): 164–68.

———. "The Stern Master and His Wayward Disciple: A 'Jesus' Story in the Talmud and in Christian Hagiography." *Journal for the Study of Judaism* 25, no. 2 (1994): 287–311.

———. "With Walter Bauer on the Tigris: Encratite Orthodoxy and Libertine Heresy in Syro-Mesopotamian Christianity." In *Nag Hammadi, Gnosticism, and Early Christianity*, edited by Charles W. Hedrick and Robert Hodgson, 287–307. Peabody, Mass.: Hendrickson, 1986.

Gilat, Yitzhak D. *R. Eliezer Ben Hyrcanus: A Scholar Outcast.* Bar-Ilan Studies in Near Eastern Languages and Culture. Ramat Gan: Bar-Ilan University Press, 1984.

Gleason, Maud W. *Making Men: Sophists and Self-Presentation in Ancient Rome.* Princeton: Princeton University Press, 1995.

Goldberg, Arnold Xavier. "Das Martyrium des Rabbi Aqiva. Zur Komposition einer Märtyrerzählung (bBer 61b)." *Frankfurter Judaistische Beiträge* 12 (1984): 1–82.

Goldin, Judah, ed. and trans. *The Song at the Sea: Being a Commentary on a Commentary in Two Parts.* New Haven: Yale University Press, 1971.

Goldstein, Jonathan A., trans. and ed. *II Macabees; A New Translation with Introduction and Commentary.* The Anchor Bible 41a. New York: Doubleday, 1983,

Goodman, Martin. *Mission and Conversion: Proselytizing in the Religious History of the Roman Empire.* Oxford: Oxford University Press, Clarendon, 1994.

———. "Nerva, the *Fiscus Judaicus* and Jewish Identity." *Journal of Roman Studes* 79 (1989): 40–44.

———. Review of *Christianity and Rabbinic Judaism*, edited by Hershal Shanks. *Journal of Jewish Studies* 44, no. 2 (autumn 1993): 313–14.

Grant, Robert M. *Greek Apologists of the Second Century.* Philadelphia: Westminster Press, 1988.

Gray, Patrick T. R. "'The Select Fathers': Canonizing the Patristic Past." *Studia Patristica* 23 (1989): 21–36.

Green, William Scott. "Palestinian Holy Men: Charismatic Leadership and Roman Tradition." In *Aufstieg und Niedergang der Römischen Welt II, Principat 19,2*, edited by Wolfgang Haase, 619–47. Berlin: Walter de Gruyther, 1979.

Gry, L. "Hénoch X, 19 et les belles promesses de Papias." *Revue biblique* 53 (1946): 197–206.

———. "Le Papias des belles promesses messianiques." *Vivre et penser* 3 (1944): 112–24.

Guha, Ranajit. "Dominance Without Hegemony and Its Historiography." In *Subaltern Studies VI*, edited by Ranajit Guha, 210–309. Delhi: Oxford University Press, 1989.

Guttmann, Alexander. "The Significance of Miracles for Talmudic Judaism." *Hebrew Union College Annual* 20 (1947): 363–406.

Hadas, Moses, ed. and trans. *The Third and Fourth Books of Maccabees*. 1953. Dropsie College Edition Jewish Apocryphal Literature. New York: Ktav, 1976.

Hadas-Lebel, Mireille. "Jacob et Esaü ou Israël et Rome dans le Talmud et le Midrash." *Revue de l'histoire des religions* 201 (1984): 369–92.

Harrison, Verna E.F. "A Gender Reversal in Gregory of Nyssa's First Homily on the Song of Songs." *Studia Patristica* 27 (1993): 34–38.

———. "Receptacle Imagery in St. Gregory of Nyssa's Anthropology." *Studia Patristica* 22 (1989): 23–27.

Hasan-Rokem, Galit. "Narratives in Dialogue: A Folk Literary Perspective on Interreligious Contacts in the Holy Land in Rabbinic Literature of Late Antiquity." In *Sharing the Sacred: Religious Contacts and Conflicts in the Holy Land First-Fifteenth CE*, edited by Guy Stroumsa and Arieh Kofsky, 109–29. Jerusalem: Yad Ben Zvi, 1998.

———. *The Web of Life—Folklore in Rabbinic Literature: The Palestinian Aggadic Midrash Eikha Rabba* (in Hebrew). Tel Aviv: Am Oved, 1996.

Hayes, Christine. *Between the Babylonian and Palestinian Talmuds*. Oxford: Oxford University Press, 1997.

Herford, R. Travers. *Christianity in Talmud and Midrash*. 1903. New York: Ktav, 1978.

Herr, Moshe David. "Persecutions and Martyrdom in Hadrian's Days." In *Studies in History*, edited by David Asheri and Israel Shatzman. Scripta Hierosolymitana, vol. 23, 85–125. Jerusalem: Magnes Press, 1972.

Hirshman, Marc G. "Midrash Qohelet Rabbah." Dissertation, Jewish Theological Seminary, 1982.

———. *A Rivalry of Genius: Jewish and Christian Biblical Interpretation in Late Antiquity*. Translated by Batya Stein. SUNY Series in Judaica: Hermeneutics, Mysticism, and Religion. Albany: State University of New York Press, 1996.

Holl, Karl. "Die Vorstellung vom Märtyrer und die Märtyrer-Akte in ihrer geschichtlichen Entwicklung." In *Gesammelte Aufsätze zur Kirchengeschichte*. Vol. 2. *Der Osten*, 68–102. Tübingen: Mohr, 1928.

Hopkins, Keith. "Christian Number and Its Implications." *Journal of Early Christian Studies* 6, no. 2 (1998): 185–226.

———. "Novel Evidence for Roman Slavery." *Past and Present* 138 (1993).

Huber, Wolfgang. *Passa und Ostern: Untersuchengen zur Osterfeier der alten Kirche*. BZNW 35. Berlin: Topelmann, 1969.

Irenaeus. *Adversus haereses*. In *Ante-Nicene Fathers*. Vol. 1. Edited by Alexander Roberts and James Donaldson. Oak Harbor, Wash.: Logos Research Systems, 1997.

Janssen, L. F. "'Superstitio' and the Persecution of the Christians." *Vigiliae Christianae* 33 (1979): 131–59.

Jardine, Alice A. *Gynesis: Configurations of Woman and Modernity*. Ithaca: Cornell University Press, 1985.

Jerome. *Correspondence*. Edited by Isidorus Hilberg. Corpus Scriptorum Ecclesiasticorum Latinorum. Vienna: Verlag der Osterreichischen Akademie der Wissenschaften, 1996.

Jones, F. Stanley. *An Ancient Jewish Christian Source on the History of Christianity: Pseudo-Clementine Recognitions 1.27–71*. Texts and Translations: Christian Apocrypha Series. Atlanta: Scholars Press, 1995.

Joyce, James. *Ulysses*. 1914. New York: Random House, 1961.

Justin Martyr. *The First and Second Apologies*. Ancient Christian Writers: The Works of the Fathers in Translation, no. 56. Mahwah, N.J.: Paulist Press, 1997.

Kalmin, Richard. "Christians and Heretics in Rabbinic Literature of Late Antiquity." *Harvard Theological Review* 87, no. 2 (April 1994): 155–69.

Kellermann, Ulrich. "Das Danielbuch und die Martyrtheologie der Auferstehung." In *Die Entstehung der jüdischen Martyrologie*, edited by J. W. van Henten, 51–75. Leiden: E. J. Brill, 1989.

Kimelman, Reuven. "Birkat Ha-Minim and the Lack of Evidence for an Anti-Christian Jewish Prayer in Late Antiquity." In *Aspects of Judaism in the Greco-Roman Period*, edited by E. P. Sanders, Albert I. Baumgarten, and Alan Mendelson. Jewish and Christian Self-Definition, vol. 2, 226–44; 391–403. Philadelphia: Fortress Press, 1981.

———. "R. Yoḥanan and Origen on the Song of Songs: A Third-Century Jewish-Christian Disputation." *Harvard Theological Review* 73, no. 3–4 (July–October 1980): 567–95.

King, Karen L. "Gnosticism as Heresy." Forthcoming.

Kinzig, Wolfram. "'Non-Separation': Closeness and Co-Operation Between

Jews and Christians in the Fourth Century." *Vigiliae Christianae* 45, no. 1 (1991): 27–53.

Koester, Helmut. "Gnomai Diaforoi: The Origin and Nature of Diversification in the History of Early Christianity." *Harvard Theological Review* 58 (1965): 279–318.

Kofsky, Aryeh. "Mamre: A Case of a Regional Cult?" In *Sharing the Sacred: Religious Contacts and Conflicts in the Holy Land First-Fifteenth CE*, edited by Guy Stroumsa and Arieh Kofsky, 19–30. Jerusalem: Yad Ben Zvi, 1998.

Koltun-Fromm, Naomi. "Psalm 22's Christological Interpretive Tradition in Light of Christian Anti-Jewish Polemic." *Journal of Early Christian Studies* 6, no. 1 (spring 1998): 37–57.

Konstan, David. "Acts of Love: A Narrative Pattern in the Apocryphal Acts." *Journal of Early Christian Studies* 6, no. 1 (spring 1998): 15–36.

Kraft, Robert A., translation and commentary. *Barnabas and the Didache*. Vol. 3 of *The Apostolic Fathers: A New Translation and Commentary*. Edited by Robert Grant. New York: Thomas Nelson, 1965.

Krauss, Samuel. "The Jews in the Works of the Church Fathers." *Jewish Quarterly Review* 5–6 (1892–93): 122–57, 225–61.

Lauterbach, Jacob Z. "Jesus in the Talmud." In *Rabbinic Essays*, 473–570. 1951. New York: Ktav, 1973.

Lawlor, Hugh Jackson, and John Ernest Leonard Oulton, trans. and eds. *Eusebius, Bishop of Caesarea, the Ecclesiastical History and the Martyrs of Palestine*. 2 vols. London: Society for Promoting Christian Knowledge, 1927.

Le Boulluec, Alain. *La notion d'hérésie dans la littérature grecque IIᵉ–IIIᵉ siècles*. 2 vols. Paris: Études Augustiniennes, 1985.

Levine, Amy-Jill. "Diaspora as Metaphor: Bodies and Boundaries in the Book of Tobit." In *Diaspora Jews and Judaism: Essays in Honor and, in Dialogue with, A. Thomas Kraabel*, edited by J. Andrew Overman and Robert S. MacLennan. South Florida Studies in the History of Judaism, 105–18. Atlanta: Scholars Press, 1992.

Levine, Lee I. *Caesarea Under Roman Rule*. Studies in Judaism in Late Antiquity 7. Leiden: E. J. Brill, 1975.

Levinson, Joshua. "Bloody Fictions" (in Hebrew). *Tarbiz*. Forthcoming.

L'Huillier, Peter. *The Church of the Ancient Councils: The Disciplinary Work of the First Four Ecumenical Councils*. Crestwood, N.Y.: St. Vladimir's Seminary Press, 1996.

Licht, Jacob. "Taxo on the Apocalyptic Doctrine of Vengeance." *Journal of Jewish Studies* 12 (1961): 95–103.

Lieberman, Saul. "The Martyrs of Caesarea." *Annuaire de l'institut de philologie et d'histoire orientales et slaves* 7 (1939–44): 395–446.

———. "Palestine in the Third and Fourth Centuries." In *Texts and Studies.* 1946, 112–77. New York: Ktav, 1974.

———. "On Persecution of the Jewish Religion" (in Hebrew). In *Salo Wittmayer Baron Jubilee Volume: Hebrew Section*, 213–45. Jerusalem: American Academy for Jewish Research, 1974.

———. "Roman Legal Institutions in Early Rabbinics and in the *Acta Martyrum.*" In *Texts and Studies*, 57–111. 1944. New York: Ktav, 1974.

———. *Texts and Studies.* New York: Ktav, 1974.

Lieu, Judith. "Accusations of Jewish Persecution in Early Christian Sources, with Particular Reference to Justin Martyr and the *Martyrdom of Polycarp.*" In *Tolerance and Intolerance in Early Judaism and Christianity*, edited by Graham N. Stanton and Guy G. Stroumsa, 279–95. Cambridge: Cambridge University Press, 1998.

———. *Image and Reality: The Jews in the World of the Christians in the Second Century.* Edinburgh: T & T Clark, 1996.

Loraux, Nicole. *Tragic Ways of Killing a Woman.* Translated by Anthony Forster. Cambridge, Mass.: Harvard University Press, 1987.

MacDonald, Dennis Ronald. *The Legend and the Apostle: The Battle for Paul in Story and Canon.* Philadelphia: Westminster, 1983.

Maier, Harry O. "Purity and Danger in Polycarp's Epistle to the Philippians: The Sin of Valens in Social Perspective." *Journal of Early Christian Studies* 1, no. 3 (1993): 229–47.

Maier, Johann. *Jesus von Nazareth in der talmudischen Überlieferung.* Darmstadt: Wissenschaftliche Buchgesellschaft, 1978.

Malamud, Martha. *A Poetics of Transformation: Prudentius and Classical Mythology.* Ithaca: Cornell University Press, 1989.

Marcus, Ivan G. *Rituals of Childhood: Jewish Acculturation in Medieval Europe.* New Haven: Yale University Press, 1996.

Markus, Robert A. *The End of Ancient Christianity.* Cambridge: Cambridge University Press, 1990.

Marmorstein, Arthur. "Judaism and Christianity in the Middle of the Third Century." *Hebrew Union College Annual* 10 (1937): 223–65.

McCue, James F. "Orthodoxy and Heresy: Walter Bauer and the Valentinians." *Vigiliae Christianae* 33 (1979): 118–30.

McGuckin, John H. "Caesarea Maritima as Origen Knew It." In *Origeniana Quinta: Papers of the Fifth International Origen Congress, Boston College,*

14–18 August 1989, edited by Robert J. Daley. BETL 105, 3–25. Louvain: Louvain University Press, Peeters, 1992.

Meeks, Wayne A., and Robert L. Wilken. *Jews and Christians in Antioch in the First Four Centuries of the Common Era.* SBL Sources for Biblical Study 13. Missoula, Mont.: Scholars Press, 1978.

Meyer, Michael W. "Making Mary Male: The Categories 'Male' and 'Female' in the Gospel of Thomas." *New Testament Studies* 31 (1985): 554–70.

Michaelson, Jay. "Antilawyerism/Antisemitism." Master's thesis, Religious Studies, Hebrew University, 1998. Photocopy.

Momigliano, Arnoldo. "Popular Religious Beliefs and the Roman Historians." *Studies in Church History* 8 (1972): 1–18.

Moore, Stephen D., and Janice Capel Anderson. "Taking It Like a Man: Masculinity in 4 Maccabees." *Journal of Biblical Literature* 117, no. 2 (summer 1998): 249–73.

Mühlenberg, Ekkehard. "The Martyr's Death and Its Literary Presentation." *Studia Patristica* 29 (1997): 85–93.

Musurillo, Herbert, ed. and trans. *Acts of the Christian Martyrs.* Oxford: Oxford University Press, 1972.

Neusner, Jacob. *Eliezer Ben Hyrcanus: The Tradition and the Man.* 2 vols. Leiden: E. J. Brill, 1973.

———. *Judaism and Christianity in the Age of Constantine: History, Messiah, Israel, and the Initial Confrontation.* Chicago Studies in the History of Judaism. Chicago: University of Chicago Press, 1987.

———. *Why No Gospels in Talmudic Judaism?* Brown Judaic Studies, no. 135. Atlanta: Scholars Press, 1988.

Niditch, Susan. *Underdogs and Tricksters: A Prelude to Biblical Folklore.* San Francisco: Harper & Row, 1987.

Odom, R. L. *Sabbath and Sunday in Early Christianity.* Washington, D.C.: Review and Herald, 1977.

O'Meara, John J., trans. and ed. *Prayer: Exhortation to Martyrdom.* In *Origen.* Ancient Christian Writers: The Works of the Fathers in Translation, no. 19. New York: Newman Press, 1954.

Ophir, Adi. "Victims Come First." Paper presented at Berman Center for Jewish Studies. Lehigh, Pa., 1994.

Oppenheimer, Abraham. *The Am Ha-ʔaretz: A Study in the Social History of the Jewish People.* Leiden: E. J. Brill, 1977.

Origen. *Origen, The Song of Songs: Commentary and Homilies.* Translated by R. P. Lawson. Westminster, Md.: Newman Press, 1957.

Pardes, Ilana. "Beyond Genesis 3." *Hebrew University Studies in Literature and the Arts* 17 (1989): 161–87.

———. *The Biography of Ancient Israel.* Berkeley: University of California Press, 1999.

———. *Countertraditions in the Bible: A Feminist Approach.* Cambridge, Mass.: Harvard University Press, 1992.

Patterson, L. "Origin of the Name Panthera." *Journal of Theological Studies* 19 (1918).

Perkins, Judith. *The Suffering Self: Pain and Narrative Representation in the Early Christian Era.* London: Routledge, 1995.

Perler, Othmar. "Das vierter Makkabäerbuch: Ignatius von Antiochien und die ältesten Märtyrerberichte." *Rivista Di Archeologia Cristiana* 25 (1949): 47–72.

Petruccione, John. "The Portrait of St. Eulalia of Mérida in Prudentius' *Peristephanon.*" *Analecta Bollandiana* 108 (1990): 81–104.

Pliny. *Pliny the Younger: Letters and Panegyricus.* Translated by Betty Radice. 2 vols. Loeb Classical Library. Cambridge, Mass.: Harvard University Press, 1969.

Porton, Gary G. *The Stranger Within Your Gates: Converts and Conversion in Rabbinic Literature.* Chicago Studies in the History of Judaism. Chicago: University of Chicago Press, 1994.

Pritz, Ray A. *Nazarene Jewish Christianity: From the End of the New Testament Period Until Its Disappearance in the Fourth Century.* Jerusalem: The Magnes Press, 1992.

Prudentius. *The Poems of Prudentius.* Translated by Sister M. Clement Eagen, C.C.V.I. The Fathers of the Church: A New Translation. Washington, D.C.: Catholic University of America Press, 1962.

Rajak, Tessa. "Dying for the Law: The Martyr's Portrait in Jewish-Greek Literature." In *Portraits: Biographical Representation in the Greek and Latin Literature of the Roman Empire,* edited by M. J. Edwards and Simon Swain, 39–67. Oxford: Oxford University Press, Clarendon, 1997.

———. "The Jewish Community and Its Boundaries." In *The Jews Among Pagans and Christians in the Roman Empire,* edited by Judith Lieu, John North, and Tessa Rajak, 9–28. London: Routledge, 1992.

Ramsey, Boniface. *Ambrose.* The Early Church Fathers. New York: Routledge, 1997.

Regnault, L. "Les Apotegmes des pères en Palestine aux Ve–VIe siècles." *Irénikon* 54 (1981): 320–30.

Reiner, Elchanan. "From Joshua to Jesus: The Transformation of a Biblical Story to a Local Myth: A Chapter in the Religious Life of the Galilean Jew." In *Sharing the Sacred: Religious Contacts and Conflicts in the Holy Land First-Fifteenth CE*, edited by Guy Stroumsa and Arieh Kofsky, 223–71. Jerusalem: Yad Ben Zvi, 1998.

Richlin, Amy. *The Garden of Priapus: Sexuality and Aggression in Roman Humor*. 2d ed. New York: Oxford University Press, 1992.

Rives, J. B. *Religion and Authority in Roman Carthage from Augustus to Constantine*. Oxford: Oxford University Press, Clarendon, 1995.

Robert, Louis. *Le martyre de Pionios*. Edited by Glen. W. Bowersock and C. P. Jones. Washington, D.C.: Dunbarton Oaks Research Library, 1994.

Rokeah, David. "Ben Stara is Ben Pantera" (in Hebrew). *Tarbiz* 39 (1969): 9–18.

Rosaldo, Michelle. "Toward an Anthropology of Self and Feeling." In *Culture Theory: Essays on Mind, Self and Emotions*, edited by Richard A. Shweder and Robert A. LeVine, 137–57. Cambridge: Cambridge University Press, 1984.

Roy, Parama. *Indian Traffic: Identities in Question in Colonial and Postcolonial India*. Berkeley: University of California Press, 1998.

Rubenstein, Jeffrey L. "Torah, Shame, and the Oven of Akhnai (Bava Mesia 59a-B)." *Journal of Jewish Thought and Philosophy*. Forthcoming.

Rubin, Zeev. "Porphyrius of Gaza and the Conflict Between Christianity and Paganism in Southern Palestine." In *Sharing the Sacred: Religious Contacts and Conflicts in the Holy Land First–Fifteenth CE*, edited by Guy Stroumsa and Arieh Kofsky, 31–66. Jerusalem: Yad Ben Zvi, 1998.

Ruether, Rosemary Radford. "Judaism and Christianity: Two Fourth-Century Religions." *Sciences Religieuses / Studies in Religion* 2 (1972): 1–10.

Safrai, Shemuel. "Martyrdom in the Teachings of the Tannaim." In *Sjaloom*, edited by T. C. de Kruijf and H. v. d. Sandt, 145–64. Arnheim, 1983.

Sagi, Avi. *The Meaning of Halakhic Discourse*. Translated by Batya Stein. Forthcoming.

Salisbury, Joyce. *Church Fathers, Independent Virgins*. London: Verso, 1991.

———. *Perpetua's Passion: The Death and Memory of a Young Roman Woman*. New York: Routledge, 1997.

Sandmel, Samuel. *Judaism and Christian Beginnings*. New York: Oxford University Press, 1978.

Satlow, Michael L. "'Try to Be a Man': The Rabbinic Construction of Masculinity." *Harvard Theological Review* 89 (1996): 19–40.

Satran, David. *Biblical Prophets in Byzantine Palestine: Reassessing the Lives of the Prophets.* Studia in Veteris Testamenti Pseudepigrapha 11. Leiden: E. J. Brill, 1995.

Schäfer, Peter. "R. Aqiva und Bar Kokhba." In *Studien zur Geschichte und Theologie des rabbinischen Judentums.* AGJU 15, 65–121. Leiden: E. J. Brill, 1978.

Scheid, John, and Jesper Svenbro. *The Craft of Zeus: Myths of Weaving and Fabric.* Revealing Antiquity, vol. 9. Cambridge, Mass.: Harvard University Press, 1996.

Schiffman, Lawrence H. "At the Crossroads: Tannaitic Perspectives on the Jewish-Christian Schism." In *Aspects of Judaism in the Greco-Roman Period,* edited by E. P. Sanders, Albert I. Baumgarten, and Alan Mendelson. Jewish and Christian Self-Definition, vol. 2, 115–56; 338–52. Philadelphia: Fortress Press, 1981.

Schirmann, Jefim. "Hebrew Liturgical Poetry and Christian Hymnology." *Jewish Quarterly Review* 44 (1953–54): 123–61.

Schneemelcher, Wilhelm, ed. and trans. "The Acts of Peter." In *Writings Related to the Apostles: Apocalypses and Related Subjects.* Vol. 2 of *New Testament Apocrypha,* edited by Edgar Hennecke, Wilhelm Schneemelcher, and R. McL. Wilson, 259–322. Philadelphia: Westminster Press, 1965.

Schoedel, William R. *Ignatius of Antioch.* Hermeneia—a Critical and Historical Commentary on the Bible. Philadelphia: Fortress Press, 1985.

———, translation and commentary. *Polycarp, Martyrdom of Polycarp, Fragments of Papias.* Vol. 5 of *The Apostolic Fathers: A New Translation and Commentary.* Edited by Robert Grant. New York: Thomas Nelson, 1967.

Scott, James C. *Domination and the Arts of Resistance: Hidden Transcripts.* New Haven: Yale University Press, 1990.

———. *Weapons of the Weak: The Everyday Forms of Peasant Resistance.* New Haven: Yale University Press, 1985.

Segal, Alan F. *The Other Judaisms of Late Antiquity.* Brown Judaic Studies, no. 127. Atlanta: Scholars Press, 1987.

———. *Rebecca's Children: Judaism and Christianity in the Roman World.* Cambridge, Mass.: Harvard University Press, 1986.

Sered, Susan, and Samuel Cooper. "Sexuality and Social Control: Anthropological Reflections on the Book of Susanna." In *The Judgment of Susanna: Authority and Witness,* edited by Ellen Spolsky, 43–55. Atlanta: Scholars Press, 1996.

Setzer, Claudia. *Jewish Responses to Early Christians: History and Polemics, 30–150 C.E.* Minneapolis: Fortress Press, 1994.

Severus of Minorca. *Letter on the Conversion of the Jews.* Translated and edited by Scott Bradbury. Oxford Early Christian Texts. Oxford: Oxford University Press, 1996.

Shanks, Hershel, ed. *Christianity and Rabbinic Judaism: A Parallel History of Their Origins and Early Development.* Washington, D.C.: Biblical Archaeology Society, 1992.

Shaw, Brent D. "Body/Power/Identity: Passions of the Martyrs." *Journal of Early Christian Studies* 4, no. 3 (1996): 269–312.

———. "The Passion of Perpetua." *Past and Present*, no. 139 (May 1993): 3–45.

Sherwin-White, A. N. *The Letters of Pliny.* Oxford: Oxford University Press, 1966.

Sigal, Phillip. "Early Christian and Rabbinic Liturgical Affinities: Exploring Liturgical Acculturation." *New Testament Studies* 30 (1984): 63–90.

Simon, Marcel. *Verus Israel: A Study of the Relations Between Christians and Jews in the Roman Empire (135–425).* Translated by H. McKeating. The Littman Library of Jewish Civilization. Oxford: Oxford University Press, 1986.

Smallwood, E. M. *The Jews Under Roman Rule from Pompey to Diocletian.* Leiden: E. J. Brill, 1976.

Smith, Jonathan Z. "Differential Equations: On Constructing the 'Other.'" Lecture. Tempe, Arizona, 1992. Pamphlet.

Stein, Dina. "Folklore Elements in Late Midrash: A Folkloristic Perspective on Pirkei de Rabbi Eliezer." Dissertation, Hebrew University (in Hebrew, with English abstract), 1998. Photocopy.

Stern, David. "Midrash and Indeterminacy." *Critical Inquiry* 15, no. 1 (autumn 1988): 132–62.

Stevenson, J. *A New Eusebius: Documents Illustrative of the History of the Church to A.D. 337.* London: SPCK, 1960.

Strack, Hermann, and Paul Billerbeck. *Kommentar zum Neuen Testament aus Talmud und Midrasch.* Munich: C. H. Beck, 1924.

Strecker, Georg. "On the Problem of Jewish Christianity." In *Orthodoxy and Heresy in Earliest Christianity,* by Walter Bauer, 241–85. Philadelphia: Fortress Press, 1971.

Stroumsa, Gedalyahu. "The Hidden Closeness: On the Fathers of the Church and Judaism" (in Hebrew). *Jerusalem Studies in Jewish Thought* 1, no. 2 (fall 1982): 170–75.

Suetonius. *The Twelve Caesars.* Translated by Robert Graves. New York: Penguin Books, 1980.

Surkau, Hans Werner. *Martyrien in Jüdischer und Frühchristlicher Zeit.* Göttingen: Vandenhoeck & Ruprecht, 1938.

Swain, Simon. "Biography and Biographic in the Literature of the Roman

Empire." In *Portraits: Biographical Representation in the Greek and Latin Literature of the Roman Empire,* edited by M. J. Edwards and Simon Swain, 1–37. Oxford: Oxford University Press, Clarendon, 1997.

Taylor, Joan E. "The Phenomenon of Early Jewish-Christianity: Reality or Scholarly Invention." *Vigiliae Christianae* 44 (1990): 313–34.

Taylor, Miriam S. *Anti-Judaism and Early Christian Identity: A Critique of the Scholarly Consensus.* Studia Post-Biblica, vol. 46. Leiden: E. J. Brill, 1995.

Tertullian. "An Answer to the Jews." In *Ante-Nicene Fathers.* Vol. 3. Edited by Alexander Roberts and James Donaldson. Oak Harbor, Wash.: Logos Research Systems, 1997.

Theodor, Jehuda, and Hanoch Albeck, eds. *Genesis Rabbah.* Jerusalem: Wahrmann, 1965.

Tilley, Christopher. "Michel Foucault: Towards an Archaeology of Archaeology." In *Reading Material Culture,* edited by Christopher Tilley, 281–347. Oxford: Blackwell, 1990.

Trevett, Christine. "Gender, Authority and Church History: A Case Study of Montanism." *Feminist Theology* 17 (January 1998): 9–24.

Urbach, Ephraim Elimelech. "The Homiletical Interpretations of the Sages and the Exposition of Origen on Canticles, and the Jewish-Christian Disputation." *Scripta hiersolymitana* 22 (1971): 247–75.

Urman, Dan. "The House of Assembly and the House of Study: Are They One and the Same?" *Journal of Jewish Studies* 44, no. 2 (autumn 1993): 236–57.

van der Horst, Pieter W. "Plato's Fear as a Topic in Early Christian Apologetics." *Journal of Early Christian Studies* 6, no. 1 (spring 1998): 1–13.

van der Klaauw, Johannes. "Diskussion: Das Phänomen des Martyriums: Versuch einer Definition." In *Die Entstehung der Jüdischen Martyrologie,* edited by Jan Willem van Henten. Studia Post-Biblica, 220–23. Leiden: E. J. Brill, 1989.

van Henten, Jan Willem. "Datierung und Herkunft des vierten Makkabäerbuches." In *Tradition and Re-Interpretation in Jewish and Early Christian Literature: Essays in Honor of Jürgen C.H. Lebram,* edited by J. W. van Henten, H. J. de Jonge. Studia Post-Biblica, 136–49. Leiden: E. J. Brill, 1986.

————. *The Maccabean Martyrs as Saviours of the Jewish People: A Study of 2 and 4 Maccabees.* Supplements to the Journal for the Study of Judaism. Leiden: E. J. Brill, 1997.

————, ed. *Die Entstehung der jüdischen Martyrologie.* Leiden: E. J. Brill, 1989.

Vessey, Mark. "The Forging of Orthodoxy in Latin Christian Literature: A Case Study." *Journal of Early Christian Studies* 4, no. 4 (winter 1996): 495–513.

―――. "*Opus Imperfectum*: Augustine and His Readers, 426–435 A.D." *Vigiliae Christianae* 52, no. 3 (August 1998): 264–85.

Von Campenhausen, Hans. "Bearbeitungen und Interpolationen des Polykarpmartyriums." In *Aus der Frühzeit des Christentums*, 253–301. Tübingen: J. C. B. Mohr (Paul Siebeck), 1963.

von Kellenbach, Katharina. *Anti-Judaism in Feminist Religious Writings.* American Academy of Religion. Atlanta: Scholars Press, 1994.

Vööbus, Arthur. *The Didascalia Apostolorum in Syriac I + II* (with English translation). CSCO 401–2. Louvain: Peeters, 1979.

Ward, Benedicta SLG. *Harlots of the Desert: A Study of Repentance in Early Monastic Sources.* Cistercian Studies Series 106. Kalamazoo: Cistercian Publications, 1987.

―――, trans. *The Sayings of the Desert Fathers: The Alphabetical Collection.* With a foreword by Metropolitan Anthony. London: Mowbray, 1981.

Wechsler, Michael G. "The Purim-Passover Connection: A Reflection of Jewish Exegetical Tradition in the Peshitta Book of Esther." *Journal of Biblical Literature* 117, no. 2 (summer 1998): 321–27.

Werner, Eric. *The Sacred Bridge: The Interdependence of Liturgy and Music in Synagogue and Church During the First Millenium.* Da Capo Music Reprint Series. Da Capo Press, 1979.

―――. *The Sacred Bridge: The Interdependence of Liturgy and Music in Synagogue and Church During the First Millenium.* Hoboken, N.J.: KTAV, 1985.

Wilken, Robert L. *John Chrysostom and the Jews: Rhetoric and Reality in the Late 4th Century.* Berkeley: University of California Press, 1983.

Yuval, Israel Jacob [Yakov]. "Easter and Passover as Early Jewish-Christian Dialogue." In *Passover and Easter: Origin and History to Modern Times*, edited by Paul F. Bradshaw and Lawrence A. Hoffman. Two Liturgical Traditions, vol. 5. Notre Dame, Ind.: University of Notre Dame Press, 1999.

―――. "The Haggadah of Passover and Easter." In Hebrew. *Tarbiz* 65, no. 1 (October–December 1995): 5–29.

―――. "Jews and Christians in the Middle Ages: Shared Myths, Common Language." In *The "Other" as Threat: Demonization and Antisemitism*, edited by Robert Wistrich, 88-107. Chur: Harvard Academic Publishers, 1999.

―――. "Passover in the Middle Ages (on Shabbat Hagadol)." In *Passover and Easter: Origin and History to Modern Times*, edited by Paul F. Bradshaw

and Lawrence A. Hoffman. Two Liturgical Traditions, vol. 5. Notre Dame,
Ind: University of Notre Dame Press, 1999.

———. *"Two Nations in Your Womb": Perceptions of Jews and Christians in the Middle Ages.* Berkeley: University of California Press, 1999.

———. "Vengeance and Damnation, Blood and Defamation: From Jewish Martyrdom to Blood Libel Accusation" (in Hebrew). *Zion* 58 (1993): 33–90.

Zuckermandel, M. S., ed. *Tosephta: Based on the Erfurt and Vienna Codices, with Lieberman, Saul, "Supplement" to the Tosephta* (in Hebrew). Jerusalem: Bamberger & Wahrmann, 1937.

Index

In this index an "f" after a number indicates a separate reference on the next page, and an "ff" indicates separate references on the next two pages. A continuous discussion over two or more pages is indicated by a span of page numbers, e.g., "57–59." *Passim* is used for a cluster of references in close but not consecutive sequence.

FIGURAE: READING MEDIEVAL CULTURE

Library of Congress Cataloging-in-Publication Data

Boyarin, Daniel.
   Dying for God : martyrdom and the making of Christianity and
Judaism / Daniel Boyarin.
      p.   cm. — (Figurae)
   Includes bibliographical references and index.
   ISBN 0-8047-3617-0 (cloth : alk. paper)
   1. Judaism—History—Post-exilic period, 586 B.C.–210 A.D.
2. Christianity—Origin.   3. Judaism—Relations—Christianity—
History—To 1500.   4. Christianity and other religions—Judaism—
History—To 1500.   I. Title.   II. Series: Figurae (Stanford, Calif.)
BM176.B65   1999
270.1—dc21   99-40509

Original printing 1999

Last figure below indicates the year of this printing:
08   07   06   05   04   03   02   01   00   99

Designed by Janet Wood
Typeset by James P. Brommer in 11/14 Garamond